GALANTHUS

SCILLA

CROCUS

LYCORIS SQUAMIGERA

LILY (BASE-ROOTING)

STERNBERGIA

DAFFODIL

D1408103

FOR SPRING BULBS SEE BACK ENDSHEET

THE COMPLETE
BOOK OF BULBS

THE
COMPLETE
BOOK
OF BULBS

REVISED EDITION

by F. F. Rockwell and Esther C. Grayson

Revised and Edited by Marjorie J. Dietz

A PRACTICAL MANUAL ON THE USES,
CULTIVATION AND PROPAGATION
OF MORE THAN 100 SPECIES,
HARDY AND TENDER,
WHICH THE HOME GARDENER
CAN ENJOY OUTDOORS
AND IN THE HOUSE

J. B. LIPPINCOTT COMPANY
Philadelphia and New York

TO JAN DE GRAAFF who, like his father and grandfather before him, has done so much to provide gardens the world over with ever increasing beauty.

U. S. Library of Congress Cataloging in Publication Data

Rockwell, Frederick Frye, 1884–1976
The complete book of bulbs.

Includes index.
1. Bulbs. I. Grayson, Esther C., joint author.
II. Dietz, Marjorie J. III. Title.
SB425.R62   1977   635.9′44
ISBN 0-397-01194-6
Library of Congress Catalog Card Number 77–4437

Foreword to the Revised Edition

Some gardening books should never be put on the shelf—the shelf that means retirement and oblivion where they can never be found by new generations of gardeners or by new gardeners of any age. Such a book is *The Complete Book of Bulbs,* written with total dedication and loving care by F. F. Rockwell and Esther C. Grayson over twenty years ago, yet still as practical and filled with inspiration today as when it was first published.

Twenty years is not really such a long interval and little has changed in the timeless rites of gardening the Rockwells have known about and practiced for so many seasons. Some of the cultivars and varieties of bulbs first recommended are still available and being grown today; others have disappeared, necessitating revisions and additions in the text and in the special lists in Chapter 22, The Gardener's Bulb Selector and Recommended Varieties of Garden Bulbs section. The trend away from total pest control with environmentally-harmful chemicals and the laws that prohibit their use have been heeded throughout this revised edition. Reasonable attention has been paid to changes in nomenclature, an example being the English bluebell or wood-hyacinth whose generic name has been changed to *Endymion nonscripta,* although many gardeners will continue to call this spring bulb by its old name, *Scilla nonscripta.*

Studying anew *The Complete Book of Bulbs,* for the purpose of making this revision, I was repeatedly impressed with the wealth of essential information the Rockwells had been able to pack within the covers of one volume. Surely this is an extremely valuable book in the world of gardening. Just how valuable is it? In the course of my research, I had need of an additional copy of the out-of-print original. While talking to one of the country's leading experts on bulbs, I mentioned that I certainly would be happy to have his copy, and indeed would gladly pay him fifteen dollars for it. To which the expert replied: "That's very interesting! Now, if you were able to offer me a thousand dollars, I guess I could consider it . . ." Perhaps he would have entertained a lower figure—but he did *not* make me a counter-offer within my budget, and I never was able to purchase his copy—or for that matter, another copy from anyone else. So, to describe the new revised edition of the Rockwells' classic as one of the "most-wanted" gardening books of our time, I honestly think is no exaggeration.

In this edition, I would like to acknowledge the assistance given by Marc Reynolds of Wallach/Reynolds/Bildersee Inc., and by Derek Fell.

MARJORIE J. DIETZ

East Hampton, New York

Foreword to the Original Edition

For some reason the group of plants commonly designated as bulbs has always held a special fascination for me. A psychologist would probably ascribe it to the fact that the very first plant I ever owned was a potted lily presented to me at an Easter church service. I remember, too, that one of my very first attempts at growing a flower was to dig up a blooming meadow lily from the edge of a hayfield where the clattering newfangled mowing machine would have caught it on the next round. Carefully I transplanted it to the dry, sandy patch of ground which had been given me as a garden of my very own; to keep me, as I came to suspect later, from getting under the feet—and in the hair—of the hired man who had to take care of the real gardens. Needless to say, the tall stalk and nodding yellow bells never appeared again.

At any rate, and for whatever reason, this group of plants has continued, through the years, to hold the interest which it so early inspired. It has been a great satisfaction, therefore, to watch the steadily growing popular appreciation of bulbous plants of all kinds, and to contribute, where opportunity offered, to this development.

When, some twenty-five years ago, I undertook the writing of a book devoted to bulbs, I was astonished to find that in the preceding quarter century there had appeared no American book on the subject. I have long felt that my original venture in this field was out of date, and have therefore welcomed the opportunity given me by my present publishers to prepare this new volume.

A lot of water has passed over the dam since those earlier days. Bulbous plants are no longer for the gardens of the few, but are represented, by one species or another, in almost every yard. The sale of bulbous plants has increased steadily, year by year. Where formerly practically all plants of this type were imported from Holland, Belgium, France, Japan, and other bulb-producing countries, millions are now grown in the United States. Notwithstanding the output of this comparatively new American industry, the importation of bulbs from abroad in 1951 reached the impressive figure of over 450,000,000.

The use of bulbs in American gardens is, however, in its infancy. Dozens of species and varieties, grown without difficulty and most rewarding to the grower, are seldom to be found in the average garden. The hardy-amaryllis and the hardy begonia—to cite but two examples—are among the most persistent and easily cared-for garden subjects to be found anywhere, and by no means new, yet one seldom encounters them.

I should like to express here my appreciation of the assistance given me from many sources in the preparation of this volume. First and foremost to my co-author and co-worker; then to many friends, among them Jan de Graaff, internationally known for his lily hybrids and daffodils; Dr. George Slate, author of *Lilies for American Gardens;* Dr. Cynthia Westcott, the Plant Doctor; Dr. P. P. Pirone of the New York Botanical Garden; and Jack Grullemans of Wayside Gardens, whose excellent catalogues have played an important part in making American gardeners more bulb-conscious; to Marjorie P. Johnson, for her assistance, beyond the call of duty, in preparing the manuscript; and to Katharine Burton, for her patient co-operation in the preparaion of the line drawings which accompany the text. The quotation from *The Poetical Works of Robert Bridges* is by permission of The Clarendon Press, Oxford. That from Mr. Slate's book is used by courtesy of the publishers, Charles Scribner's Sons.

It is with the hope that this new volume may bring to other gardeners something of the great pleasure that the growing of bulbous plants, outdoors and in, has brought to us, that I and my co-author pass along, within these pages, such information as we have gained.

F. F. ROCKWELL

GrayRock
West Nyack, New York

Contents

PART ONE: BULBS FOR YOUR GARDEN
AND HOW TO USE THEM

Why you need bulbs no matter what else you grow; extending
the season of color; garden pictures with bulbs—for terraces
and patios, in borders, for landscape groups, for naturalizing,
in the rock garden.

You can enjoy bulbs even without a garden; bringing spring
indoors with forced bulbs; bulbs as house plants; for porches
and window boxes.

Bringing the bulbs picture into focus; hardy, half-hardy, and
tender bulbs—types for different purposes; spring-, summer-,
autumn-, and winter-flowering.

PART TWO: THE MORE IMPORTANT GROUPS OF BULBS

A. SPRING-FLOWERING

B. SUMMER- AND AUTUMN-FLOWERING

PART THREE: THE CATALOGUE OF BULBS

(with references to preceding chapters) of more than 100 species—Achimenes to Zephyranthes.

Lists of bulbs for special purposes; for the border, for naturalizing, for shade; for dry, hot situations; for fragrance; for the rock garden; for landscape effects; for edgings; for patio and terrace containers, planters; for window boxes; for moist locations; for cutting; for arrangements; by season of bloom; by height.

COLOR ILLUSTRATIONS

(*Color photographs by Malak, Ottawa on Plates 1–6, 10, 11, 15, 18, 19, 22; elsewhere, by the authors*)

LINE ILLUSTRATIONS

By Katharine Burton

HALFTONE ILLUSTRATIONS

CREDITS, Halftone Photographs

Associated Bulb Growers—53, 76 (top), 163, 167, 172, 184, 186, 281; Boutrelle—108 (bottom), 194, 195; Cassebeer—49, 230; Gottscho-Schleisner—20, 28; J. H. McFarland—24, 177, 257, 261, 265; Monkmeyer—51; Roche—34; Rockwell and Grayson—35, 36, 48, 56, 57, 69, 75, 76 (bottom), 102–106, 108 (top), 140, 150, 169, 170, 197, 206, 221, 248, 249, 256, 258, 273, 278–280; Richard Averill Smith, 204; Steenson & Baker—99, 101, 182; George Taloumis—54, 62, 64, 78, 82–84, 90, 91, 93, 107, 125, 133, 161, 226, 243–246, 294, 303

PART ONE
—BULBS FOR YOUR GARDEN
AND HOW TO USE THEM

Daffodils naturalized under birches. For this purpose it is best to use individual varieties or types rather than a general mixture.

CHAPTER *1. Make Your Garden More Beautiful with Bulbs*

Why have bulbs in your garden?

First of all because a garden without bulbs is only half a garden. Bulbs provide whole groups of flowers for which there are no substitutes, not even poor ones, among annuals or perennials. The garden pictures which you can readily create with them can be achieved in no other way.

But the one clinching argument for having bulbs, and having them in abundance, is that they provide a month or more of heart-lifting color before perennials, annuals, and all but the earliest shrubs are giving more than a promise that eventually they will break the shackles of their prison-keeper, winter, and again be set free to beautify the earth.

We have just come in from an around-the-garden stroll, between showers, on a day in April. It would have been a disheartening trip indeed but for the cheerful flowers from bulbs and corms that greeted us along the way, just as their still earlier companions have been doing for nearly a month past.

All but the most laggard of the tulip species—which in most springs seem to be everlasting—have finally dropped their weather-beaten petals along the curving main path through the rock garden. But *Tulipa tarda's* golden stars, tipped with white light, and the brilliant flames of *T. eichleri* are still in their prime, with the dainty candlestick and the weirdly twisted petals of *T. acuminata* still to carry on.

Another spot of glorious color, now in its third week, is a collection of half a dozen varieties of Early Tulips; old varieties, but still as desirable as ever. So colorful are these that from the living-room windows they make a patch of sunshine even on a dreary day; and so fragrant that visitors, noticing the sweet scent, look around to see where it could come from, not realizing that there are such things as fragrant tulips.

In the rock garden there is still plenty of interest: the later-flowering little bulbs such as grape-hyacinths, and snowflakes, with camassias thrusting up their tall spikes that later will bear blue and white stars set off by golden stamens, and the late wood-hyacinths. But if this area of the garden produced not another flower from now until next spring, it would have proved worthwhile. In March, April, and early May it is a sort of sun trap, sloping to the southeast and protected on the northwest by hemlocks, pines, and rhododendrons— the earliest of our several outdoor living rooms to become really comfortable and inviting. *And its attractiveness is due chiefly to bulbs.*

It is in the hardy borders, however, that bulbs make their most extensive, varied, and colorful displays. Here, long before the rock garden has lost its interest, the daffodils and tulips, in groups spaced between the various types of perennials, bring sudden life and color to the long stretches where but a few days before were only brown earth and bits of budding greenery. Many of the other bulbous flowers will help carry on here, too, through midsummer and even into autumn. The wide range of hardy lilies begins with the dainty coral lily and chaste madonna in June, continues with the towering spikes of various lily hybrids in midsummer, and ends with *L. tigrinum* and *speciosum* and their hybrids in August or September. The lilies are especially desirable because their upright habit of growth gives much needed contrast to the rounded or spreading forms of most garden flowers.

And then there are the half-hardy and tender bulbous plants of many kinds from many climes. It is reassuring to know that after the tall bearded and Siberian irises are gone there will still be the bulbous irises to take over and continue to make available this flower, so delightful in any of its many forms, in arrangements as well as in the garden. The exotic ismene and the spire-stalked galtonia provide notes of pure white, especially welcome during the season when they are in bloom. (The heavy, strap-leaved foliage of ismene is so useful in arrangements all summer long that it would be well worth growing even if it never flowered.)

And after these, of course, come the summer-flowering tender bulbs—gladiolus in all its rainbow range of colors, with the delightful little miniatures and "babies" for the table-size arrangements; dahlias in all kinds of shapes, sizes, and hues; montbretia, fountain-like and sprightly, sending up one spike after another for a long season; tigridia, unsurpassed in brilliancy and a variety of dramatic color combinations.

WHERE CAN YOU USE THEM?

With such a treasure chest of plant jewels to choose from, it is small wonder that the inexperienced gardener will find himself bewildered. But it is an easy matter to make a beginning and then gradually increase, in variety and numbers, the range of bulbous plants that will add so greatly to the beauty and character of your garden. Most of the hardy bulbs and many of the tender ones, when given even moderate care, will propagate themselves so readily that in a few years' time you will have, from a very modest start, all of any one species or variety you are likely to be able to use. And yet, unlike most of the more persistent perennials, they do not demand frequent taking up, dividing, and replanting.

When you are ready to add bulbous plants to your garden, the first step should be to make a survey of locations in which you can use them, and then select the kinds that will best fit into these areas. The way *not* to start is to go through the bulb catalogues, with their gorgeous close-up photographs of individual flowers, and pick out at random those which, in color and size, are most dramatically presented. Such photographs usually convey little or no conception of the habit of the plant and, as they are not in uniform scale, fail as a guide even to the size of the individual blooms.

Let us then take a walk about the place, about *your* place, and try to get an idea of where the various types of bulbs could be used to best advantage. Unless your property is of considerable size, it is not likely that you will have available all of the types of locations we shall consider, but on even the smallest place there will be several of them.

Outdoor Living Areas—the Terrace or Patio

The porch or spacious veranda, once such an important adjunct to every home dwelling, is now mostly a relic of nostalgia. It has been replaced by the terrace or patio, a much more private area, usually open to the sky and located toward the rear of the house. While the terrace is indeed an outdoor living room with appropriate furnishings for relaxation and entertaining, it can also be an extension of the garden. In fact, on small properties, the terrace can serve as the major gardening area, allowing the homeowner to practice gardening activities in the same environs in which the "fruits" of such labors can later be enjoyed at leisure and from a comfortable lounge.

Since most outdoor-living areas are designed—or should be designed—to provide some shade as well as sunshine, a wide variety of plants is available for both exposures and their variations, and bulbous plants are certainly among the most important.

The first kinds of bulbs to select for terrace decoration are the spring-blooming ones—crocuses, daffodils, hyacinths, tulips, and

A tulip border edged with pansies. Curving design of bed, with hedge at rear, sets off the blooms to the very best advantage.

others. A great advantage to using spring bulbs on the terrace or in beds adjacent to it is that their flowers can be seen and enjoyed from indoors during those wet, chilling storms that inevitably accompany the spring season over much of the country. If your terrace does not have the space for extensive beds of tulips or other bulbs (which can be followed by masses of petunias, marigolds, wax begonias, and other low-growing plants for summer color), you may have space for a few bulbs around a tree planted on the terrace to provide shade; or you may have earth insets or "islands" in the terrace paving which have been deliberately left open for various planting combinations. A third choice for spring bulbs is in containers—pots, boxes, tubs. The bulbs can be planted in them in the fall or carefully transplanted from the open ground in early spring just as new growth emerges.

The summer season, though, is when outdoor living is at its peak and again, bulbous plants offer the beginning as well as more experienced gardener infinite possibilities for decorating a terrace. Tuberous begonias and caladiums are our favorites among the summer bulbs, and both are superb subjects for pots and containers, although they can also be planted in the open ground. Other bulb-type plants for summer bloom that are uniquely suited to the shelter afforded by most outdoor-living areas are achimenes and gloxinias, both very glamorous relatives of the African-violet. Both achimenes and the pendulous forms of tuberous begonias can be set out in hanging containers. The bulbs mentioned so far appreciate some shade, but for terraces (or decks especially) that are bathed in sunshine most of the day, there are the low-growing dwarf dahlias which do not grow over 1½ feet tall. Plant them individually in large pots, or for masses of color plant several tubers in open beds alongside the terrace or in large planters.

Landscape Groups

Before discussing this method of employing bulbs, it will be worthwhile to mark the distinction between landscape groups and "naturalizing"—a term that is too loosely used. To be really naturalized, bulbs—or any other type of plant material for that matter—should be planted in such a location and in such a way, both as to numbers and distribution, as to simulate a natural growth, unplanned by the mind, and largely untended by the hand, of the gardener; in a word, a passable substitute for a work of nature. To be convincing, the setting—the terrain and the companion plants used—must be in accord with the plants that are to be naturalized. In most cases this requires more space than many of us possess, and the use of bulbs in large quantities.

The landscape group, on the contrary, makes no pretense of having, like Topsy, "jist growed." It may occupy a space of but a few square feet. Its purpose is to create a pleasing "little picture," a highlight or accent point in the general garden scheme. Its success will depend upon the gardener's skill in selecting the right thing for the right place. It *may* have the appearance of having been a happy accident of nature (which will be a credit to the gardener's cleverness), but that is not at all essential.

In the landscape group, as in naturalizing, a keen sense of composition is all-important. A circle of daffodils set in the middle of a lawn does not constitute a landscape group. Yet the same daffodils rearranged in a kidney-shaped drift beneath a tree or spreading out from a shrub planting would comprise a landscape grouping that would increase in beauty spring after spring.

Here again the degree of success attained will be commensurate with the care used in selecting materials. If one desires informal effects, avoid the giant Darwin tulips, huge trumpet daffodils, exhibition hyacinths, large-flowered gladiolus and dahlias. Those which make the most attractive landscape groups are the species and hybrids of tulips and daffodils, small-flowered daffodils in general, crocuses, both spring- and autumn-flowering, and many of the lilies.

Landscape groups are arranged according to the setting and the plants to be used. Often the soil where such a group is to be grown can be left in grass or permanently mulched. This is a great advantage in growing hardy bulbs, for the foliage always should be allowed to mature. Then a planting, which is a decided point of accent in the spring, just automatically disappears and is forgotten after the flowers fade. Landscape groups are most easily done and, on the whole, most successful when but a single variety of bulb is used.

Making a group planting is an excellent way of spotlighting some out-of-the-ordinary or unusually attractive species or variety. During its period of bloom it may attract more attention in the garden than a whole border full of larger flowers competing with each other. *White* flowers, showing up more conspicuously against their green or dark backgrounds than most colored flowers, are especially effective in group plantings.

One word of caution! A group planting is an exclamation point! The too-free use of kinds that flower at the same time will, like a page of print sprinkled with exclamation points, defeat its own purpose! If care is taken to provide for bloom *at intervals through the season,* a large number of landscape groups can be arranged even on a small place.

Naturalizing

Where a sufficient area is available and local conditions are suitable, many of the hardy bulbs make extremely satisfactory plants for naturalizing. Daffodils in particular, because of their permanency, their freedom from insect injury and disease, and the fact that they bloom early in spring, while sunshine still floods the ground under deciduous trees, are ideal for the purpose.

One need not possess acres of ground to have a satisfactory naturalized planting. Wherever a bit of woods or meadow, a natural slope or a rocky bank, a few old fruit trees, a bit of stream or a garden pool suggests a suitable setting, bulbs of one sort or another can be used to create an intriguing view.

What has already been said about selecting appropriate types and varieties for landscape groups applies also, but with even greater force, to naturalized plantings. The effect desired simply will not come off if the flowers planted look foreign to their setting. This by no means implies that only native material should be used. One does not think of a field of dandelions or of roadside day-lilies covering a bank as being exotics, although both are immigrants from other lands. The point is that they *look* as though they belonged naturally where one finds them. Just so with the simpler types of daffodils, the tulip species, the grape-hyacinths, the lilies, and the many other bulbs and bulbous plants which are well adapted to naturalizing.

Another highly desirable, if not essential, quality required in plants for naturalizing is that they be permanent or self-perpetuating. An advantage possessed by many bulbs adapted for use in naturalized plantings is that they pretty much take care of themselves, increasing in numbers by division and by self-seeding, while on the other hand they do not spread so rapidly and vigorously as to drive out everything else—a serious fault of many perennials.

The prime objective in naturalizing is to get a finished planting that will look natural. To achieve this, avoid using too many different varieties of a single kind in one area, and avoid placing the bulbs in anything approaching a regular pattern.

A naturalized planting need not involve a very heavy original outlay. Bulbs will have to be used, of course, in greater numbers than would be required for planting small groups in borders. But many of

Daffodils naturalized in the landscape. Scattered planting, with areas left unplanted, is more pleasing than a solid mass of bloom.

the older and least expensive varieties are perfectly satisfactory, and most of them will multiply rapidly. If one is content to have a somewhat thin effect for three or four years, the allotted spaces will soon fill up. The wise gardener will not be tempted by cheap mixtures containing many varieties offered for naturalizing. Daffodils are frequently sold in this way. Even if the bulbs are good, the result is a hodgepodge that looks anything but natural. The "naturalizing" of a

collection of varieties is a compromise which the collector may be willing to make. If pains are taken to keep varieties of the same general type together, the result will not be so regrettable—from the artistic point of view—as otherwise it might.

In Foundation Plantings

On the small property, where lack of room presents a problem, another possibility is to place bulbs in, or just in front of, the foundation planting about the house. Often such plantings are composed entirely of dwarf evergreens—although in most instances a combination of evergreen and deciduous shrubs would be better. In either case, almost any of the spring-flowering bulbs can be used to add interest and color. They should be planted in groups rather than in a straight line or border, as they often are. The maturing foliage can usually be pretty well concealed under low branches or by pot-grown annuals set in to provide color later in the season.

The Flower Garden

One of the most traditional ways to use bulbs of many kinds is in the flower garden in company with perennials, such as peonies and day-lilies; with biennials, such as sweet William and hollyhock; and with annuals, such as petunias and marigolds. This is the "mixed border" of garden lingo and bulbous plant material should have a prominent place in such a border. Bulbs are essential for early color accents and highly desirable for medium-to-tall spire material during the summer.

A logical place for a flower border on today's often limited properties can be in the foreground of a fence, hedge or shrub planting along the boundaries of the property. Or such gardens can be planned around the outside edges of the terrace, as suggested earlier. Although most flower gardens are located in the backyards of home properties, don't overlook the possibilities of making a dooryard garden. We know of one such garden on Cape Cod, enclosed in a white picket fence, which has given pleasure to passersby for years, beginning in spring when several clumps of daffodils and tulips bloom to summer when dahlias and gladiolus mix their flowers with perennial phlox and annual zinnias.

No matter where you locate your border, it is where the more familiar bulbs, such as daffodils, tulips, hyacinths, some of the more robust-growing minor bulbs and the more vigorous hardy lilies, can best be used to advantage. Here, too—though they are seldom so employed—may well go such tender bulbs as dahlias (of moderate size), gladiolus, summer-hyacinth (*Galtonia*), and tigridias.

In the Rock Garden

The very term "rock garden" is likely to scare off the beginner with a small place or limited means. The picture of a rock garden that comes to mind is based upon what has been seen in books, magazines, or at botanical gardens and flower shows—rock gardens, to be sure, but rock gardens on a much grander and more elaborate scale than is at all essential. A rock garden is primarily a garden made among rocks, and such a garden can be made on an area of a few square yards and with very few rocks. Your real rock-garden enthusiast may condescendingly refer to such a setup as a "rockery" rather than a rock garden, but that does not change the fact that it provides growing conditions and a setting quite different from those in the flower bed or border.

The point is stressed here because many of the smaller spring bulbs find conditions more to their liking, and are displayed to much better advantage, when they are planted among rocks. If there is available a natural outcrop or a stony slope or bank, so much the better; but wanting that, a rock garden of some sort can usually be provided without too much expense or labor. It can even be constructed on a level surface to simulate a natural outcropping. In constructing any kind of rock garden, try to remember how the rocks are placed in nature. Be sure to bury a good portion of the rock in soil.

Among the bulbs especially suitable for growing among rocks are the species and hybrids of tulips and daffodils, and the smaller bulbs already mentioned. Others will be found in the list on page 346.

Where the rock garden is sufficiently large, or a bank or sloping wall may be utilized to provide height somewhat above surface level, the smaller bulbs can be enjoyed not only for their general effect but for the beauty of the individual flowers, much of which is lost when they must be looked down upon at one's feet. By all means provide, if possible, a rock setting for some of your bulbs.

One might continue almost indefinitely concerning the garden possibilities of this greatly varied group of bulbous plants for gardens large or small. A pool, a stream, a winding path through a bit of woods—these and a dozen other locations not already discussed present alluring possibilities. And the wonderful part of it is that the initial expense for almost any of these adventures need not be great. With few exceptions, the colony of plants increases more or less automatically once you get a start.

In a word, your garden will be more beautiful, interesting, and varied if you accept the help that bulbs so generously offer.

A drawback to the use of some bulbs—especially tulips and daffodils—is the fact that the foliage should be left to mature, and during its dying-down period becomes unsightly. For this reason, on large properties and estates where many bulbs are grown, these are often placed in a special bulb border or borders where they can be left until time to take them up; or interplanted with annuals or bedding plants to conceal the dying foliage and provide later color. In the mixed border, however, using suitable perennials and annuals near and in front of the groups of bulbs will keep the foliage from being too obtrusive.

Bulbs which are best *not* used in the mixed border include low-growing sorts, such as crocus and grape-hyacinths, and the various delicate-flowered little fellows: snowdrops, snowflakes, glory-of-the-snow, and the like. In the bare soil of the flower border, these are likely to become beaten down and mud-spattered and more or less lost amid the fast-growing foliage of larger bulbs and perennials. Being so low-growing, they display themselves to much better advantage if they are planted, where possible, at an elevation somewhat above the general ground level, as at the top of a low retaining wall or in planting areas on a terrace or patio.

Such bulbs as are used in the mixed flower border are best placed in small groups, somewhat irregular in form and at irregular distances. Otherwise they will present very conspicuous and spotty patterns when in bloom. As few as five or six tulips or daffodils of a single variety, or even three lilies, will make an attractive spot of color the first season, though double these quantities are desirable. In a large border, of course, more should be used in each group, to be in scale with the general planting design.

Let us take a look at what bulbs can do in providing beauty and interest within the house. Here you can enjoy them, in one form or another, from the first week in January to the last in December.

The ways in which bulbs serve to provide enjoyment indoors are (1) as cut flowers for decoration; (2) forced in pots for winter bloom; and (3) as house plants that are grown indoors the year round, except for their summer vacation in the open.

As cut flowers the spring bulbs provide an ample supply for decorations at a time when few other flowers are available. They last well and combine charmingly with branches of such early shrubs as may be in bloom (or may readily be forced indoors), adding needed color and emphasis in arrangements. Later in the season the summer-flowering types, including the many July and August lilies, furnish tall spikes to accompany the annuals and perennials in bloom at this season. And from midsummer on, gladiolus, dahlia, montbretia, and others are available during that period when perennial borders usually have little to offer until the chrysanthemums come in. If you have a cold frame, daffodils, early tulips, and many of the other hardy spring bulbs, grown in pots, flats, or directly in the soil, may be had for cutting a month or more ahead of the same varieties in the garden. With a small greenhouse the flowering dates of some sorts may be advanced to New Year's or shortly thereafter.

Forced bulbs for flowering indoors constitute one of the easiest and most certain of all types of flower growing. Everyone, even the city apartment dweller, is familiar with the 'Paperwhite' and the similar yellow-flowered 'Soleil d'Or' narcissus which can be bought in garden centers and from other outlets including mail-order concerns, and can be grown in pebbles and water, without benefit of soil. A number of others, including hyacinths, colchicums, and crocuses can be treated in the same way.

Those which are grown in soil or compost—tulips, daffodils, and a

Forced bulbs of various kinds add color and cheer to the indoor garden from Christmas time to Easter. Growing them is not difficult.

whole group of the early hardy bulbs—require little more work, for they are merely potted up in late fall, stored away in the dark at a cold temperature (like so many packages of food in a freezer), and then brought into the house, one or a few at a time, to flower. In this way it is possible to have, from January to April, as much of a bulb garden indoors as you can provide space for. And in addition to this winter show, most of these bulbs, after being forced, can be transferred to the garden and there will establish themselves and flower during succeeding years.

Winter-flowering tender bulbs make satisfactory house plants or

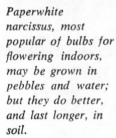

Paperwhite narcissus, most popular of bulbs for flowering indoors, may be grown in pebbles and water; but they do better, and last longer, in soil.

Veltheimia, excellent long-lived house plant, thriving in a kitchen window. This flower spike began to open on December 20, was photographed a full month later.

greenhouse subjects to be grown in pots the year round, or placed out-of-doors during summer and brought in again in late autumn. Best known of these perhaps is the amaryllis (*Hippeastrum*) with its giant, spectacularly colored blooms. In other days varieties of amaryllis and oxalis, with its cheerful, simple flowers and shamrock-like leaves, were to be found in almost every farmhouse collection of house plants, "swapped" among neighbors and passed on to every daughter who was setting up housekeeping on her own. They are still deservedly popular.

In the Small Greenhouse

The possession of a greenhouse, even a very small one, increases tremendously the pleasure which may be had from bulbous plants.

Florists' cyclamen, a favorite gift plant, continues in bloom for weeks if kept in a cool (40° to 50°) temperature, and can be saved for another season.

With "glass" one can enjoy many kinds that cannot be handled in the house or that are not practical to attempt. Also, bulbous plants wanted for house decoration can be cared for in the greenhouse until they come into flower, and returned to it afterward. Thus such window space or other locations as may be available for plants can be constantly replenished with blooming material. In our own small greenhouse, for instance, bulbs are brought in and started into growth under a bench, grown on to flowering stage on a bench, then transferred—as many as we have room for—to living room, dining room, or kitchen. After flowering they are returned to under-bench space in the greenhouse, where the foliage is allowed to mature. But even without a greenhouse a very satisfying number may be grown.

So you see that, though you may possess little garden space, there are many ways in which you can have a lot of fun growing bulbous plants. And as most of them may be kept from year to year, the expense of having them is very reasonable indeed.

CHAPTER *3.* *The Various Types of Bulbs*

Up to this point we have talked only in a very general way about bulbous plants and what they can do to help make the garden more beautiful and to bring cheer and color into the house. We have spoken of "hardy" bulbs and "tender" bulbs, without providing any definition of just what those terms mean; and of summer-flowering and winter-flowering ones just as though they might be different varieties of the same species. It is time now to observe more closely the members of this great group of plants and to learn something of the habits, possibilities and limitations, advantages and disadvantages of each.

This knowledge is essential for two reasons. It is necessary to enable us to know *where* and *how* to use the different types about the garden or indoors; and it also helps us to *grow* them successfully after we have decided which bulbs we would like to use.

The botanists' system of arranging bulbous plants in groups or categories is to classify them according to family relationships. Of more immediate importance to you, the gardener, however, is information concerning their behavior in the garden, window, or greenhouse.

You will want to know, first of all, whether they are hardy, semi-hardy, or tender: whether they can be left in the ground without protection in winter; whether they will come through if they are protected; whether they must be taken up and stored over the winter in a frostproof place or must be grown as pot plants the year round.

You will want to know also the season of the year when each blooms—spring, summer, autumn, or winter. And of course the size or height of the plant will be a determining factor in where to place it in the garden.

Let us take a quick glance at some of the more familiar bulbous plants and get an idea of how they fit into groups based on the characteristics indicated above.

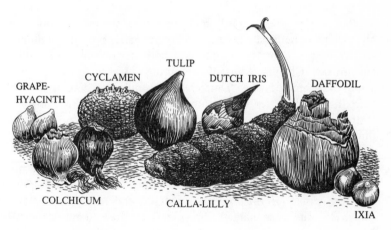

PLANTS SOLD AS "BULBS"

HARDINESS

If by the term "hardy" we mean capable of living out-of-doors through the winter, it is obvious that many plants are hardy in the

South which are not hardy in the North. The term as applied to plant material in general designates a species or a variety that will survive out-of-doors, without protection, in sections where the temperature drops to zero or occasionally well below. It is not an exact and definite term, for many plants commonly survive in areas where temperatures drop lower than those encountered in other areas where frequently the same plants perish during the winter. The reason for this, of course, is that temperature is only *one* factor of the several involved. Some of the others are: protection by snow that remains for most of the winter; exposure to high winds; the amount of moisture in the soil (determined by rainfall and drainage conditions); and the degree to which new growth has matured as it goes into the winter season.

Hardy

When we speak of a hardy bulb, therefore, we refer to one which, once planted and established, under normally good conditions will survive in cold climates—in our Northern tier of states, for instance, and up into Canada. Most of the spring-flowering bulbs are hardy. This group includes the "Dutch" bulbs—tulips, hyacinths, crocuses, daffodils—with a few exceptions—muscari (grape-hyacinths), galanthus (snowdrops), leucojums (spring snowflakes), scillas, and others. Another large group of the really hardy bulbs takes in most of the lilies, such as regal, madonna, turkscap, Canada or meadow, and the new hybrid sorts. In addition to these there are many native bulbous plants, such as Jack-in-the-pulpit (*Arisaema triphyllum*), dogtooth-violet (*Erythronium*), camassia, and Mariposa-lily (*Calochortus*). The last named, however, is often temperamental in Eastern gardens.

Semi-hardy

This group includes those which, while hardy in somewhat milder climates, or in moderate winters, or under unusually favorable conditions in the North, still cannot be relied upon to withstand near-zero temperatures unless given adequate protection. Well-known examples of these are the cluster-flowered narcissus ('Paperwhite' and 'Soleil d'Or', and a few others), anemones, ranunculus, and bulbous irises. These are hardy, in general, in the latitudes of Philadelphia, Louisville, Oklahoma City, and south, and on the West Coast to Portland and Spokane.

Tender

This group, again, includes those bulbs which will not tolerate hard freezing and can be left in the ground only in warm climates. In chillier sections they must be taken up when early frosts kill back their foliage and be stored over winter, or treated as pot plants and taken indoors. Among the tender bulbs are such popular ones as dahlia, gladiolus, canna, montbretia, tigridia, tuberous-rooted begonia, ismene, and galtonia (summer-hyacinth), all of which are stored; and, usually grown as pot plants, amaryllis, calla, amarcrinum, caladium, eucharis, and gloriosa.

SEASON OF BLOOM

There are some bulbs which will bloom, outdoors or in, almost any week in the year. Few of us, however, can have any very complete collection of bulbous plants, and hence it becomes important to make sure that those we do procure will give us as wide a spread as possible in time of flowering. We can classify them roughly, so far as blooming season is concerned, into four general groups: spring-, summer-, fall-, and winter-flowering. If a few species or varieties are selected from each of these groups, with a very moderate investment we can enjoy flowers from bulbous plants pretty much the year round.

Spring-flowering

This group is made up chiefly of the "Dutch" bulbs, so called because Holland has been the main source of supply for them. Far from being natives of Holland, they came originally from many parts of the world. The Dutch bulbs include tulips, daffodils, hyacinths, crocuses, and numerous smaller flowering genera—snowdrops, grape-hyacinths, squills, and others.

In addition to these, there are our own natives, such as trillium,

Jack-in-the-pulpit, spring beauty, and camassia. All of these, and the Dutch bulbs mentioned above, are perfectly hardy.

There are also a few semi-hardy bulbs that will give spring bloom in the Northern states if grown in frames or under specially favorable conditions: anemones, ranunculus, brodiaea, for example.

Summer-flowering

The summer-flowering (June to September) bulbs include two distinct types, some reliably hardy in cold climates and some that, except in warm climates, must be taken up and wintered over in protective storage.

Among the former, the hardy lilies comprise by far the most important single group. They provide, in the various species and hybrids, an almost uninterrupted succession of bloom.

In addition to the lilies, among the hardies are the hardy-amaryllis (*Lycoris squamigera,* the hardy begonia (*B. evansiana*), the blackberry-lily (*Belamcanda chinensis*), lily-turf (*Liriope*), and a few others that are hardy in milder climates.

The tender bulbs which provide our summer gardens with flowers are numerous and include several genera in which the named varieties and hybrids run into the thousands. Dahlias lead in diversity of form and coloring, with gladiolus a close second. Popular, too, are tuberous-rooted begonias, now grown by the thousand where they used to be grown by the dozen. Others are canna, tigridia, montbretia, tuberose, caladium, zephyranthes, and the less well-known but well worthwhile ismene (Peruvian-daffodil), *Lycoris radiata,* galtonia, acidanthera, and chlidanthus.

Still another group of summer-flowering bulbs includes several species usually grown in the greenhouse or indoors, but which can be set out in the ground during warm weather, or kept out of doors (or on a terrace) in pots or tubs. Typical of these are the dramatic blue lily-of-the-Nile (*Agapanthus africanus*), the Amazon-lily (*Eucharis grandiflora*), glory-lily (*Gloriosa*), gloxinia, and achimenes.

Fall-blooming

For most of our fall-blooming bulbous plants we come back again to the hardy group. Hardy bulbs which bloom in autumn are, incidentally, one of the most useful and most neglected of all groups of plant material.

Among these we have a fine array of *Crocus* species and varieties —sufficient in themselves to provide a whole garden of color, in a final defiant thumbing-of-the-nose at oncoming winter. And then there are the crocus-like colchicums, and *Sternbergia lutea* to add a touch of gold.

Late-planted gladiolus (you can put them in up to the Fourth of July in most regions), montbretia, and tigridia will carry on into the fall; and of course the dahlia, canna, and tuberous-rooted begonia will keep on flowering until Jack Frost cuts them down.

Winter-blooming

Here again we have two distinct groups—the tender bulbs for house or greenhouse that normally bloom in winter (in the Northern Hemisphere), and the spring-flowering hardy ones that can be forced into winter bloom.

Among the former are such bulbs as amaryllis, calla, clivia, cyclamen, freesia, morea, and veltheimia. Among the latter are practically all of the spring-flowering hardy bulbs, though with some (Darwin tulips, for instance) it is necessary to use *early* varieties. Many bulb catalogues indicate which varieties are most suitable for forcing.

HEIGHT

To plan for the most effective use of bulbs of any kind in the garden, one must have a knowledge of their heights. Otherwise very dramatic or very lovely delicate kinds may be almost completely hidden from sight behind taller ones, or lost among more robust-growing companions. Typical examples of such possible misplacement are most of the tulip and daffodil species and many of their hybrids.

Tall

Some of the taller kinds—2 feet or over—are a few of the late tulips, cannas, dahlias (except dwarf types), gladiolus, galtonia, most of the lilies, tuberoses, and the towering foxtail-lilies (*Eremurus*), some species of which reach a height of 8 feet or more. All of these should be kept well to the back in border plantings or in mixed landscape groups.

Medium

For the middle border use species and varieties of medium height —12 to 24 inches. Into this group fall most of the garden tulips and daffodils, camassias, bulbous irises, the dwarf lilies, wood-hyacinth or Spanish bluebell, *Fritillaria meleagris,* Jack-in-the-pulpit, and Solomon's-seal, among the hardy ones. Some tender bulbs of medium height are montbretia, tigridia, tuberous-rooted begonia, caladium, calla, and morea (generic name, *Moraea*).

Low

Along or near the front of the border, for edgings along terrace and patio areas or in pockets left in the pavement, along paths, in the foreground of naturalized plantings, or by themselves where ground-carpeting masses of color are wanted and in rock gardens, the various low-growing bulbs find their places. Here there is a wide choice indeed: crocuses (spring- and autumn-flowering), colchicums, almost all of the minor Dutch bulbs (grape-hyacinths, snowdrops, snowflakes, squill, scillas, and the like), lily-of-the-valley, and lily-turf (*Liriope*). Several of the tulip and daffodil species and their hybrids are less than a foot tall—some under 6 inches. Then, too, there are the dogtooth-violets (*Erythronium*) for shaded places, and the early-blooming winter-aconite (*Eranthis*).

So it becomes amply evident that whatever your limitations of space, your local conditions or requirements, you can find a goodly number of bulbous plants ready to accommodate themselves to your needs and to grace your garden with additional beauty.

In the specialized lists of bulbs (beginning on page 337) you will find more complete and detailed information, arranged to help you select just the species and varieties that will best provide the flowers you want for any location or season.

Now let's see how to get the best results from these accommodating bulbs once you have planned to add them to your garden.

CHAPTER *4. What Is a Bulb?*

You, the gardener, starting out on this great adventure into the world of plant life and the management of growing plants, quite naturally assumes that anything you purchase from a bulb catalogue, or pick out at the garden center's intriguing display of bins and trays in the section of the store devoted to bulbs, will be a bulb.

Like Alice in Wonderland, however, you will not have traveled far into this strange new realm before you discover that not everything is exactly what at first it seemed to be, and that there are many complications to be unraveled. Perhaps you have already had the experience of asking a more knowledgeable neighbor how deep to plant gladiolus bulbs, or if it is yet warm enough to put dahlia bulbs in the ground, and been informed that these are not bulbs but, in the one case, "corms," in the other, "tuberous roots."

Your reaction to this information may well be: "I don't give a damn what they are called. All I want is to grow some good flowers."

The point is that to grow good flowers, and particularly to keep on getting good flowers *after the first year,* it helps to have some knowledge of the growth habits, the life cycle, of the plant that is to produce the good flowers you wish to grow. It may surprise you to learn, for instance, that the daffodil bloom which you hope to display proudly to friends or perhaps win a blue ribbon with at the local flower show begins its career some ten to twelve months before it opens its white or golden petals to "take the winds of March with beauty."

BULBS, CORMS, AND TUBERS

Bulbs, corms, and tubers are alike in one particular. They are all in reality *buds* (or underground roots or stems bearing buds), in a state of dormancy, awaiting, to resume growth, only the right season

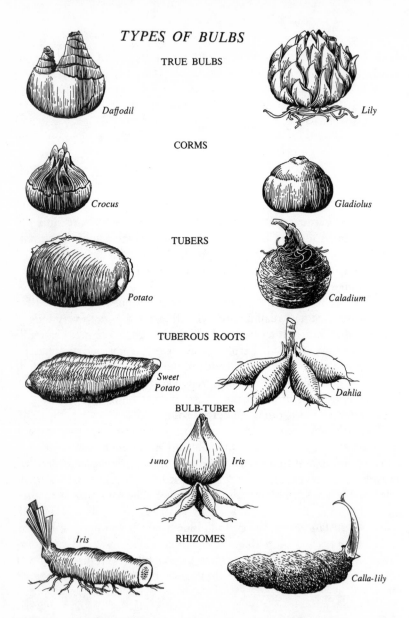

TYPES OF BULBS

TRUE BULBS

Daffodil

Lily

CORMS

Crocus

Gladiolus

TUBERS

Potato

Caladium

TUBEROUS ROOTS

Sweet Potato

Dahlia

BULB-TUBER

Juno *Iris*

Iris

RHIZOMES

Calla-lily

or the proper conditions of temperature and moisture. In this respect they resemble the leaf buds and flower buds on a forsythia or lilac bush. In many other respects they differ from such buds: they are formed underground; they are self-contained—that is, each is the nucleus of an entire plant, not just a part of a plant; and they are so constructed as to serve as storehouses of food that will support the plant for a considerable period when it renews growth. (Hyacinths grown in pebbles and water, and colchicums that will bloom even if pinned up on a curtain in the window, are examples of bulbs and corms capable of producing flowers, when growth is renewed, with no additional supply of food.)

Unlike the bud on shrub or tree, these bulbous, underground buds produce new sets of roots without an intervening stem or trunk that remains a permanent part of the plant's structure. In shrubs and trees the reserve food supply is stored in branches, trunks, canes, and roots; in perennials (which die back to the ground) it is in the crowns and in the roots, which in numerous species are so enlarged or swollen as to resemble bulbs, but still remain only parts of a larger organism.

Without getting into botanical technicalities, it may be explained that the food stored in any underground root, stem, or bud, to be carried over the dormant period as a reserve supply, is first taken up by the feeding roots, carried to the leaves to be elaborated or processed, and then returned to dormant-season storage quarters. In a word, the foliage plays a very vital part in preparing the reserve food supply.

The practical point for the gardener to learn from all this is that the bulb, corm, or tuber cannot develop normally to its full size, or its maximum flower-producing capacity, unless the leaves of the plant are allowed to complete, under favorable conditions, their full growth.

That is lesson number one in the culture of all bulbous plants.

True Bulbs

Coming from the general to the more specific application of the word "bulb," we may define a true bulb as being an underground stem with a growing point (or bud) surrounded by fleshy layers of tissue containing a stored-up food supply. These layers may be closely wrapped around the growing point or bud at the center, as is the case with an onion, a daffodil, or a tulip. Or they may be loosely placed, fleshy scales, as in a lily. All of these are true bulbs.

In the case of all of these, too, the layers or scales are held together at the base by a disk of hardened stem tissue known as the "plate." When growth is renewed, new roots develop from around the edge of this plate. If you have ever grown onions, you know how, when the foliage dies down, the roots at the base of the onion bulb also die off, so that the slightest pull will remove the onion from the soil. It is then in its dormant state, and if properly "cured" and stored may be kept through the winter. (Onion "sets" are merely very small onions which, because of late planting and overcrowding, have not attained their normal size. They are, however, true bulbs, just as fully grown specimens are.)

Cross sections of daffodil bulb show complete embryo flower developed at center. Dark spot (extreme right) is new offset forming.

Conical sections of tulip bulb, showing thick fleshy tissue. Embryo flower, well developed, apparent at center—right.

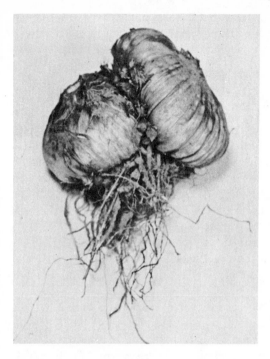

Second-year gladiolus corm at harvesting. Group of cormels have developed near bases of large corms.

Corms

A corm differs from a true bulb in that it is made up of a solid mass of fleshy tissue. Usually incipient buds on the top surface of the corm are visible, indicating where new growth will start. As with true bulbs, there is a distinct bottom or basal plate around the edge of which roots start when growth is renewed. Unlike a true bulb, however, a corm is a temporary storehouse for food and withers and disintegrates as this food is used up. A brand-new corm (sometimes two or more) forms on top of the old one. Gladiolus and crocuses are typical corms.

Tubers

A tuber, like a corm, is composed of solid tissue but does not have a basal plate: it is really a modified stem. Like corms, also, tubers have discernible "eyes" or buds that develop into new growth shoots. In some cases they shrivel and disintegrate as the new plant matures. Potatoes, caladiums, and elephant's ears (*Colocasia*) are typical tubers.

Tuberous Roots

These resemble tubers in that they are made up of solid tissue and do not have basal plates. Unlike tubers, however, they are formed of *root* tissue instead of stem tissue; in other words, they are modified roots. The dahlia, usually called a tuber, is more accurately a tuberous root. In some instances the tuberous root has eyes or buds at intervals over its surface; in others the eyes are limited to the neck of the tuberous root, where it is joined to the old plant stem. The former type can be cut into numerous pieces (each with an eye), all of which will grow—as with the sweet potato. On the contrary, a dahlia root, unless it carries a piece of the old stem bearing an eye, will not sprout at all.

Still another form of tuberous root may be called a bulb-tuber, as it is an unusual combination of a real bulb with short, fat tuberous roots attached to it. The Juno iris is an example. It is quite different from the more generally known bulbous irises—the English and Dutch irises of the catalogues—which are true bulbs. The long, fleshy roots of ismene bulbs persist through the dormant period (in the ground or in perfect winter storage) and are important in aiding the new growth. To a less extent, the same is true of many lilies.

Rhizomes

Forming a sort of halfway link between tubers and perennial roots are rhizomes. A rhizome consists of solid tissue (stem tissue), but instead of being rounded in shape, like a tuber, it is elongated and often branching. In some cases—as with bearded irises and rex begonias—rhizomes grow just in or along the surface of the soil; in others—calla-lily and Solomon's-seal, for instance—the rhizomes form underground. Another characteristic of most rhizomes is that the roots develop along the lower surface, while the leaves and flower stalks rise from buds (eyes) on the upper surface.

So you see that the term "bulb" as employed in the trade, and

Rhizomes of calla-lilies during dormant period after foliage has matured and died. Flower buds will develop with new leaf growth.

even by many gardeners, really covers several groups of plants, many of which are not, accurately speaking, bulbs at all. They do have some common characteristics. The most important of these, from the gardener's viewpoint, is this: in their resting or dormant period they become self-contained bits of suspended plant life that will survive for weeks or months without benefit of soil or moisture. They thus lend themselves particularly well to being transported long distances or stored for long periods with little attention.

When—after the proper resting period—soil, moisture, and a congenial temperature are provided, they are ready and eager to take up active growth again and reward the gardener's efforts with beauty in a thousand forms and many colors, and at any season of the year you may elect to have them serve.

But just as there are *structural* differences among true bulbs, corms, tubers, tuberous roots, and rhizomes, there are also differences in the *way they grow* during their life cycles. And so our next step, in progressing toward the goal of achieving success with bulbs, is to get some understanding of their habits, and particularly of *what goes on underground* during the periods when ordinarily we give them no thought or attention. And that is quite as fascinating, if not as spectacular, as what goes on above it.

CHAPTER 5. *How Bulbs Grow*

Plants adapt themselves to the conditions under which they have to grow. This is not to say that if you set out in a hot dry place a plant that ordinarily grows in a bog it will at once change its structure and its method of life to conform to its new environment. On the contrary, it will probably perish quickly.

But by gradual evolution during hundreds or thousands of years, each species has developed a structure and a time for growing and for resting which fit into the conditions of soil, moisture, temperature and seasonal changes that constitute its natural habitat.

The changes which the plant undergoes from the time it starts into active growth until it begins again the following year are known as its *growth cycle*. The growth cycle includes what happens underground and even the changes which may take place within the plant itself, as well as those obvious changes which you see taking place before your eyes aboveground.

These changes are far more extensive than the gardener is likely to suspect. When we carelessly speak of a plant's being in a "dormant" state, we usually mean that it is not making any visible growth aboveground. But its roots may be in active growth, and most important changes may be going on in its physical structure and in its chemical composition. Perhaps you have noticed the difference between a branch of a flowering shrub in late fall, when it enters its so-called dormant period, and the same branch, still "dormant," just before its buds break into leaf or flower. You may also have observed that the same spray, cut and placed in water indoors, in December will remain dormant for many weeks; while cut in March or April it will—often within a matter of days—burst into bloom. What has happened during the interim? The growth cycle, in nature's secret, potent ways, has continued at work.

Placing a bulb in the ground, you think of it as a dormant thing which can be forgotten until next spring, when—according to the

Stages in development of a hyacinth grown in plain water. Embryo flower spike, already formed within bulb, draws its sustenance from the bulb.

habit of bulbs—it will start to grow. What really happens is something quite different. When planted, it immediately sends out roots and, somewhat later, a stem or stems from the top. In most cases the top growth will remain safely underground until spring, although it may have pushed up several inches to a point just below the surface of the soil. Or, as with the familiar madonna lily, it may form a rosette of foliage in the fall that persists through the winter.

Not all bulbs, however, follow this pattern. Colchicums and autumn-flowering crocuses will often bloom without having been placed

A few weeks after gladiolus corms are lifted in autumn, the stalks should be sufficiently cured to be cut off close to the corms, as shown.

The old dried and shrivelled corms at the base of the new corms are useless for propagation or further growth, so are twisted off and discarded.

in the ground at all, even in a paper bag on a shelf. And if they are then planted they will produce roots, but sometimes no foliage until the following spring.

These infinitely varied growth patterns, could we trace them all back, would be found connected with the conditions existing where the various genera and species developed. In sections where summer months are hot and rainless, making vegetative growth impossible, they have come to adapt themselves to such conditions—like fenestrarias, the "windowed" plants of South Africa, which have learned to live largely underground, with merely a peephole to admit a sufficient amount of sunlight to keep them alive. In our own gardens, where we bring together bulbous plants from all over the world, we cannot expect to reproduce all the variations of soil, climate and treatment which best suit the individual genera and species. But the more we do know about their normal environments and growth habits, the closer we can approximate their maintenance in the style of living to which they are accustomed. Fortunately for us, most of them are willing to co-operate and strive to do their best under such conditions as we can provide.

METHODS OF REPRODUCTION

The annual growth cycle of a plant that lives for more than a year is but part of its longer life cycle from birth to death. This brings us to the matter of the method of *reproduction* employed—of how it perpetuates itself. Bulbs, corms, tubers, tuberous roots and rhizomes, under favorable conditions, can go on producing new plants asexually—that is, without the production of seeds. Some bulbs do this by "division"—that is, the original bulb splits up, forming small new bulbs which in time separate themselves from it. (The daffodil and the madonna lily are familiar examples of this type.) Others increase by "multiplication"—the old bulb or corm disintegrates, leaving in its place several new ones of various sizes. Tulips, crocuses and gladiolus are examples of this type.

In the case of some tubers, the old tuber disappears, leaving a cluster of new tubers in its place. This happens with stem tubers and root tubers—the white potato and the dahlia are examples. In others, such as the tuberous begonia and the gloxinia, the original tuber per-

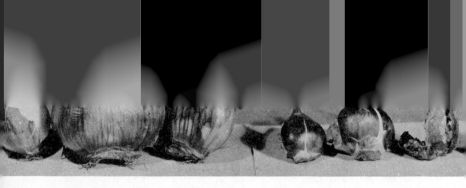

LEFT: *Original bulb of daffodil has produced two offsets or "splits" which readily separate from it.* RIGHT: *Original tulip bulb has disintegrated, leaving merely a husk; the three bulbs are* new *growths.*

sists, producing additional eyes but not splitting up to form separate new plants.

Rhizomes, during the annual growth cycle, may branch, each branch producing a new eye or growing tip; or they may continue as single horizontal fleshy roots, each year's new growth starting at the tip of the old rhizome. Bearded iris and false Solomon's-seal are examples of these two types.

Bulbils and Cormels

In addition to what we may term direct propagation from the bulbs, corms, or tubers planted in our gardens, there are other, indirect means by which the plants propagate themselves. The first of these, of course, is the production of seeds: but with that, for the moment, we are not concerned.

Some of the lilies, in addition to forming offsets underground, also develop secondary aerial bulbs, called *bulbils,* in the axils of the leaves. These sprout readily and, when grown on for a year or more, produce flowering-size bulbs. The tiger lily and certain of its offspring, like the Mid-Century Hybrids, are examples of this type of reproduction. Bulbils are occasionally formed also by tulips.

Cormels are miniature corms, formed at the ends of fleshy stems sent out from the base of a corm. They are pointed, hard-shelled, and quite different from the new corms which form at the surface of the old one. Like bulbils, they must be grown on for at least one season before being capable of producing a flower. The gladiolus is a typical cormel bearer.

Very small tulip bulbs (left) produce merely one big leaf, no flower. The following season they will bloom and begin to form new bulbs, as at right.

Clump of daffodils toward end of season's growth. Foliage still attached, but at this stage they can be lifted, separated, and replanted.

IMPORTANCE OF FOLIAGE DEVELOPMENT

Attention has already been called to the fact that many of the true bulbs, especially those flowering in early spring, contain completely formed flowers when they are planted in autumn. (See page 48.) The food supply to support the amazingly rapid growth and production of flowers in the spring is drawn largely from the bulb. The same is true of early-flowering tubers and corms.

With such plants as these, the growth cycle is not drawing to a close when they reach the flowering stage. It is, in fact, just getting into its stride. The production of the following spring's bloom depends entirely on what happens *after* this spring's flowering.

The foliage constitutes the factory in which is processed the food to be stored up in the growing bulbs, corms, or tubers. If the foliage is not allowed to mature, or if it is starved for lack of adequate nourishment in the soil, the growing bulb underground is bound to suffer as a result.

GROWTH CYCLES

Growth cycles, in diagrammatic form, of a few typical bulbs, corms, and tubers are presented on the following pages: 136, 165, 174, 201, 223, 232, 247, 259, 263, and 284.

CHAPTER *6. Cultural Requirements*

The horticultural varieties of bulbs, many of which are of such mixed ancestry that no one knows just what species and sub-species went into their making, are of course better adapted to uniform garden conditions than are the original wild kinds from which they have descended. Most of the tulip species, for instance, will thrive in soil so dry that their giant-flowered descendants would languish and perhaps perish if planted alongside them.

But bulbs are, on the whole, extremely adaptable to growing under widely diversified conditions. Tulips, daffodils, hyacinths, crocuses and a host of others gladden the hearts of winter-weary gardeners from Maine to British Columbia, and from far above the Canadian border down to our southernmost states, where temperatures do not go low enough to provide the required period in cold ground during which root systems are developed before the tops make growth. Dahlias, originally from Mexico, and gladiolus, hailing from South Africa, thrive side by side over the same areas.

Notwithstanding their general tolerance of growth conditions, however, they do have individual preferences and also vary greatly in their tolerance of conditions other than those under which they will do their best. As you become a wise bulb gardener, you will learn to depend upon the species and varieties which really like the conditions you can provide. At the same time you will find it worthwhile to grow some of the others, both for their intrinsic beauty and for the thrill which any gardener feels in bringing through a difficult subject.

Soil

So far as the physical character of soil is concerned, the majority of bulbs are less particular than many other plants. With few exceptions they do well in fairly heavy clay, loam, or sandy loam, provided the proper nutrients are available. The preferred soil for most bulbs, however, is a medium sandy loam, which does not remain wet and sticky after heavy rains, nor, on the other hand, dry out too quickly. The relatively small areas usually required for bulb plantings—except where they are naturalized on a relatively large scale—can readily be brought to a condition that will result in good normal growth.

A traditional treatment for heavy clay soils has been the addition of sifted cinders, such as will pass through a ¾-inch screen. (Softcoal ashes, which form a soggy mass when wet, only aggravate the condition instead of improving it.) However, since few homes burn coal today, the cinder supply is limited. Very coarse sand or fine gravel serves the same purpose as the cinders. A layer of at least 2 inches, and preferably more, should be dug in. A more thorough job of mixing will result if half the amount is spread and dug well under and the balance then spread and cultivated in.

The chief trouble with light sandy soils is that they dry out too quickly. The basic treatment here is to add quantities of organic matter, such as well-rotted stable manure, leafmold, seaweed, compost, or peat moss. All of these are moisture holders and help greatly in maintaining an adequate supply of water in sandy soils. Any of them can be applied in a layer 3 inches or so deep and forked in to a depth of 8 inches. These humus-forming materials are also valuable in improving clay soils, making them more open.

The physical condition of both clay soils and sandy soils is bettered by the addition of ground raw limestone (agricultural lime). The only condition, in our experience, where lime will not prove beneficial is on alkaline soil (with a pH of 7 or over) in which plants that prefer such a soil are to be grown.

Drainage

Tolerant or indifferent though most bulbs may be as to soils, when it comes to *drainage* it is quite a different story. With very few exceptions they simply refuse to do well in soils that retain a water level close to the surface. Water that the roots can reach is all right—as witness the bulb fields of Holland with their drainage ditches maintaining a water level at a fixed depth below the surface; or the more familiar example of a hyacinth growing in a vase filled with water just *up to* the base of the bulb, or 'Paperwhite' narcissus in pebbles that hold them just above the water in the bottom.

Any place in your garden that remains wet for long periods after rain, or becomes more or less of a bog during winter and early spring, is no place for the general run of bulbs.

The task of remedying poor drainage conditions is often more difficult than that of improving the soil. If possible, it is better to sidestep it by planting bulbs only where the drainage is naturally good. If this cannot be done, you may as well face the fact that you have a difficult job on your hands—and then do it thoroughly to start with. Such makeshift efforts as putting a handful of sand under each bulb, as is frequently advised, will accomplish little or nothing. Even excavating the soil to a depth of 2 or 3 feet and putting in a layer of small stones or some similar drainage material may prove to be wasted effort, for unless the water which collects in the space thus provided can drain off to some lower level, nothing is gained.

The first step in correcting poor drainage is to discover its cause. It may be due to a layer of hardpan—compacted clay subsoil—through which surplus water from the topsoil above cannot percolate. Often it is possible to break up such a hardpan subsoil with a pick, thus permitting the water to pass down to more open soil below. The most certain method of correcting poor drainage, however, is to install drain tile as described in the following chapter.

Sun and Shade

Most of the spring-flowering bulbs like full sun—the more the better. This does not, however, restrict their planting to areas that are in full sun the year round. As they bloom before deciduous trees and shrubs have donned summer raiment, they get plenty of sun at this season of the year even in locations where there may be considerable shade later on. This is not the case under evergreens or to the north or northwest of hedges, buildings, or fences. The *foliage* will continue to develop, after the flowering season, with a little direct sunshine; but shade so dense that it results in thin, weak foliage is of course to be avoided.

The majority of summer-flowering bulbous plants—dahlia, gladiolus, glory-lily, most true lilies—require as much sunshine as possible, but happily for those who must do their gardening on a partially shaded terrace or must contend with some hours of shade in their gardening areas, there are beautiful tuberous begonias, whose flowers

Hyacinths flowering at the base of an ornamental crabapple.

mimic roses and camellias, and caladiums, with foliage colorations more brilliant than many flowers. Then there are any number of summer-blooming gesneriads (the family that includes African-violets)—gloxinia (*Sinningia*), achimenes, the dainty temple bells (*Smithiantha*) and cardinal flower (*Rechsteineria cardinalis*)—which prefer the "high" shade described below.

The gardener should learn that there is a great difference, so far as plant growth is concerned, between "high" shade and "low" shade. The foliage of many types of plants will function normally without direct sunshine if the *light* is sufficiently strong. To get an idea of the difference there is between high shade—from branches well above the ground—and low shade, under shrubs or low-growing tree branches, make a few tests with your camera light meter. You will find the light reading from two to five times as high under the former condition as under the latter. The growth of the plants themselves, however, is the surest test. If the foliage remains vigorous and green until it matures and the second year's flowering of spring bulbs seems all right, you can be pretty sure you have nothing to worry about.

Another advantage of high shade is the much better air circulation near the surface of the ground. Bulbs, in common with most other plants, like to breathe freely. A confined, dead atmosphere not only makes them unhappy, but also creates conditions favorable for many diseases, especially blights and mildews.

A list of bulbs which prefer some shade, or at least tolerate it, will be found on page 343. Check also the list of bulbs for woodland conditions that follows it.

Protection

In the culture of many bulbous plants, protection in one form or another is very important. It may be needed for purely mechanical reasons, to keep flower stems from being broken or knocked down by high winds, and to prevent low-growing flowers from being disfigured by spattering mud.

Or protection against too low temperatures may be required for kinds that, in any particular locality, are on the questionably hardy list. In the latter case it will enable you to grow a number of very desirable, attractive subjects that otherwise would be too uncertain to be worthwhile.

Fortunately the early spring-flowering bulbs leave the gardener little to worry about so far as the frost-hardiness of buds and flowers is concerned. We have had snowdrops, blooming in late January, come out as cheerful and smiling as ever after nearly a month's incarceration in frozen snow and ice. Even daffodils in bloom have reappeared, uninjured, from under a fleecy blanket of April snow.

Mechanical injury from driving March and April storms is another

The popular Easter lily (Lilium longiflorum), *sold by florists as a pot plant, can later be set out in the garden where it should give many seasons of late spring flowers. A variegated form of a shrubby dogwood is at the right of the lilies.*

matter. Protection by low evergreens or shrubs, a hedge or a fence, will frequently save tall tulips or daffodils from being damaged when those in the open take a beating or are completely wrecked.

Ground covers of growing plants and mulches of various sorts provide a degree of protection against low temperatures for bulbs that are on the danger line as to winter-hardiness. They also minimize the alternate freezing and thawing of the surface soil, which in bare ground will sometimes damage newly planted small bulbs that are not covered deep and may be literally heaved out onto the surface. The greatest value of ground covers and mulches, however, is that they provide a background against which the little bulbs show up to greater advantage and prevent the mud-spattering from heavy rains that so frequently disfigures them.

The lilies—a most important group among bulbous plants—appreciate protection of another sort: they benefit by having a not-too-dense carpet of creeping or low-growing plants about their feet through which the flowering stalks can push up to the light and air. Such ground covers—or, in place of them, a suitable permanent mulch—will keep the soil about the roots several degrees cooler than it would be if fully exposed to the sun.

This drift of daffodils is set off by a peaceful stream in the background. The variety is 'Scarlett O'Hara', a beautifully colored daffodil highly recommended as a cutflower.

Plate 1

A joy of the spring garden near the house is that the flowers can be appreciated from indoors, an advantage during inclement weather.

Plate 2

Plate 3

All the major spring bulbs—daffodils, tulips, hyacinths, crocuses—make cheering pot subjects for indoor windows at a time when winter-weary gardeners need evidence that spring is near. If daffodils and hyacinths mature properly, the bulbs may be set outdoors later.

Plate 4

Whether seen in vast drifts as in this meadow or in scattered groups in a rock garden, in soil pockets in a terrace or at the edge of a woodland path, the yellow hoop petticoat daffodil Narcissus bulbocodium is an eye catcher despite its diminutive size.

Plate 5

Daffodils are suited to almost any garden situation. Here trumpet daffodils decorate a board fence. The variety is 'Music Hall'.

Plate 6

Indicative of the great range in size and form among daffodils are the giant trumpet 'Golden Harvest' and the dainty species, N. minimus.

Plate 7

'Irena Baranova', a well-proportioned daffodil in the large cup class.
Plate 8

In the entire circle of the year's garden operations there is none more pleasurable than that of planting hardy bulbs. Here indeed are happily met the time, the place and the undertaking. And added to these is the assurance that one's efforts will end in success. In no other type of gardening can the operator be quite so certain that the results of his work will come up to his expectations.

On one of those crisp, sunny autumn days, you gather up your bags of bulbs—each with its previously prepared label—your strongest trowel, and other favorite tools. Then begins the happy ritual of getting into the ground these little brown and tan bombs, of various shapes and sizes, which, with the coming of spring, each in accord with its own built-in timing device, will explode into a pattern of heart-lifting beauty.

It is to be assumed that your ground has been prepared well in advance and your bulbs ordered sufficiently early so that they are now on hand. Then you can pick your weather for planting and do as much or as little of it at one time as you prefer. The planting period extends from mid-August until the ground freezes too hard to be dug. This will vary, in normal seasons, from mid-October in the general latitude of New York, Cleveland, or Kansas City to two or three weeks earlier farther north, and several weeks later farther south and along the Pacific Coast.

Some bulbs—such as the madonna lily, autumn-flowering crocus, colchicum, and winter-aconite—are available considerably in advance of the general run of tulips, daffodils, and small-flowered spring bulbs. With few exceptions—tulips being the most important one—it is best, as a general rule, to get the bulbs into the ground as soon as possible after receiving them.

In any event, all bulbs, corms, or tubers should be opened immediately upon receipt and carefully examined. If complaints are to be made, now is the time to make them. Bulbs purchased from a reputable dealer, at a fair price, seldom give any cause for dissatisfaction. If they cannot be planted for a week or longer, keep the bags containing them in flats or on a shelf in a cool, well-ventilated place where the air is not dried out by artificial heat. If the only storage place available is very dry, keep the bags covered with moist peat moss or wet newspapers. *Any condition causing the bulbs to shrivel will injure them.* Any cut or bruised bulbs should be immediately dusted with sulphur, captan, or some similar fungicide. Rats, mice, and squirrels are extremely fond of most bulbs. (Daffodils are an exception to this rule.) Protection from rodents is necessary, therefore, when bulbs are stored for even a short period.

START WITH GOOD BULBS

Before discussing the actual planting of the bulbs, let us take a moment to consider the question of the *quality*. What constitutes a good bulb, and how is it to be distinguished from a poor one?

Of course there *are* such things as bulb bargains, just as there are sometimes bargains in most of the other things one buys. But "bargain bulbs" are something else again, and the gardener will do well to mark the distinction clearly.

Genuine savings in bulbs may be had by taking advantage of pre-season offers from reliable dealers. The logical reason for such offers is that it actually costs the dealer less to handle your order. Advance orders help him to determine accurately what quantities of bulbs to buy, and sizable orders can be packed by the grower before shipping, thus saving the dealer the expense of rehandling them. And one can often buy small-sized bulbs (but large enough to bloom) at lower prices than top-sized ones. But usually these are available only in mixtures and will not produce top-size flowers the first season.

Another opportunity to get good bulbs at a bargain sometimes comes late in the season, when reliable dealers find themselves with surpluses to dispose of. Such bulbs may or may not be in first-class condition—but you, the buyer, can pretty well determine that if you can actually see and handle the bulbs. With many kinds, such as tulips, daffodils, hyacinths and crocuses, you can even see if they will flower. A perpendicular cut through the center of the bulb will reveal the embryo flower, completely formed. If it is blackened, dried up, or lacking, although the bulb may grow, there will be no bloom from it the first year. (See illustration, page 48.)

Bargain bulbs—the kind offered at absurdly low prices in extravagant newspaper and magazine advertising during the height of the planting season—are sometimes an uncertain commodity and the buyer should beware!

What Makes a Good Bulb?

The quality—and the value—of a bulb does not depend upon size alone. There are cases in which size is a controlling factor in what you will get for your money, but these are exceptions to the general rule. Assuming that a bulb of a given species or variety is of a size capable of producing normal flowers, the other factors affecting its "goodness" are:

Firmness: The layers of tissue or the scales, if it is a true bulb (such as a tulip, daffodil, or lily), or the flesh, if it is a tuber, corm, or rhizome (such as a dahlia, crocus, or calla), should be plump and fairly hard. In the case of true bulbs, the layers or scales should be firmly adpressed, so that there is little or no feeling of squashiness or looseness when it is compressed in the hand.

Weight: Most good bulbs present a distinct effect of being fairly heavy. This of course goes along with firmness, but even bulbs (of the same kind, of course) that feel equally firm may vary considerably in weight.

Condition: The skin or coating (in the case of tulips, hyacinths, and others) should be smooth, bright, and free from mechanical injuries. Some varieties of tulips shed their coats readily, and if the flesh beneath is not badly bruised, no injury may result; but as a rule badly skinned bulbs have been carelessly handled and will show corky spots or even fungus growth on the scales. Such are to be avoided.

With most bulbs, the base or basal plate (the corky layer or disk at the base, which holds the layers or scales together) is most likely to show injury from disease—such as the basal rot of daffodils. Any indication of trouble here means that the bulb may rot or disintegrate after it is planted. Mechanical injuries (cuts or bruises) will usually heal without diseases gaining a foothold if dusted with flowers of sulphur, captan or other fungicides.

The quality of any bulb depends, first, upon how it was grown; secondly, upon how it is handled after harvesting. Assuming good, true-to-name stocks to start with, careful culture and a reasonably favorable season will produce good bulbs. But after they are once removed from the ground, almost anything can happen. Improper or careless curing may result in soft or even diseased bulbs. Overheating in transit, as in the hold of a vessel, or poor storage facilities may blast the embryo flower, so that the bulb, while it will grow, fails to produce a bloom the first season after planting.

Then there is the matter of grading. Imported bulbs of most species are graded on a basis of centimeters (cm.) in circumference. In catalogues they are often listed as "top size"—a rather loosely applied term. Really top-size tulips, for instance, are 11 to 12 cm. for some types and varieties and 12 cm. or over for others. Extra-size bulbs are larger than top or first size. As a rule, it is best to know the centimeter size if one is ordering by mail. Species and hybrids of many bulbs—tulips and daffodils in particular—are not graded by circumference because the normal bulb sizes vary so greatly that such grading would mean little.

Bulbs of many kinds will flower satisfactorily even though smaller than extra, top, or first size. Sometimes these are offered as "bedding" size. With hyacinths, for instance, the largest bulbs (18 cm. and over) are less desirable for garden planting than the "miniatures" (14 to 15 cm.) and the bedding (16 to 17 cm.). The very large bulbs are used for show purposes (usually forced) and produce very tall, dense spikes that under garden conditions are readily broken by wind or rain and are much less graceful than the more slender and more open spikes of the same varieties from smaller bulbs.

The proper handling, curing, packing and transporting of bulbs constitute a large part of the cost of getting them into the hands of the gardener in first-class condition. This should be kept in mind by the purchaser when making a comparison of price.

PROVIDING PERFECT DRAINAGE

In discussing the cultural requirements of bulbs, we stressed the fact that, with very few exceptions, one of the most important is thorough drainage.

ABOVE: *When you buy bulbs, consider quality. Here are good tulip bulbs (left) compared to "bargain" bulbs costing exactly the same.* RIGHT: *The result: one puny flower from the 100 "bargain" bulbs; an armful from the top-size ones.* BELOW: *And the harvest: from the top-sized bulbs, more than twice as many as were planted; from the bargain bulbs, fewer than were planted—and all runts.*

If the only space available for planting bulbs lies low and cannot be sufficiently well drained, two courses are open. The first is to raise a bed or border 6 to 12 inches above the general soil level, the sides being held in place by stones, railroad ties, boards, sod, bricks, or thin cement blocks.

The second method is to install drainage tile. A single line of 4-inch agricultural tile placed 18 to 24 inches below the surface will drain an area 10 to 20 feet wide if the soil above the tile is fairly porous. The drain tiles (available at any building-supply house) are laid end to end with open joints. The drainage ditch is dug with a slope, from the highest point to the exit from which the water will run off, with a pitch of 6 inches or more to 100 feet. A layer of sand, gravel, or cinders along the bottom of the trench makes it easier to lay the tile on a uniformly even slope. Strips of tar paper or of old burlap bags placed over the joints prevent soil from silting into the tile after the trench is filled in. Test the system before refilling to make certain that everything is working properly. If there is no low spot to which the water from the tile can drain off, it may be necessary to dig a dry well—merely a wide, deep hole filled with stones, with a layer of soil over the surface—into which it can flow.

It is not often that any of these measures for improving drainage will have to be resorted to. They have been given emphasis because, in the growing of bulbs, inadequate drainage, where it is encountered, may be the one obstacle preventing success.

SOIL PREPARATION

Preparation of the soil for growing bulbs differs little from that of preparing it for vegetables, roses or perennials. The soil should be in good mechanical condition, so it will readily admit water and air and be well supplied with such nutrients (plant foods) as are needed to support vigorous growth.

There are, however, two respects in which the ordinary procedure of preparing soil for planting may have to be departed from.

The first of these is in the use of animal manure. Unless it is so thoroughly decomposed as to have become humus, *animal manure should never be used where it will come into contact with dormant bulbs, tubers, or corms in the soil.* Also, manure should not be used

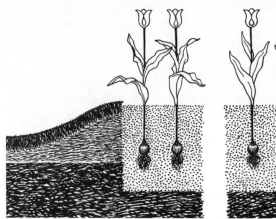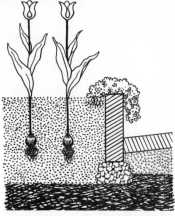

Two methods of making a raised bed on poorly drained soil: left, with turf; right, with edging of boards, brick, blocks, stones, or railroad ties.

as a mulch over any bulbous plants subject to botrytis or fungus diseases. This applies particularly to tulips and to lilies, the two groups most frequently injured seriously by botrytis.

The second is the possibility of having the soil too rich. Most horticultural varieties of bulbs—types or clones which have been developed through the years—accept a rich diet or may even insist upon it. The familiar giant May-flowering tulips are an example; to produce solid top-size bulbs from year to year, they must be grown in heavily fertilized soil. Many of the natural species, however, do better with a moderate or even a rather lean diet. Overfed, they may be injured and in any event are not improved, for their charm lies largely in their delicately refined proportions.

The chances are that your soil is already in good condition for planting bulbs—that is, it is friable and well supplied with humus and plant food from previous gardening efforts. If your property is brand-new or if you are to make a border in soil that formerly grew grass or other cultivated or uncultivated plants, more elaborate preparations are needed than merely spreading fertilizers over the ground's surface, lightly forking them in and planting the bulbs.

The first step in preparing a new garden area is to mark out the outlines of the border and then clean off the surface debris, if any exists. If this debris consists of overgrown weeds, which could be the case in summer or early fall, several passes over the area with a rotary mower (set the cutting height low) should chop up the weeds after which they can be raked, gathered and thrown on the compost heap. If the area has been under grass, you will want to skim off the sod, an inch or so deep, leaving bare ground. The turf can also go into your compost heap, the best place for it unless it is topnotch lawn grass, in which case save it to surface the sides of the bed, if it is to be a raised one, as illustrated on page 71.

Some new gardens must be prepared in areas that are covered with brush or woody growth, making preparation of the soil a more arduous task. Such a situation calls for heavy gloves, strong pruning shears and sturdy hand tools to hack out the intertwining roots and stems.

You are now ready to cultivate the soil and unless the area under preparation is of limited size or you especially enjoy digging soil by hand, by far the easiest and quickest way is to use a rototiller. Even if you don't own one, the possibilities for obtaining one on a temporary basis are good—either from a friendly neighbor or on a rental basis from a garden center or lawn mower dealer.

After working over the soil as many times as needed with the rototiller, the fertilizers and humus-forming materials recommended below can be spread over the surface. A second, thorough tilling will mix these ingredients with the soil; after a raking to even the surface, the area should be ready for planting.

The following directions are for those who prefer to prepare their soil with a spade or fork—some gardeners like the former implement and some the latter.

Dig the bed over to a depth of 8 inches or more. To do a good job, remove all soil from a strip 12 inches wide across one end of the bed, leaving an open trench. Turn the next strip over into this, inverting it, breaking up lumps, and throwing stones and roots to the surface. This will leave a second open trench into which the next strip can be turned. This procedure is continued to the end of the plot or border being prepared, leaving an open trench at that end. Next stones and roots are removed and the surface roughly leveled. A prong hoe is better than a rake for this job, as it will catch any debris down to 3 inches or more below the surface and is more convenient for breaking up any remaining clods of soil.

After this first digging, any manures, humus materials, or fertilizers to be used are spread on the surface. The bed is then dug over again, in the reverse direction, but to the same depth. This mixes the added materials thoroughly through the soil and *gets them down deep,* where the bulb roots will be searching for food. This second digging will go quickly and leave the soil loose and mellow, so that the work of planting will be a pleasant task, accomplished in a small part of the time it would take in hard, ill-prepared ground.

Humus and Fertilizers

In addition to having the soil in good mechanical condition for planting, we need of course to provide the ingredients—plant foods and plant-food activators—that will enable them to make vigorous growth.

Humus: There are very few soils, either clay, loam, or sandy, which are not materially improved by the addition of a large amount of humus or of humus-forming materials. Real compost—not soggy, half-rotted leaves and grass clippings—is ideal, but seldom is the compost heap sufficiently large to supply the quantity needed. Well-rotted animal manure is even better, but that, in most sections, can be difficult to procure, unless you live near a dairy farm or neighbors who keep a few riding horses. The material most widely available and most uniform in quality is horticultural-grade peat moss. This we have used for years in the preparation of bulb beds and have yet to find anything better. The ordinary application is a layer 2 to 3 inches thick, spread evenly over the surface, then dug into the existing soil. Rotted animal manure can go on at the same rate.

Lime: Like humus, lime is not considered a direct plant-food element, but—in common with humus—its addition to the soil usually results in more vigorous growth. This is due both to improvement of the mechanical condition of the soil, and to making more available for use by plants the chemicals already in the soil. *The use of lime is generally beneficial even when it is not required to make the soil less acid.* If a soil test shows reaction of less than pH 6, it should be used to reduce the acidity, except for bulbs which require a definitely acid soil.

The form of lime generally employed, and the one which should be used when applied at the same time with fertilizers or just before bulbs are to be planted, is raw ground limestone, commonly known as agricultural lime. The rate of application is 5 to 15 pounds per 100 square feet. If a large area is to be covered, it is well to use a mechanical spreader such as those available for fertilizing lawns.

Fertilizers: Bulbs, like other types of plants, require the three essential elements—nitrogen, phosphoric acid, and potash—and the minor or trace elements which, in most soils, are available in sufficient amounts.

In general, we prefer to use organic fertilizers rather than chemical ones for bulbous plants, especially when preparing the soil for planting. However, all-purpose, commercial fertilizers, such as 5–10–5 or 5–10–10, can also be used, and have the advantage of supplying all nutrients needed by plants in one application.

Nitrogen, for bulbs planted in the fall, is relatively less important than for most bulbs or plants set out in spring. In soil which has been under culture during the summer—as in the hardy border—there is likely to be a sufficient residue. In newly prepared ground, manure (if it has been applied) or one of the commercial dehydrated manures—available in nurseries and garden centers—will provide all that is needed. There is also a small amount of nitrogen (about 2 to 4 per cent) in bone meal, used principally to supply phosphoric acid. Nitrate of soda, dried blood, and other quick-acting high-nitrogen fertilizers, excellent for many purposes, not only are unnecessary but will be largely wasted if used in fall bulb planting. Apply dehydrated manures at the rate of a minimum of 10 pounds per 100 square feet, and two or three times that amount on poor soil.

Phosphoric acid can be supplied by bone meal or superphosphate. Bone meal, a favorite of organic gardeners, is slower acting than superphosphate and also contains a small percentage of nitrogen. There are good reasons for using either of these fertilizers. It should be noted that the slower release of nutrients from bone meal is an advantage when such bulbs as daffodils, tulips and hyacinths are likely to remain in the same place for many years. We have always used bone meal, applying it at the rate of 5 pounds per 100 square feet. Superphosphate can be applied at the rate of 3 to 4 pounds per 100 square feet. When planting large bulbs individually, allow a very scant handful of either fertilizer per generous hole, mixing it thoroughly with the existing soil before placing the bulb.

Potassium is of particular value in providing strong stems and good flowers and also in developing firm, heavy bulbs for the following year. Unleached wood ashes and tobacco stems supply potash in moderate amounts—(3 or 4 per cent) and can be used generously—up to 15 pounds or more per 100 square feet. As ashes are not al-

Planting in groups: soil is dug out to proper depth, bulbs placed irregularly, hole filled, area marked off, labels put in place.

ways available, the usual source of potassium is muriate of potash. This contains 50 per cent of potassium and is applied sparingly—½ to 1 pound per 100 square feet. In most soils there will be sufficient potash present for the initial root growth, and this element can be provided in the general fertilizer applied the following spring.

Our own method of fertilizing new beds before planting is to apply (after the first rough cultivation) the lime, bone meal, and wood ashes, finishing up with the dried manure, and then forking these all in deep. If the soil is dry and planting is not to be done at once, the bed is given a thorough watering to settle it and to start the breaking-down of the fertilizer materials in the soil. If chemical fertilizers (5–10–5, 5–10–10, or similar) are employed, soil preparation and watering well in advance of planting are even more important. Apply 5–10–5 fertilizer at the rate of 3 pounds to 100 square feet.

In preparing spots for group plantings, much the same procedure is followed, but on a smaller scale. Where bulbs are to be naturalized in very poor soil, it may be advisable to loosen it by thrusting in a fork and working it back and forth to open up small holes. The plant foods are then spread on the surface and washed in as thoroughly as possible with a heavy watering.

PLANTING

There are two methods of actually getting the bulbs into the ground. The first is to remove the soil to the desired depth, set the bulbs in place on the exposed surface, and then replace the soil.

Planting in formal or display beds: soil is removed, bottom leveled and marked off, and bulbs placed in exact design.

Planting from surface: soil is prepared to proper depth, bulbs spaced as wanted. Bulbs are planted individually, beginning with those nearest the operator.

The second is to make a hole in the soil, with trowel or dibber, for each individual bulb, placing it at the bottom and then filling in soil over it.

The former method, which was in vogue when tulips and hyacinths found favor in formal landscaping for the creation of "design" gardens laid out in geometrical patterns of contrasting colors, is now seldom practiced. In making designs it was important that all the bulbs should be spaced at accurately regular distances and flower at the same height and at the same time. Excavation planting (see photograph, page 76) assured such results. In the more informal landscaping of today, in mixed borders, decorative groups, and naturalized plantings, such uniformity is not only unnecessary but distinctly undesirable.

Whether excavation or surface planting is to be done, each lot of bulbs should be laid out before the actual planting is begun. For a formal bed, it is helpful to prepare a planting stick, with notches or pegs the desired distances apart for accurate spacing. For an informal planting as in a mixed border, the spacing may be estimated, and results are more pleasing if any regular pattern is avoided. In naturalizing, best effects are achieved by scattering the bulbs more or less at random, somewhat closer together at the center, or at one side of the colony, and thinning out toward the edge, as though they had spread from an original small group.

Depth

The depth to which the bulbs are covered varies with species and varieties, with the soil, with the exposure, and to some extent with how one wants them to behave. Details may be found under the notes on individual genera and species.

Here are some general rules to follow where more definite information is lacking.

Planting depth (from *top* of bulb to soil level): 2 to 3 times greatest diameter of bulb for large bulbs—2 or more inches in diameter; 3 to 4 times greatest diameter of small bulbs.

Distance apart: for large bulbs, 1½ to 2 times the planting depth; for small bulbs, 2 to 3 times the planting depth.

In light sandy soils, planting may well be somewhat deeper—an inch or two—than in average soil, especially in sunny exposures. Ex-

Planting hyacinth bulbs in the fall around a flowering crab-apple. The bulbs are spaced about 6 inches apart and covered with 5–6 inches of soil.

tra-deep planting will delay flowering to a slight extent but not nearly so long as has been claimed. Planting in a northern exposure is a much more effective way to delay flowering. Gardeners who make something of a specialty of exhibiting daffodils, for instance, can well make two plantings of important varieties, thus extending the period of bloom of each sort for a week or more.

With the soil well prepared—as it always should be—before planting is begun, the best tool for planting is a trowel, or trowels, for more than one shape of trowel will be found convenient if bulbs of different types are being set out. The large-bladed trowel with a long one-piece shank is best for large bulbs such as tulips, daffodils, hyacinths, and lilies, while a narrow-bladed trowel is much handier for small bulbs. Notches cut in the trowel handles, indicating varying depths from the soil's surface to the tip of the trowel, are helpful in planting. However, after all that has been said about planting depths —and more will be said under discussions of individual bulbs—the exact planting depth is not as critical as might be supposed! Bulbs seem to be able to adjust to almost any depth—within reason—at which they are planted.

For planting in turf, various kinds of planters can be found in garden centers which remove a circular piece of sod and a core of soil beneath it. After the bulb is planted, soil and sod can be returned. Under certain conditions these can be useful tools.

If the soil is newly prepared and loose, it may be advisable to use a wide piece of board on which to stand or kneel when distributing the bulbs and planting. With a pointed stick the area for each variety can be marked off. The label is then put in place and the bulbs distributed on the surface. Planting then proceeds, working from the front to the back of the area, so that any packing of the soil occurs over bulbs already planted.

A word about labels may not be amiss at this point. Most bulbs will remain for many years, and the time to provide *permanent* labels is when they are planted. Ordinary wood labels are likely to be heaved out of the soil during the first few weeks after planting, and even if they last until spring, it is almost certain that many of them will be broken off. Substantial metal labels cost more but are well worth the difference.

If the soil is dry, by all means give a thorough watering as soon as planting is finished. Rapid development of roots will anchor the bulbs firmly in place and thus lessen the danger of injury by heaving during winter.

Mulching

Whether or not newly planted bulbs should be mulched is a much debated question. It cannot be answered by an unqualified "yes" or "no." Here are the facts upon which, in any particular case, to base your decision:

The really hardy bulbs—tulips, daffodils, crocuses, and the general run of early spring-blooming bulbs—do not need protection from hard freezing once they are established. If, however, they are planted very late, mulching is beneficial in two ways: it extends the period during which root growth can develop in the soil, and it keeps the surface of the soil frozen and thus prevents heaving. A mild winter, with alternate freezing and thawing, is more likely to be injurious to newly planted bulbs—and to other plants, for that matter—than a very severe one.

Another use for mulching is to *keep from freezing* ground that has been prepared for bulbs that cannot be obtained until late in the season—many of the hardy lilies, for instance. After the planting is done and the soil has frozen an inch or two, the mulch can be replaced, but it should be removed in spring before growth starts.

For sorts that are not reliably hardy, mulching is of course desirable. The cluster-flowered (polyanthus) types of daffodil (*Narcissus tazetta*), galtonia, montbretia, bulbous irises, anemone, and ranunculus can, by providing thorough mulching, be grown outdoors in many sections where usually they are not grown. (See pages 256–60, and 295.)

CAUTION: In any event, however, mulching should never be put on over newly planted bulbs until the soil has frozen an inch or so deep. Otherwise it affords an ideal place for mice, shrews and other rodents to nest, thus providing them with both board and lodging in one convenient package.

As to materials for mulching bulbs, we consider evergreen boughs (used or leftover Christmas trees are one source) at the top of the list. The branches are readily applied, lie flat, don't blow away, catch and hold light falls of snow, and present a pleasant appearance during most of the winter; and in spring they can be removed in a matter of minutes. Pine needles are excellent and of an unobtrusive color, as are also buckwheat hulls. Dry leaves will answer but usually must be held in place with branches and boards.

The fact has already been stressed that bulbs, corms and tubers are among the most easily grown of all decorative plants. There are, of course, some exceptions, and not every bulb will find everywhere conditions to its liking. The ease with which many bulbous flowers can be grown frequently leads to neglect by the gardener. If a plant can take care of itself, why bother?

Furthermore, much of the life of most bulbous plants goes on while the tops are dormant, and then it's the old story of "out of sight, out of mind."

But if you want your bulbs to provide their maximum beauty in the garden and in your home, then you must co-operate by giving them at least a reasonable amount of attention. So let us investigate what may be done to assure better than average blooms and to secure the permanence of your bulb plantings.

The first principle to be kept in mind, and one which cannot be stressed too often, is this:

Assure vigorous, healthy and well-matured growth of the foliage, and the flowers will take care of themselves.

Whatever you do in the way of culture, then, should be aimed at this objective. If you can produce a crop of good strong bulbs, the bulbs will produce the blooms. With bulbs that you buy and plant, the bulb grower has already done this job for you, so your first crop of flowers is assured. After that it is up to you.

CULTIVATION

For our first lesson in cultural requirements, let us go back to the humble onion. This succulent and delicious true bulb, which is usually grown from "sets" (small, immature bulbs), is considered one of the easiest and surest crops for the beginner *if* the plants are kept free of weeds. If they are not, the crop will be a failure no matter how rich the soil.

So the initial step in growing good bulbs is to make sure that they do not suffer from too much competition with weeds and grasses. As soon as the tops have made 3 or 4 inches of growth in the spring, the surface of the soil should be gone over lightly with a small hoe, or with a claw weeder, to break up the hard crust which may have formed during the winter and to destroy all sprouting weeds. As the spring-flowering bulbs make very rapid growth, one thorough cultivation is usually sufficient to keep them clean until the foliage shades the soil thoroughly. After flowering, they may need a second going over, but usually this is not required. The handiest tool we know of for cultivating among bulbs which grow close together and are spaced irregularly is the small triangular-bladed "all-purpose" hoe.

With tender bulbs planted in the spring, cultivation is given as soon as the plants are large enough to be readily distinguished. It should be repeated at intervals so long as weeds threaten serious competition.

Once planted, daffodil bulbs can be relied upon to flower spring after spring. Although new varieties are introduced each year, such old varieties as 'King Alfred' justly retain their popularity.

Even the smallest garden has space for a few spring bulbs, such as these early white fosteriana hybrid tulips. Pansies which like the same cool weather as spring bulbs are appropriate flowering companions.

FERTILIZING

Maintaining the food supply of most bulbs (other than those grown in pots as house plants) is an easy matter.

Our method with the hardy spring-flowering sorts grown in bulb beds or in a mixed border is to make one application in early spring, immediately after cultivation to eliminate weeds. If we get time for it, a second application is made in late summer or early autumn, when new roots are beginning to develop underground. We feel that the second application is desirable but not essential, especially if the plants have made normally vigorous growth after flowering.

The fertilizer we use is a mixture of three parts (by weight) of dehydrated manure, such as is available in garden centers, and one part of bone meal. This supplies nitrogen and phosphoric acid and a moderate amount of humus. It is scattered between the sprouting plants at the rate of 8 to 10 pounds per 100 square feet. To this is added once every two or three years, to maintain the potash content in the soil, wood ashes at the rate of 10 to 15 pounds per 100 square feet, or muriate of potash, 1 to 2 pounds per 100 square feet. In many soils, however, most bulbs will thrive without applications of potash.

Many bulb plantings are maintained in good condition with general-purpose chemical fertilizers, such as those with an analysis of 5–10–5, 5–10–10, or 4–12–4. Only in very exceptional cases is it necessary to use a quick-acting high-nitrogen fertilizer like tankage or nitrate of soda. If the foliage is weak in growth and lacking a healthy, normal green color, a nitrogen application may be advisable. Trying it first on a few plants in liquid form (one tablespoon of nitrate of soda to a 10-quart watering can) will indicate in the course of a few days, by the response of the plant, if the trouble is due to lack of nitrogen.

If any chemical fertilizer is used, exercise care to prevent it from lodging on the foliage where it can cause burning; or, better, give a thorough watering immediately after applying.

MULCHING

The advisability of mulching after planting has already been discussed. (See page 79.) This applies to mulching for winter protection. Mulching *as a part of general cultural practice* is quite another matter. In bulb literature other than that concerning lilies, there is little on this point. Even with lilies it is the desirability of using a ground cover of growing plants, rather than actual mulching materials, that is stressed.

Crocuses in bloom above a mulch of redwood chips. Although redwood chips usually must be purchased from garden centers, other mulching materials can often be collected locally.

So far as lilies are concerned, there is small doubt that mulching is beneficial. (See Chapter 15.) In regard to the hardy spring-flowering bulbs and summer-flowering bulbs in general, we feel certain that mulching could advantageously be used to a much greater extent than has been the general practice.

There are three distinct advantages to be derived from mulching: weed control, conservation of moisture and prevention of deface-ment of the flowers from mud spattering.

We have emphasized repeatedly the importance of *growing a good crop of foliage*. This applies to all types of bulbs, corms and tubers. Preventing the competition of weeds, which use plant foods, moisture and sunshine needed by the bulbs, is decidedly a step toward this end. Weeds can of course be controlled by cultivation, as they are in the commercial plantings of bulb growers. As bulbs are grown about the home, in borders, groups, or naturalized, cultivation is difficult and fraught with some danger of injury to the plants aboveground, or to roots below. Adequate mulching, which can easily be maintained year after year once it has been established, is an answer to the weed problem.

Soil under a mulch tends to remain moist. For most species of bul-bous plants, the amount of water received in home-garden plantings is more likely to be too little than too much. The few exceptions in-clude some of the wild species which, in their native habitats, get a real sun baking in the soil during a rainless period. (This applies es-pecially to many of the tulip species and to some of the bulbous irises.) But even with these a mulch can work both ways, for some materials prevent ordinary rains from penetrating the soil. We have never experienced unfavorable results with any of the bulbous plants we have mulched. If the drainage is what it should be, there is no need to fear excessive moisture from mulching.

Mulching materials are of many kinds. What the gardener will use depends largely upon what is available. In recent years we have leaned more and more to pine needles, which we can gather locally. They have the advantage of being easily applied, of "staying put," of remaining loose and open enough to admit water and air readily, and, having much the color of soil, are not conspicuous. A flaw is they can be favored as nesting headquarters by rodents. Buckwheat hulls, now generally available as a commercial mulch, have the same good qualities; no other commonly obtainable material makes quite so neat a mulch or more closely resembles good brown soil. Rough compost, about half decomposed, is good but may contain weed seeds that are still viable. We prefer digging this into the soil, in preparing beds for planting, rather than using it as a mulch.

Of quite different consistency, but also useful, are peat moss and *rotted* sawdust. The former, if put on too thickly, has the double disadvantage of becoming almost impervious to rain if it gets completely dry, and of tending to remain wet and soggy if it becomes thoroughly soaked. It is better when mixed into the soil as a source of humus. Sawdust, if of a sufficiently coarse grade and well rotted, remains porous, and it practically inhibits weed growth.

Bog- or salt-marsh hay and straw are fine if you don't garden in semi-rural regions with high rodent populations.

Mulches used for winter protection are put in place only after the soil has frozen an inch or more. Summer mulches we like to put on in beds or borders just after the spring cultivation, weeding and feeding, or after flowering. For naturalistic plantings, they may be applied at any time.

Loose, springy mulches, such as pine needles, hay, or hardwood leaves, can be 3 to 5 inches thick; more compact materials—buckwheat hulls, sawdust, or peat moss—about half that depth.

WATERING

In most sections of the United States there are in any year periods during which growing plants will be greatly benefited by occasional watering. Mulches help to conserve the reserve of moisture already in the soil but cannot add moisture to it.

Many a gardener makes the mistake of assuming that, since spring-flowering bulbs grow and bloom during a season when rain is likely to be plentiful, there is nothing to worry about so far as these are concerned. But an early hot dry spell may result in premature dying of the foliage of daffodils, tulips, and other spring subjects, with the result that the bulbs do not fully develop. And the *next* spring's flowers will suffer for it.

The extensive bulb plantings of Holland are grown on soil where the water table remains constant, not far below the surface, within easy reach of thirsty roots. Commercial bulb growers in America provide irrigation for their vast fields in order that they can be sure to produce full-size bulbs that in turn will bloom satisfactorily the first season after they are planted.

The home gardener no less than these expert plantsmen should, within the limits that it is possible for him to do so, make provision for giving his bulbous plants additional water when they need it. The fact that they may be able to survive without it should not satisfy him.

When and how should water be supplied?

As a general rule, water in generous amounts is needed most by bulbous plants from the time the flower buds begin to develop until they come into bloom. In the case of those which do not develop their foliage fully until after flowering—daffodils, tulips and most of the early spring bulbs—the supply of moisture should be plentiful until the foliage has had a chance to mature. With the relatively few species that mature their foliage first and bloom at a later period—lycoris, colchicums, autumn-flowering crocuses, for example—the important period for abundant moisture is *while the foliage is growing*. Most bulbs of this type will come to flower even in bone-dry soil.

For most bulbous plants, the method of watering is not especially important. Any sprinkler that applies the water in a fine rain, and slowly, so the soil can be thoroughly saturated without making the surface a mass of mud is satisfactory. In exceptional cases, where it is desirable not to wet flowers or foliage, the porous "soil-soaker" is the answer, or water may be allowed to run slowly from the open hose. As in all watering, the aim should be to get the soil thoroughly moist to a depth of several inches. Mere sprinkling is likely to do more harm than good.

Tulips are one of the exceptions to overhead watering; if there is any danger of "fire" (botrytis) being present, overhead watering may help to spread it. Another exception is tuberous begonias; the large flowers may become spotted or even break off as a result of careless heavy watering, and foliage may spot or "burn" if exposed to strong sunshine while wet.

The gardener who grows bulbs on a scale at all extensive will find it a paying investment to extend pipes to strategic points, so that watering can be done conveniently and quickly. Plastic freeze-proof pipes that need be buried only 2 or 3 inches deep are available.

PROTECTING FLOWERS

With spring-flowering bulbs, and to a lesser degree with summer- and autumn-flowering ones, much of the beauty which the gardener has been waiting for weeks or months to enjoy is lost as the result of a sudden windstorm or a driving, mud-spattering rain. This possibility should be anticipated and all practical means taken to prevent it.

For low-growing plants such as hyacinths and the minor spring bulbs, and most of the species of tulips and daffodils, a mulch of some sort is the best protection. Buckwheat hulls or peat moss are particularly good here; a very light covering will prevent splashing. Even the taller-growing daffodils and tulips are not safe from mud spattering if they are growing in bare soil.

Many of the taller summer bulbs—dahlias, lilies, summer-hyacinths—are subject to injury from being whipped about or broken by windstorms. Planting them in a protected location will do much to lessen this danger; but the use of supports to which the plants are secured is more certain, and especially advisable where flowers are wanted for show purposes. Bamboo stakes, which are available in lengths up to 8 feet, are commonly used for this purpose. We have found heavy (8- or 9-gauge) galvanized-wire stakes both more convenient to use and less conspicuous. They have a distinct advantage, too, in that they sway slightly in a heavy wind, thus making less likely the breaking of the plant's stem. With reasonable care they last indefinitely.

In staking lilies or other tall plants—we have had the summer-hyacinths go over 5 feet—tying should begin when they are about two-thirds grown. Good-sized soft twine or raffia is used, a knot being tied tight around the support and then a loose loop tied around the plant stem. Or use one of the several plastic plant-ties, available under various trade names, in place of twine or raffia. Very tall plants should be secured, as they grow, at two or more points.

Low-growing plants which have a tendency to make numerous side shoots—such as semi-dwarf and bedding dahlias—can be inconspicuously supported with small twiggy branches of birch, gray dogwood, or something similar. Whatever method of support is used, the important thing is to provide it early. A plant which has once fallen or blown over, even though it may not be broken, can rarely be made to resume a natural appearance when it is tied up.

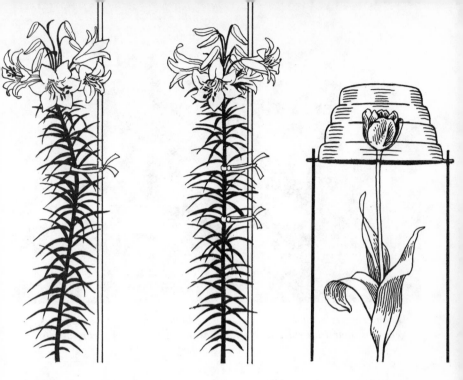

LEFT: *Supporting a tall plant: (left) wrong—one loop at one point;
(right) correct—double loops at two or more points.* RIGHT: *Protection
for individual bloom: plastic dome supported on stakes.*

Flowers being grown for show purposes will of course be given
special attention in regard to preserving the blooms in perfect condition; otherwise the results of meticulous care during a whole year
may be lost in an hour's heavy rain.

A not-too-difficult method of protecting low-growing plants, such
as tulips and daffodils, is to stretch plastic sheeting over tent wire
frames. Such miniature waterproof tents make a good covering for a
fair-sized group of bulbs.

For beds or for plants grown in rows, stout stakes with wires
stretched between them make a support for plastic sheeting. The
ideal way to grow daffodils and tulips for show purposes is in a deep,
unheated frame. Thus, in addition to protection from the weather,
timing can be controlled to some extent. Where the show schedule
calls for flowers grown in the open, such methods, however, are not
permissible.

When space is available, planting spring bulbs, such as these daffodils, in generous quantities will make a long-lasting, heart-lifting spring display.

CUTTING

The cutting of the flowers of bulbous plants is an important point in their cultivation. There is some disagreement as to how much the development of seed pods affects the growth of bulbs underground after flowering, but it is well established that it does reduce the size of the bulbs produced. It is the universal practice of commercial bulb growers to remove the flowers. Some allow the buds to develop sufficiently to be cut for sale, as this brings a by-product income. It is considered better for the bulb crop, however, to remove them before blooming or just as soon as they show enough color to be "rogued" —a term applied to the pulling up of all plants that are not true to the variety or the type being grown.

In the garden, flowers that are wanted for decoration should be cut as soon as they are safely beyond the tight bud stage. According to species and variety, most of them will then remain in good condition from a couple of days to a week or more. Too often they are left until they have passed full bloom, and then cut and brought in, without benefit of hardening, to fade or collapse within a few hours.

In cutting flowers of bulbous plants which have thick, fleshy stems

The stately tulips are unsurpassed for use in special tulip borders. The color display in such borders can be continued over summer by sowing seeds of annuals—or setting out young plants—among the tulips as they pass into dormancy. The tulip bulbs can be left in place or lifted and stored until fall.

with leaves attached, such as those of tulips, gladiolus, or lilies, most of the foliage should be left to grow. Foliage is the mechanism which manufactures food to be stored in the old bulb or corm remaining in the ground, or in the new ones being formed. Bare-stemmed flowers —daffodils, ismenes, amaryllis, and the like—are cut to the ground.

To have them last well in bouquets and arrangements, cut the flowers early in the morning or late in the afternoon, plunge the stems at once into deep fresh water, and store for several hours or overnight in a dark, cool place—the cooler the better, down to 40 degrees. If straight stems are wanted, they should be kept vertical or nearly so. Most fleshy stemmed flowers will tend to turn upright at the tips—even in the dark—if they are placed with much of a slant or if laid horizontally in boxes. Flower arrangers often take advantage of this fact to secure desired bends or curves in stems.

Blooms that are left to finish their allotted span of life in the garden should be snapped off as soon as they fade. The few exceptions are those which produce attractive seed pods, berries, or fruits—such as an occasional lily or iris, Jack-in-the-pulpit, blood-lily (*Haemanthus*), or blackberry-lily (*Belamcanda*).

CARE OF FOLIAGE

For reasons already explained, the foliage of all plants producing bulbs, corms, or tubers should be encouraged to keep growing as long as it will. This means maintaining soil moisture, and possibly additional feeding, after the flowering period is over.

In the garden such foliage growth is often a nuisance. Gradually yellowing tulip leaves, the sprawling, messy green ribbons of daffodils, and the great bunches of herbage of colchicums do offer something of a problem.

For the sake of the bulbs—and *next* year's bloom—the foliage should be left intact. The practice of plaiting or knotting the long strong foliage of daffodils is no longer recommended, as some of the leaves are bound to be injured—to the detriment of next year's flowers. Seedlings of fast-growing annuals—either home-grown or purchased—can be planted in front of and between groups of tulips. Dwarf marigolds and zinnias, petunias and dwarf dahlias are a few of those which are excellent for this purpose. We like especially the too little-known star of Texas (*Xanthisma*), which withstands early frosts and goes on cheerfully producing its hundreds of starry golden flowers long after the others have been cut down.

In a mixed border, the well-planned placing of certain perennials adjacent to groups of bulbs can do much toward making their ripening foliage inconspicuous.

Where for any reason the unsightly foliage must be removed—as was often the case with tulips and hyacinths in the days of "design" beds in formal gardens—the bulbs can be lifted immediately after flowering and replanted. If they are just carelessly heeled in and forgotten, the foliage will die back almost immediately; but if taken up with adhering soil, planted close together in a trench in partial shade, with plenty of peat moss in the soil, *and kept watered,* they will attain much nearer normal development. The bulbs may be smaller than normal, but perfectly usable. However, if the work of salvaging them must be done by hired labor, the cost, with tulips, is likely to be little less than that of purchasing new stock.

REPLANTING

With the most easily grown hardy bulbs, the time will arrive when, through normal increase, they have become so overcrowded as to

Daffodil and tulip bulbs, when they have become crowded, can be lifted after flowering and temporarily replanted ("heeled in") in a trench so the still-green foliage can properly mature. After the foliage browns and withers, the bulbs can be lifted again and stored in a dry garage until autumn.

give fewer and inferior blooms. This stage can be postponed by good care and generous fertilizing, but not indefinitely. And putting off replanting only makes it more difficult when it is undertaken, with a larger percentage of undersized bulbs.

The period until replanting becomes necessary varies greatly with different types and species, and even with varieties. Some daffodils, 'Peeping Tom' for instance, are giving us satisfactory bloom after sixteen years, while others make such dense clumps that they should be taken up and divided every three or four years. Others, such as the hardy-amaryllis (*Lycoris squamigera*) and the colchicums, which propagate slowly, can be left undisturbed almost indefinitely.

The work of replanting is best undertaken at the beginning of the dormant period, just after foliage has died down, but while it and new offsets, cormels, or bulblets are still attached to the bulbs. Using a broad-tined digging fork, thrust it down deep in a vertical position, well away from the clump (to avoid spearing any of the bulbs); then lift the clump out, turning partly over to expose the bulbs on the surface of the forkful of soil. Grasping the foliage at the base with the left hand, after the soil is thoroughly loosened, often enables the operator to lift the clump out neatly, with small bulblets or cormels adhering to the parent plant. Separating the bulbs from the soil, place each lot in a flat with a label. Stack these flats crisscross to provide free ventilation in an open shed or garage. With the exception of daffodils, *they should be carefully protected from mice or other rodents.*

With proper storage conditions, bulbs of most sorts can be kept out of the ground for many weeks. If they are of a type developing offsets—daffodils, for instance—these will separate from the "mother" bulbs much more readily after they have cured for a considerable time. However, in replanting for one's own use, there is little object in doing this, except in cases of varieties which it is desired to increase rapidly.

In replanting hardy bulbs of any kind, we like to get them back into the ground as soon as possible. In this we do not make an exception even of tulips. Immediate replanting has several advantages: it permits root growth to start again whenever the bulb is ready to break dormancy; it saves the bother of storing over a long period; and it greatly lessens the danger of losing or mixing up labels.

The bulbs, corms, or tubers you take up will be of varying sizes. All are good for replanting, but of most kinds there will soon be more than you can accommodate. Then it becomes necessary to select the largest and best; the smaller ones can be grown on in a nursery row, used for naturalizing, or discarded.

In general it is best not to replant in the same spot. This is especially true of tulips, which are subject to fire-blight disease, and of lilies. Needless to say, the soil for replanting should be just as thoroughly prepared as for planting new bulbs.

Tender bulbs that are grown in the garden, of course, must be replanted annually, so there is little danger of their becoming overcrowded. But it can happen. The inexperienced gardener who sets out, intact, a clump of dahlia roots which he has carefully preserved through the winter will find himself with a dense growth of stalks and foliage and few and inferior blooms. The same is true of canna, ismene, and others that tend to remain in clusters unless separated. Separation should be done, where necessary, with a knife.

But while most hardy bulbs increase in number as rapidly, or even more rapidly, than you wish them to, there are occasions when you will want to hasten the process. Or, once you become an enthusiast, you may even wish to try your hand at developing new varieties. And so, in the following chapter, we shall consider the intriguing matter of propagation.

CHAPTER *9. Propagation*

Much of the pleasure to be had in growing any plant is to know how to increase your stock of it. With the propagator's skills at your finger tips, you can afford to purchase many things that might otherwise seem too expensive. Starting with an individual plant, which in itself scarcely would make a worthwhile display, you can, with no additional outlay, soon possess as large a planting as you wish.

Then, too, it is always nice to feel that you have a few surplus plants of choice things to spare for a friend or neighbor, or to swap for some desired plant that you do not yourself possess.

With no helping hand save that of old Mother Nature, many bulbs, corms and tubers increase so rapidly that they soon present an embarrassment of riches. There are others which come along nicely with just a little encouragement from the attentive gardener. A few, however, are really obstinate in their wish to remain the sole representative of their kind in your garden. With these, very persuasive measures must be used—even to the extent of putting them under the knife. Many kinds that normally self-propagate at a slow rate can be increased much more rapidly when special methods are used to hurry them. A knowledge of such methods, indispensable to the commercial grower, is also of definite advantage to the amateur.

METHODS OF REPRODUCTION

Members of the great group of bulbous plants have many ways of propagating themselves. Increase by seeds is known as sexual propagation; other means, such as the formation of offsets or of bulbs and bulblets (see pages 96–98), are termed asexual. A basic difference between the sexual method and all asexual methods is that plants raised by the former are seldom entirely uniform, while the latter are. Very literally they are chips off the old block. All the 'Clara Butt' tulips in the world are direct descendants of the one original plant—just as all the Koster's blue spruces are pieces, through successive generations, from the original seedling which old Peter Koster selected, because of its exceptionally fine color, from a batch of seedlings of Colorado blue spruce. Such a plant, descended from a *single* parent, is known as a "clone" or "cultivar."

Seeds

The method of reproduction most familiar to gardeners is of course the growing of plants from seed. *Species* of plants "come true" from seed; horticultural varieties seldom do. If, for instance, you plant seeds of the regal lily, the resulting seedlings will be regals. They may vary somewhat in height, time of bloom, shape of the flowers, but they will all be regals. If you sow seeds from a named hybrid lily, however, you will get a great variety of plants, most of which will be definitely not the same as the parent variety. The same would be true of a named horticultural tulip, such as the venerable but still sought-after 'General de Wet', the seedlings of which would vary like those of a hybrid lily's seedlings.

In addition to the fact that garden varieties of bulbous plants do not come true from seed, there is another drawback which deters both commercial growers and home gardeners from using seeds, except infrequently, as a means of propagation: that is the length of time required to get plants to blooming size. There are a few, such as the dwarf bedding dahlias and tuberous begonias (if started in January or February), which will flower the first season; but most bulbous plants require two or three years, on up to five or six—as with daffodils, for instance. Growing bulbous plants from seed, therefore, is in general a matter of concern chiefly to the hybridist, professional or amateur, interested in developing new varieties.

Asexual Methods

For the sake of making a distinction between two different types of asexual propagation, we may say that bulbous plants increase themselves by *multiplication;* or may be increased, at the hands of the gardener, by *division.*

To illustrate: if you plant a 60-watt tulip bulb in October, you may dig up, the following June, a couple of 40-watt bulbs and two or

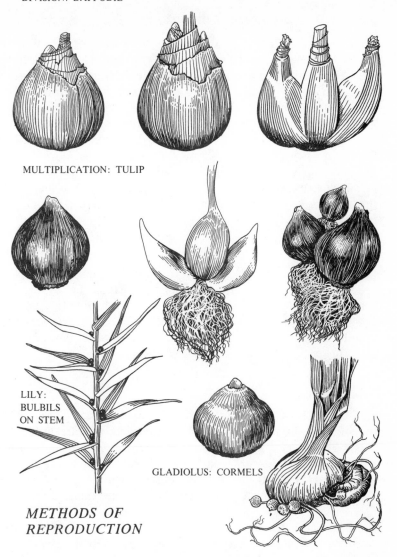

DIVISION: DAFFODIL

MULTIPLICATION: TULIP

LILY:
BULBILS
ON STEM

GLADIOLUS: CORMELS

METHODS OF
REPRODUCTION

three 25-watters! If you plant a single daffodil bulb, you will find, after three or four years, a whole shovelful of individual bulbs of various sizes. In neither case will you have had anything to do with the matter.

If, on the contrary, you plant a dahlia tuber in the spring, you take up in the autumn a clump of many fleshy roots, but they will all be joined to one stem; and the only way you can get more than one plant is to divide this clump by cutting the stem into sections—each with an "eye" and attached to a root. If you plant a tuberous begonia tuber, you take up in the fall the same tuber—grown larger, perhaps —and that is all you will ever get, no matter how many times you replant it. But this tuber can be divided by cutting it into sections, each with an eye or bud.

Under "division" we might also place the propagation of bulbous plants by stem cuttings. Not many of them are subject to increase by this method, but there are a few. Dahlias and tuberous begonias are examples.

PROPAGATING OPERATIONS

So much for the several methods of propagation. Let us now take a look at the way each of them is put into practice. In describing these operations, typical examples of each are used. Where variations from these exist, they are mentioned in the cultural methods for each genus or species given in succeeding chapters.

Seed

In catalogues comparatively few bulbous plants are offered in the lists of seeds. In gardens many of them produce seed freely, and the amateur who wishes to try his hand at raising his own plants will find plenty of material to work with.

In general, bulbous plants are no more difficult to grow from seed than are those of other groups—except for one thing. That is the time element. It does involve a great deal more attention and work, and considerably more space, to carry through to maturity a plant requiring several years than one which will reward the grower with its first flowers within a season or two. And the chances of loss through injury or accident are correspondingly increased. These facts the grower should face before embarking on the venture of growing bulbs from seed.

As in sowing seeds of any sort, it is advisable to use a prepared mixture rather than ordinary garden soil. The various soilless mixes, such as Redi-Earth, Jiffy Mix, that are available in garden centers, are convenient and clean. However, we have found entirely satisfactory our regular seed mixture of one part each of soil, compost (or leaf-mold), and peat moss, with sufficient sand added to give it a slightly gritty texture. This is run through a half-inch mesh screen. For extremely fine seed, such as that of tuberous begonias, a half-inch layer or more of very finely sifted compost, or of peat moss or shredded sphagnum moss alone, is used on top of the regular mixture.

The time for planting seeds will depend upon the type of seed and upon the facilities available. As a general rule, the sooner they are sown after gathering, the better. Seeds of most hardy sorts, ripening in summer or autumn, are usually sown in flats or in a frame. Many of these seeds will not germinate until the following spring, or even the second spring after sowing. Seeds of tender types are best started in a greenhouse or in the house under fluorescent lights in January or February; or a month or two later, when the weather has moderated sufficiently, in a hotbed or cold frame.

The seeds that germinate quite promptly—dahlia, canna, ismene, tuberous begonia, gloxinia, and some lilies, to mention a few—are started in pots, bulb pans, or flats, with a half inch or so of coarse drainage material under the prepared soil. Those which require a long period to germinate are better sown in substantial flats, 4 inches deep, with an inch of drainage material in the bottom; or directly in a frame. Polyethylene bags—the kinds used for food storage—have become as useful to the gardener as to the cook. Large seeds, such as those of some of the faster-germinating lilies, germinate within a few weeks when enclosed in plastic bags. The seeds are mixed with a handful or so of moistened vermiculite. The bags must be kept from

Ismene seeds sprouting.

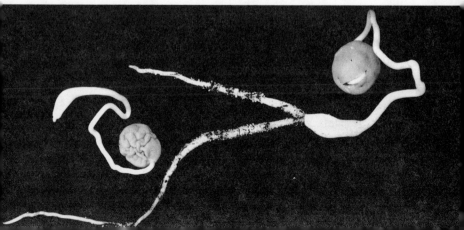

direct sunshine or the inner temperature will become too warm for the seeds or seedlings.

Seeds of some species will not germinate, or will give only partial germination, until after freezing. These may remain in the soil a year or more before sprouting. Daffodils, tulips and some alliums are examples. Some lilies germinate but make only a bulblet the first season, no leaf appearing above the soil until the following season. It is evident, therefore, that seeds of this character should be sown where they can be both kept track of and protected until ready for their first transplanting.

As a rule, the earlier transplanting can be done, the better. By the time there is sufficient top growth to make it possible to handle the seedlings, the root system will have made a good start—often a surprisingly vigorous one. The smaller the plant, the less the shock in transplanting it; and if seedlings have come up thickly, the longer they remain untransplanted, the greater the danger of loss by damping-off or other diseases.

The first transplanting is usually made into flats, as they occupy much less space and require much less attention than individual pots. Some vigorous, rapid-growing plants, such as dahlia and canna, can go directly into 2½- or even 3-inch pots, and then either into 4-inch pots or into the open ground.

The soil mixture used is similar to that in which the seed was started, but with a larger proportion—about one half—of soil, with bone meal added at the rate of a pint to a bushel of the mixture. An inch layer of rough compost or old, thoroughly rotted manure in the bottom of the flat will provide a happy feeding area for growing roots.

The seedling plants are set 2 to 4 inches apart each way, according to the type of plant being grown. Plants with cotyledons (seed leaves) are set deep enough so these are just above the soil; others, slightly deeper than they have been growing. Flats are best watered from the bottom, and provided with shade from hot sun for a week or so. If even with shading the seedlings wilt, mist-spray the foliage two or more times daily, but never enough to keep the soil soaking wet.

Lilies and other hardy bulbs are often carried over the first winter in the seed flats, with the protection of a frame. Let them freeze, and then mulch or shade to keep them frozen, and thus avoid alternate

Ismene seedling;
first true leaf,
and bulb beginning
to form.

freezing and thawing which might bring them to the surface.

Tender subjects, such as dahlias, gladiolus, tuberous begonias, is-menes, etc., are of course taken up and stored in the usual way over the winter (see page 225), to be replanted the following spring. *Small-sized bulbs, corms and tubers being grown from seed should be given special care in packing and an occasional examination during the storage period to make sure that they are not drying out and shrinking.* Bulbs that have begun to shrivel can be restored to their original plump, firm condition, if the process has not proceeded too far, by being placed in damp peat moss or vermiculite for a few days. After this they should be repacked as before for storage.

Offsets

An offset—sometimes called a "split" or a "spoon"—is a small bulb which develops within the mother bulb, as with the daffodil; or at the base of the mother bulb, as with the ismene. Starting as a bud, it gradually increases in size until it breaks away from the mother bulb and is on its own, to produce, in time, its own progeny. The mother bulb remains, to become a grandmother or a great-grand-mother bulb.

Nature often comes to the assistance of the gardener, but where offsets are involved the gardener can be of assistance to her, becoming, in a sense, a green-thumb midwife. For the offset baby bulbs, left undisturbed, become a dense clump, with even more offspring com-

Madonna lily bulbs as dug—from original planting of six bulbs.

ing along to increase the overcrowded conditions, until finally there is not space or food enough underground, nor sufficient air or sunshine above it, for all of them to develop properly.

Here the gardener now steps in, takes up the old clump, and separates, grades, and replants, so all the progeny will have a full opportunity to grow as they should.

The time from planting the original bulb until replanting is necessary varies with species, varieties and growing conditions. But if it is desired to increase the number of plants as rapidly as possible, then, with few exceptions, the lifting, separation and replanting should be done every year or every second year.

For purposes of propagation it is best to plant both large bulbs and young offsets in rows in very well-prepared soil, in the vegetable plot or the cutting garden, if you have one, where they can be cared for, cultivated, fed, and, if necessary, watered. Small offsets can be grown quite close together; daffodils, for instance, 2 to 4 inches apart, in rows 18 to 24 inches apart. Replanting immediately after digging (after the foliage has died down), or as soon as the stock can conveniently be cleaned, separated and graded, is advisable for most types of hardy bulbs.

LEFT: *Veltheimia—offset originating on old bulb.* RIGHT: *Haemanthus (blood-lily)—offsets originating from fleshy stolons.*

New Bulbs or Corms

New bulbs or corms, such as those produced by tulips, crocuses and gladiolus, differ from offsets in that the original bulb or corm, at the end of the season's growth, will have dried up or disintegrated entirely, leaving a new bulb, or several of them, in its place. Some of these new bulbs will be as large as the original bulb, or at least of flowering size. Usually others are much smaller and require growing on for a season or two before reaching flowering size. In some instances these new bulbs are formed at the end of underground roots or runners, at a distance from the parent bulb or below it (as the "droppers" of tulips and crocuses), and to secure all of them, great care in digging is required.

With new bulbs, as with offsets, if they are hardy, replanting can be done at once or delayed. If tender, they are stored over winter for spring planting.

Cormels or Bulblets

Cormels or bulblets (see illustration, page 97), which in some species are produced along with the new bulbs or corms, are embryo forms, much smaller in size, which must be grown on for from one to three years before they become flowering-sized bulbs. They may develop in large numbers—we have had gladiolus of some varieties produce as many as thirty to forty from one corm—and thus they offer a means for very rapid propagation.

The trick in successful propagation with bulblets and cormels is to keep them in good condition through the winter, so that a thick and vigorous stand will result when they are planted. Storing dry in grocery paper bags is sometimes recommended, but we have been more successful in using *slightly* moist peat moss or vermiculite in polyethylene bags. Here again an occasional examination is advisable. Cormels of gladiolus and montbretia, once thoroughly dried, become almost as hard as buckshot. A soaking of 24 to 48 hours in tepid water before planting will both hasten and increase new growth.

The bulblets and cormels may be sown like peas, in a broad, flat-bottomed furrow, and covered about 3 inches deep. Avoid weedy soil, as they must be kept clean to allow the grass-like juvenile foliage to get a good start. When the foliage dies down, dig, dry off—without too much exposure to hot sun or to wind—and later clean, grade and store for winter.

The number of new bulbs or bulblets produced may in some cases be increased by artificial means. With lilies, for instance, removing the flower buds before they open often results in the production of more bulbs and bulblets than would otherwise form. Sir Daniel Hall reported that, with some varieties of tulips, the production was increased 300 per cent by disbudding. (See pages 162–64.) Some growers claim that bent stems bear more bulblets, and plant bulbs on their

Madonna lily bulbs—separated and graded for replanting.

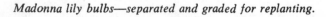

Lily (L. bulbiferum) *with bulbils formed in axils of leaves.*

sides to obtain a crook at the base of the stem. Removing and layering the stem is a more certain process.

Bulbils are tiny aerial bulbs which form along the stems or in the leaf axils of some species or varieties of plants. Some lilies, notably *Lilium tigrinum,* the tiger lily, regularly produce bulbils, and they occasionally occur in tulips. They may be planted as soon as readily detached from the parent stem, in deep flats or directly in a frame.

Increase by Division

In the several methods of propagation discussed above, you, the gardener, have had a minor part. In those that follow you assume the leading role, and nature becomes *your* assistant. The technique starts with an operation, in which some section of the parent plant is removed. This piece is then induced to form roots and becomes a new plant.

Simplest of the several methods of attaining this end is that in which the bulb, tuber, corm, or rhizome is cut into two or more

Ismene: bulb at center (against pot) as dug; others separated. Fleshy roots are left on in storage.

pieces, these being planted directly, just as the original would have been. A universally known example of propagation by division is the Irish potato. Other typical ones are the dahlia and canna. Many cormous plants, ordinarily grown from seed or from small corms or cormels, can be increased by dividing a large corm. Gladiolus and crocuses are examples.

In making the divisions it is essential that there be a growing point (a bud or "eye") on each piece. With cormous plants there must also be a section of the basal plate. Make the cuts with a clean sharp knife. It is good practice to dust over the cut surfaces with powdered charcoal or with one of the seed and bulb disinfectant powders. In any event, they should be allowed to dry sufficiently to form a slight

Not a flock of geese, but new corms of colchicum.

Cutting off the dried stalk of ismene, also called Peruvian-daffodil, in autumn. The fleshy roots must be left intact.

film of scar tissue over the cut before being planted. If they are to be started in pots, flats, or a frame before being set out in the open or repotted, a rooting medium of soil, peat moss, and sand will be of advantage.

Scales

Some of the true bulbs can be propagated rapidly by an operation known as "scaling." Many lilies are often grown in this way. Any good gardener can succeed with it, even though it may sound a bit mysterious to one who has not tried it.

The thick fleshy scales are removed from the outside of the bulb, care being taken not to bruise them or the bulb unduly and to retain the base of each. If the heart of the bulb is left intact, that can be replanted for further growth. In fact, scales can be removed from a growing bulb without the necessity of first lifting the bulb and disturbing its roots. A careful unearthing of the bulb is necessary to prevent injury; then a few scales are gently removed and the soil is replaced around the bulb. The scales can be placed in a plastic bag in moist (but not saturated) vermiculite, as with seeds, described above. Or the scales can be set in rows in a flat, in sand or a sand-

Propagation of lily by scaling. Scales are placed on sand, or mixture of sand and vermiculite. Plastic dome protects from rain and rodents. Heart of bulb (at left) can be replanted for further growth.

peat moss mixture, and covered about 2 inches deep. *Excellent drainage is essential!* Or they may be placed directly in a frame. Keep covered against rain, *and only moderately moist,* for 20 to 25 days, until miniature new bulbs begin to form at the bases of the old scales; then moisture can be somewhat increased.

As a temperature of 60 degrees or thereabouts should be maintained, a greenhouse or other space where the temperature can be controlled is helpful. In a humid atmosphere a temperature of 75 to 80 degrees has given quicker results.

When scales are started in February or March, the flats are then

New baby bulbs forming at bases of scales and sending out vigorous roots.

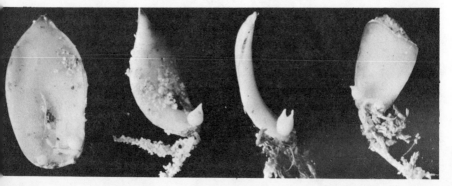

plunged out-of-doors in April or May and left undisturbed until the bulbs are planted out the following spring. Light is not necessary while the new bulbs are forming. If one must depend on a frame, the early and mid-season varieties can be scaled. The operations should be done as soon as the plants have bloomed. The lovely June-flowering madonna lily is readily propagated by scaling.

Stem-layering

Easier and quicker than scaling, but producing fewer new plants, is the method known as stem-layering. This develops bulblets in greater numbers than they would normally form, or where they could not form at all under normal conditions.

Stem-layering is accomplished by removing the stem from the bulb, just as the last flowers wither, by giving it a *quick* pull or jerk with a twisting motion. Don't try to be gentle about it, or you're likely merely to uproot the plant. A foot placed near the base of the stem, if the soil is light or sandy, will be an additional safeguard. The stems so gathered are heeled in, to about one-third their length, in well-drained sandy soil or a half-and-half mixture, by bulk, of sand and peat moss. Placing the stems on a slant will permit covering them with sash in an ordinary cold frame—an advantage with late-flowering varieties, as they can be held over in the frame until spring. When these heeled-in stems of early varieties have withered, they can be cut back to the soil, and the bases of the stems, with the newly formed bulblets still attached, set out in a nursery row to grow on for another year before being transplanted.

A modification of this method is to cut the stem back to 1 or 2 feet, remove all leaves, and layer in sand or sand-peat moss, covered a couple of inches deep, in a frame until the bulblets have formed.

Cuttings

Very few of the bulbous plants lend themselves to propagation by cuttings, but two notable exceptions are dahlias and tuberous begonias.

In the case of the former, the roots—usually in undivided clumps, just as they were dug in the fall—are started in March or April in the greenhouse or in a frame. Deep flats, filled with a peat moss-sand mixture, will accommodate them. The new shoots, grown in full sun but fairly cool so the stems will be firm and short-jointed, are allowed to form four or five sets of leaves. Then they are cut *just* below the second node, leaving the first set to form side shoots. (If cut between nodes, the stems will root, but the resulting plant will never form tuberous roots to carry over winter.) The cuttings, with the lower leaves shortened about one-half, placed in sand or sand and peat moss, root easily and produce husky plants soon ready for potting or for setting out-of-doors.

Leaf cuttings of the gloxinia, like those of their relative, the African-violet (*Saintpaulia*), root readily. Mature leaves are taken, with all of the stem, and inserted a couple of inches deep in sand or sand-peat moss. Baby plants start near the base of the stem and are grown on in small pots until ready for shifting to a larger size.

Scooping

A type of propagation which is sort of halfway between cuttings and scaling is practiced with some bulbs. Commercial growers employ it in propagating garden hyacinths, as these increase but slowly by offsets.

A cone-shaped incision is made through the base of the bulb, leaving the scales (layers of fleshy tissue) exposed at the cut edges. The hollowed-out bulb is then placed in sand, covered 2 or 3 inches deep, and stored for about three weeks in a temperature of 60 to 70 degrees, to callus. The bulb is then placed in any dark, cool place, such as a cellar or under a greenhouse bench, where the small new bulbs form. At the approach of autumn, these are removed and planted 3 to 4 inches deep and protected, after the soil begins to freeze, with a mulch of hay or pine needles.

A modified form of scooping, easier to follow, is to cut a couple of deep grooves at right angles across the basal plate. In this process, known as "scoring," the subsequent treatment is the same as for scooping. There will be fewer baby bulbs, but they will average larger in size.

In trying any method of propagation for the first time, it is advisable to start on a small scale. Do a little experimenting as soon as you can, just to get the swing of it, and then you'll be ready, when the occasion arises, to go about the job with confidence.

CHAPTER *10.* *Pests and Diseases*
and Their Control

By and large, bulbous plants are far less troubled by insects and diseases than are those of most other groups. This is good news for those for whom Rachel Carson is a respected household name and who wish to use as few poisonous sprays and dusts as possible. However, despite the claims of some catalogue compilers and writers, there is no plant that isn't susceptible to some pest or trouble—and the bulbous group certainly has its share.

Glancing through this chapter, you may get the impression that a sea of possible plagues surround bulbous plants and that the statement above puts the case—to say the least—very mildly! But be assured that you will probably never encounter more than a fraction— if that—of the troubles discussed, and even those that do plague you will not all appear in any one season. Both plant pests and diseases are more likely to be of serious danger to the commercial grower who is handling bulbs by the hundreds of thousands. And by the time the bulbs reach the homeowner, most serious pests and diseases have been controlled by the grower.

OVER-ALL PRECAUTIONS

Three definite measures the gardener can take to minimize greatly his troubles with pests or diseases:

Sanitation

The first is to keep his bulb plantings *clean.* Many weeds are host plants for insects or diseases, either during the summer or as sheltering material for their over-wintering stages. Fallen petals or foliage, old plant stalks—any miscellaneous litter in general—may serve the same purpose. Dead, dying, or diseased leaves on plants should be removed and destroyed. Don't let them lie around until dry; bury them with quicklime, or deposit with the trash. A basket—frequently disinfected—kept handy for the particular purpose of gathering such material will help.

Observation

Cultivate the habit of *looking* for anything abnormal in the growth of your plants. A curled leaf that might pass unnoticed for days unless your eye was kept peeled for just such an abnormality may shelter a colony of aphids that has not yet begun to spread to other parts of the plant. *At this point* such an initial "cell" of some insect pests may be eliminated by rubbing it off with your fingers, or, if you are squeamish, use a few squirts from an aerosol spray can. Not all insects, of course, are so easily controlled as are aphids. Most diseases will have obtained a strong start before their symptoms become apparent. Prompt identification of the trouble, however, and the removal and destruction of one or a few diseased plants will often prevent the infection of others.

Prompt Action

The third step in the successful control of any pest or disease is to lose no time, once it has been identified, in applying the proper remedy or control. A day or two may mean all the difference between success and failure.

The "proper remedy or control" may be as uncomplicated as the method suggested above—simply destroying the pest- or disease-ridden leaf, flower or entire plant by allocating it to the trash bin (not the compost pile!). If a bulb is soft or just doesn't look healthy, don't plant it. A more complicated trouble may require the application of insecticides or fungicides—chemicals you probably already possess for general garden use. (A general list of the various sprays, dusts and disinfectants is given on pages 121–24.)

CAUTION: In using any insecticide or fungicide, *follow the manufacturer's directions accurately*. Failure to do so may result not only in poor results but also in actual injury to plants—or to you!

PESTS

APHID, GREEN PEACH: A pale yellowish-green, soft-bodied sucking insect. Attacks many bulbous plants, feeding on the under-sides of the foliage. It is dangerous, also, because it transmits mosaic disease.
Control: Rotenone, nicotine sulphate, pyrethrum, malathion, Cygon, diazinon.
Attacks: Crocus, dahlia, lily, tulip.

APHID, LILY: Yellow and black. One form is found only on lilies (see Chapter 15). Another, *Myzus circumflexus,* feeds on terminal buds and shoots of many bulbous plants, turning the foliage yellow and deforming them. Also transmits mosaic disease.
Control: Rotenone, nicotine sulphate, pyrethrum, malathion, Cygon, diazinon.
Attacks: Anemone, cyclamen, freesia, iris, lily, oxalis.

APHID, MELON: Small, dark green, brown, or black. Feeds on undersides of foliage, which curls and turns yellow. Transmits mosaic disease.
Control: Rotenone, nicotine sulphate, pyrethrum, malathion, Cygon, diazinon.
Attacks: Begonia, cyclamen, lily.

APHID, POTATO: Pink and green, wingless. Feeds on succulent young foliage.
Control: Rotenone, nicotine sulphate, pyrethrum, malathion, Cygon, diazinon.
Attacks: Gladiolus, oxalis.

APHID, TULIP BULB: Small, whitish, powdery, with black head. Colonies appear on foliage, in leaf sheaths of growing bulbs, especially in a greenhouse, causing discoloration and distortion of leaves. Found also on bulbs in storage or in the ground.
Control: Soak tulip bulbs in nicotine sulphate solution (1½ teaspoons to 1 gallon of water) with soap or in pyrethrum solution for ½ hour before planting. Or dip bulbs in a malathion solution of 2 level tablespoons per gallon of water; or dust bulbs with 4% malathion before storing or planting. Spray foliage of growing plants with nicotine sulphate.
Attacks: Gladiolus, iris, squill, tulip.

BORER, EUROPEAN CORN: Flesh-colored caterpillar, 1 inch long with black dots. Enters stems and shoots, causing upper portions to wilt. Hole is visible where borer entered.
Control: Cut below affected part, or dust stalks with Sevin as preventive. Destroy all dead refuse in fall.
Attacks: Dahlia, gladiolus.

BORER, STALK: Brown caterpillar, 2 inches long, with white stripes. Attacks plants as does the European corn borer (above).
Control: As for European corn borer.
Attacks: Dahlia, lily.

BUG, TARNISHED PLANT: Inconspicuous brown bug, ¼ inch long, flattened, oval, mottled. Sucks plant sap, causing drooping and malformation of shoots and buds.
Control: Dust with methoxychlor, Sevin, pyrethrum, or sulphur; or spray with nicotine sulphate solution. Keep weeds down. Burn or destroy trash in autumn to prevent wintering over. Difficult to control.
Attacks: Dahlia, gladiolus.

CATERPILLAR, CONVICT: Black, 2 inches long, with cream bands around body. Leaves are skeletonized; stalks eaten.
Control: Sevin or use the biological control, *Bacillus thuringiensis*.
Attacks: Amaryllis, hymenocallis, daffodil.

CUTWORMS: Soft, fat, black, brown, or green worms. Attack newly-set young plants, cutting the stem at or near ground level. Usually can be found coiled in the surface soil near where damage has been done.
Control: Place tar-paper collars around newly-set plants or young shoots.
Attacks: Dahlia, gladiolus.

FLY, LESSER BULB: Wasp-like, about size of common house fly.

FLY, NARCISSUS BULB: Resembles small bumblebee. Bulbs, attacked by larvae of fly, are reduced to a soft brown, decayed mass.
Control (*for both*): See Chapter 11.
Attacks: Amaryllis, daffodil, galtonia, hyacinth, lily, tulip.

LEAFHOPPER, POTATO: See Chapter 16.

LEAF ROLLERS, CANNA: Mostly in the South. There are two forms, the larger being a greenish caterpillar with dark orange head and narrow neck; the lesser, a yellow-white caterpillar, becoming greenish. Both roll the leaves, the caterpillar being found inside.

Control: Hand-pick, or crush insects inside leaves, or spray or dust with Sevin or *Bacillus thuringiensis* in early summer.

MEALYBUGS: Small, oval, scale-like sucking insects covered with a woolly white substance which extends beyond their bodies. Affected plants appear unthrifty; with white woolly tufts at joints and axils.

Control: In greenhouse, fumigate with Cyanogas (for professional use only). Indoors and outdoors, paint individual colonies with small brush or cotton swab dipped in rubbing alcohol; or spray with rotenone or malathion.

Attacks: Amaryllis (*Hippeastrum*), begonia, calla, cyclamen.

MITE, BULB: Minute whitish mite. Burrows in roots, especially of rotting bulbs; seldom encountered in home garden.

Control: Discard rotting bulbs. Prevent rotting by storing bulbs at 35 degrees. Dip slightly affected bulbs in nicotine sulphate solution (see aphid, tulip) at 122 degrees for 10 minutes: or in hot water at 110 degrees for 2½ hours; or dust bulbs with Floral Dust or similar all-purpose pesticide available at your garden center, or 2 per cent nicotine dust and store for several days in closed paper bags; or use malathion dip, 2 tablespoons per gallon of water.

Attacks: Amaryllis, calla, crocus, freesia, gladiolus, hyacinth, lily, daffodil, tulip.

MITE, CYCLAMEN: Minute whitish pest (not visible to naked eye). Causes stunting of plant, especially at growing tips; malformation of leaves; blackening and distortion of buds.

Control: Destroy badly infested plants. Spray with Kelthane, Tedion, Dimite or a 1–200 rotenone solution. Avoid contact between affected and healthy plants.

Attacks: Cyclamen, gloxinia, tuberous begonia.

NEMATODE, ROOT-KNOT: Microscopic worm; male thread-like; female white, swollen, size of pin point. Causes knots or galls on feeding roots, yellowing of foliage, wilt, die-back.

Control: Treat fallow soil with DD mixture, or with Soilfume Caps, 2 weeks before planting. Punch holes 10 to 12 inches apart, 5 to 6 inches deep; use ⅓ ounce DD or 1 Soilfume Cap per hole. Steam-sterilize greenhouse soil.

Attacks: Begonia, cyclamen, dahlia, gladiolus, tuberose.

NEMATODE, STEM AND BULB (Eelworm or Ring Disease): Seldom found in home garden. Microscopic thread-like worm, this nematode lives in soil and decaying vegetable matter. Infestation causes irregular markings along leaf edges, stunt, failure to bloom. Leaves are twisted, with yellowish swellings. When bulb is cut, it shows black rings.

Control: Soak bulbs 3 to 4 hours in water at 100–112 degrees, with formaldehyde added at the rate of 1 pint to 25 gallons. Replant at once. Destroy badly infested bulbs. Disinfect all equipment by dipping in water with formaldehyde added, 1 part to 9 of water; sterilize soil with Soilfume Caps, tear gas, or DD.

Attacks: Amaryllis, anemone, chionodoxa, daffodil, galanthus, galtonia, hyacinth, iris (bulbous), muscari, tulip.

RODENTS: Mice, especially field and pine mice, rabbits and chipmunks are enemies of some kinds of bulbs, and it is not an easy task to keep them under control in regions where they are prevalent. Rural areas that have only recently been developed, especially pine barrens with their sandy soils, are bound to harbor various rodents. (Moles do not eat bulbs as they are carnivorous.)

Control: Keeping a cat or cats which are good hunters will virtually eliminate rabbits and chipmunks as well as cause a dent in the mice population. If you are only planting a few bulbs, place them in wire baskets made from hardware cloth; or edge tulip beds with ½-inch hardware cloth sunk 8 inches below ground and extending 2 inches above. Dusting bulbs before planting with thiram is reputed to repel mice and deeper-than-usual planting depths are recommended for tulip bulbs. (See Chapter 12.) The various baits, traps and bombs listed in mail-order catalogues may give partial or less control. Some are highly poisonous. It's comforting to know that mice populations fluctuate from year to year and that it is a rare spring when they have destroyed every last tulip, hyacinth or crocus bulb.

Attack: Tulip, lily, crocus, gladiolus, dahlia and other irids.

SLUGS: Resembling snails without shells, they are chewing creatures which hide in the dark (usually under old boards or other debris) by day, and feed at night, eating foliage and leaving a slimy, silvery trail behind them.

Control: Trap slugs under old shingles or thin boards under which they will be found by day. Remove any other litter under which they may hide. Use one of the poison baits containing metaldehyde sold under various trade names, such as Snarol and Slugetta.

Attacks: Dahlia, lily and other bulbous seedlings.

THRIPS, GLADIOLUS: Tiny black or brown winged insects to $\frac{1}{16}$ inch long. Cause silvery streaks in foliage, followed by browning and dying leaves; deformed flowers, streaked white. Dormant corms become sticky, corky, browned.

Control: After drying corms, from which all foliage and stems are removed, dust thoroughly with malathion or lindane before storing. In growth: start spraying methoxychlor, lindane, Sevin, diazinon or Cygon, when foliage is 6 inches high. Avoid spraying when flowers are showing color.

Attacks: Amaryllis, daffodil, freesia, gladiolus, iris (bulbous).

THRIPS, GREENHOUSE: Tiny blackish-brown insects $\frac{1}{24}$ inch long, with network of lines over head. Infested leaves look silvery or papery; wilt; die-back; leaves drop off or are marked with reddish-brown dots.

Control: Dust with pyrethrum, lindane or malathion.

Attacks: Alstroemeria, amaryllis, begonia, calla, cyclamen, dahlia, gloxinia, hymenocallis, nerine.

THRIPS, ONION: Tiny, yellow to brown insects $\frac{1}{25}$ inch long. Infestation is marked by whitish blotches on foliage, then distortion of leaf tips, followed by withering and browning of the plant, which falls to the ground.

Control: Spray with malathion or lindane, starting when plants are very young. Repeat weekly. Dust corms of gladiolus with lindane or malathion before storage.

Attacks: Dahlia, gladiolus.

WIREWORMS: Dark, smooth, hard-shelled wiry worms (the larval form of click beetles), which feed on roots, corms or bulbs. They are most prevalent in recently cultivated land which has been in sod.

Control: An old-fashioned method is to place cut potatoes, pressed 3 or 4 inches into the soil at 3-foot intervals, in an infested area. After a week or so dig them up and destroy the worms which are found attached to them. Spray or dust soil with diazinon, then dig into 6 inches of soil. Spray or dust bulbs before planting. Spray growing plants with malathion.

Attacks: Tuberous begonia, dahlia, gladiolus.

DISEASES

BLIGHT, GRAY MOLD (*Botrytis cinerea*): Symptoms vary with plants attacked.

> Amaryllis: Grayish mold on foliage; mostly in South, outdoors after a chill.
>
> Anemone: Rotting of crown.
>
> Tuberous Begonia: Dead spots on flowers and leaves, rapidly enlarging, turning dark and covered with grayish mold.
>
> Dahlia: Dark spots covered with grayish mold on buds and blooms.
>
> Gladiolus: See Chapter 17.
>
> Lily: Grayish mold on leaves, but see Chapter 15 for more serious botrytis blight caused by *Botrytis elliptica.*
>
> Daffodil: Occasionally troublesome, causing grayish mold on leaves.

> *Control:* Gather all infected leaves or flowers into bag as soon as noticed, and destroy. Destroy plants which show rot of crowns or bulbs. Provide good ventilation and wide spacing of greenhouse plants. Avoid syringing. Spraying with Bordeaux mixture will help in most cases.

BLIGHT, LILY (*Botrytis elliptica*): See Chapter 15.

BLIGHT, NARCISSUS FIRE (*Botrytis polyblastis*): See Chapter 11.

BLIGHT, NARCISSUS LEAF SCORCH and RED BLOTCH OF AMARYLLIS: Tips of daffodils appear to be suffering from frost injury for several inches and are separated from the healthy part of the leaf by a yellow margin. Secondary infection consists of very small yellowish or watery spots which become scabby and dark reddish-brown. These spots may also appear on stems and flower petals. On amaryllis (*Hippeastrum*) red spots appear on leaves, stems of flowers, and flower petals. Leaves and stems are deformed.

> *Control:* Discard seriously affected bulbs. Disease is spread by syringing and heavy watering. Spray with zineb.
>
> *Attacks:* Amaryllis, crinum, daffodil, eucharis, haemanthus, hymenocallis, leucojum, nerine, sternbergia, vallota, zephyranthes.

BLIGHT, SNOWDROP (*Botrytis galanthina*): Causes black dots to appear on outer scales of bulbs.

> *Control:* Remove affected scales before planting.

BLIGHT, SOUTHERN (*Sclerotium rolfsii*): Also known as "mustard seed fungus" because of characteristic mustard seed-like sclerotia attached to white threads of mycelium found in soil around rotting roots and bulbs. The sclerotia are first white, then turn tan or brown. Often first sign of trouble is sudden wilting and yellowing of the plant. A closer examination will show sclerotia and mycelium threads in the soil, often at the surface. Bulbs and roots will be partially or completely rotted. Most prevalent during warm and rainy weather.

Control: Destroy affected bulbs and the soil about them as soon as noticed. Treat soil area with Terrachlor.

Attacks: Amaryllis, canna, daffodil, gladiolus, ornithogalum.

BLIGHT, TULIP FIRE (BOTRYTIS BLIGHT) (*Botrytis tulipae*): See Chapter 12.

MILDEW, POWDERY: See Chapter 16.

MOSAIC, DAHLIA: See Chapter 16.

MOSAIC, IRIS: This disease so far is confined to the Pacific coast, where plants attacked show mottled foliage and dwarfing, with flower colors darker than normal; transmitted by potato and peach aphids.

Control: Keep free of aphids. Destroy diseased bulbs.

Attacks: Babiana, iris (bulbous).

MOSAIC, LILY: See Chapter 15.

MOSAIC, NARCISSUS: See Chapter 11.

MOSAIC, ORNITHOGALUM: Causes young foliage to become mottled light and dark green; mature foliage gray or yellow. Stems are marked and blotched. Transmitted by the cotton, lily and peach aphids.

Control: As above for iris mosaic.

Attacks: Galtonia, hyacinth, lachenalia, ornithogalum.

RING DISEASE: See stem and bulb nematode, page 116.

ROT, BASAL, OF NARCISSUS: See Chapter 11.

ROT, BASAL FUSARIUM, OF NARCISSUS: See Chapter 11.

ROT, BLUE MOLD: Causes brown, sunken lesions on corms in storage; edges of lesions are water-soaked, greenish. Blue mold develops when moist.
   Control: Dry rapidly at 80 degrees for two weeks after digging; then store in cooler temperature.
   Attacks: Crocus, gladiolus, montbretia, scilla.

ROT, BROWN, OF GLADIOLUS: See Chapter 17.

ROT, DRY FUSARIUM, OF GLADIOLUS: See Chapter 17.

ROT, FUSARIUM, OF LILY: Brown rot occurs at base of scales next to basal plate of bulb. Affected scales fall away.
   Control: Soak bulbs 30 minutes in formalin solution, 1–50. Soil can be disinfected with formalin or methyl bromide (professional use only).
   Attacks: Crocus, freesia, lily.

ROT, FUSARIUM YELLOWS, OF GLADIOLUS: See Chapter 17.

ROT, NARCISSUS SMOULDER: See Chapter 11.

SCAB, GLADIOLUS: See Chapter 17.

SMOULDER, NARCISSUS: See Chapter 11.

VIRUS DISEASES: See mosaics, page 119.

WILT, SPOTTED (VIRUS): Foliage becomes spotted, streaked, or ringed with yellow, brown, or purple, followed by death of leaves.
   Control: Destroy affected bulbs or corms. Disease is transmitted by thrips. To destroy these, dust bulbs with malathion or lindane. (See thrips, page 117.)
   Attacks: Amaryllis, begonia, calla, dahlia, gloxinia.

YELLOWS, FUSARIUM: See Chapter 17.

INSECTICIDES AND FUNGICIDES

Chemicals used for the control of pests and diseases are constantly being reviewed and studied for their effects on mankind, animals and the environment in general. This means that state or federal agencies can prohibit further manufacturing and use of a chemical that is found to be detrimental, or limit its availability and application to specially trained, licensed personnel. At the same time, research continues for more effective and safer pesticides, or even alternatives to them, such as biological controls and improved gardening techniques that will outfox the pests or at least keep them at low levels. While it is reassuring that the U.S. now has an Environmental Protection Agency and that its officials as well as others in the state and federal governments are concerned over the short-term and long-range problems of dangerous chemicals, it does complicate the compilation of a list of current garden chemicals. A second complication is that many states have their own environmental protection agencies and subsequent regulations so an insecticide that may be legal in one state may be banned in another. One way for gardeners to keep abreast of the changes and developments that may occur in pesticides and fungicides is through the Cooperative Extension Association, usually listed in the telephone book under the county government. The experts in these offices—they were once known as "county agents" but are now called "extension specialists"—can help in identifying plant troubles and can make specific control recommendations that are compatible with local and state ordinances.

Note: The relative toxicity of all "icides" (insecticides, fungicides, herbicides, and rodenticides) is expressed in a ratio. This ratio compares the body weight of a group of test animals to the amount of the chemical compound required to kill one-half the population of that test group.

The abbreviation for this nomenclature is known as the LD50 of the compound. The lower the LD50 the more toxic the compound is to man and other animals. In general, a compound with an LD50 of 600 or above is safe to applicator and his environment. However, even with these compounds, care must be exercised. For comparison, some of the LD50s of the insecticides and fungicides that follow are given.

Insecticides

AMIPHOS: For control of aphids and mites (LD50–500).

BACILLUS THURINGIENSIS: Trade names, Dipel, Thuricide-HDC. Effective biological control of caterpillars. Safe for all mammals.

CARBARYL: See Sevin, below.

CYANOGAS: Insecticide and rodenticide which forms a deadly gas on contact with air and moisture. To be used with great caution and by professionals only.

CYGON: Effective against mealybug: may cause injury to tender plants (LD50–215).

CYTHION: More refined malathion odor. Does not irritate as much as malathion.

DD MIXTURE: A soil fumigant for control of root-knot nematodes, wireworms and other soil-borne pests. Contact with human flesh may cause serious burns.

DIAZINON: Control of wireworms (LD50–125).

DICHLORVOS: Trade name, Vapona. Control of mites, aphids, white fly (LD50–56–80).

DIMITE: Effective on all stages of mites, destroying eggs and adults (LD50–600).

DRAMITE: Effective on all stages of mites, destroying eggs and adults (LD50–600).

KELTHANE: All-purpose miticide (LD50–575).

LINDANE: Control of aphids, mites (Trade name, Isotox) (LD50–125).

MALATHION: Contact insecticide for aphids, mites, white fly and variety of other insects (LD50–1000–1200).

NICOTINE SULPHATE: An insecticide effective against sucking insects. Poisonous to man.

PYRETHRUM: Organic insecticide effective for very short periods of time. Safe. (LD50–1000.)

RESMETHRIN: Synthetic pyrethrum for white flies.

ROTENONE: Organic insecticide. Use as contact; short residual action. Toxic to fish. (LD50–250–1000.)

SEVIN: General insecticide. Harmful to bees. Replacement for DDT. (LD50–500–700.)

SOILFUME CAPS: Soil fumigant in convenient capsule form. Used for nematodes and wireworms.

TEDION: Specifically for mites. Doesn't harm beneficial insects. Short residual action (LD50–1500).

Fungicides

ACTI-DIONE: Antibiotic for control of powdery mildew (LD50–100).

BENLATE: Trade name for benomyl, a fungicide with systemic action.

BORDEAUX MIXTURE: Zinc-copper fungicide with long history in grape vineyards. Leaves residue on leaves.

BOTRAN: Effective against botrytis. Safe.

CAPTAN: General fungicide for control of many diseases.

CORROSIVE SUBLIMATE: Used as dip for prevention of diseases—highly toxic (professional use only).

DACONIL: General fungicide (LD50–8000).

FORMALDEHYDE: Trade name is Formalin used as soil sterilant. Will kill plant tissue as well; must be used on fallow areas or greenhouse benches.

METHYL BROMIDE: Soil fumigant to be used with great caution.

POTASSIUM PERMANGANATE: Soil sterilant.

SULPHUR: Control of powdery mildews.

THIRAM: Used for seed and bulb disease prevention.

Caution! IN USING ANY INSECTICIDE OR FUNGICIDE, FOLLOW MANUFAC-TURER'S DIRECTIONS ACCURATELY. Failure to do so may result not only in poor results but also in actual injury to plants, animals, human life and the environment.

*PART TWO
—THE MORE IMPORTANT
GROUPS OF BULBS*

CHAPTER *11. Daffodils*

"Take the winds of March with Beauty"

All winter our pleasantest dreams of the coming of spring are built around the certainty that the golden sunshine of daffodils will cascade down our garden slopes, break in creamy foam against stone terrace walls, and run off in rivulets along paths and into flower borders. Whatever the weather, bugs and germs, the unkindly hand of late winter, or just plain sulks may do to other flowers, we know that the ever-dependable daffodils will come through with colors flying.

Sounds as though we must have bought them by the thousand? Not a bit of it; not even by the hundred. They have all come from original plantings of from three to a dozen bulbs, and the only propagation we have done is an occasional replanting. Remember the old story about the blacksmith and the king's horse—one penny for the first nail, tuppence for the second, fourpence for the third, and so on? Daffodilian progression—that's the answer. Every year now we add a few bulbs of each of a few new varieties, in the hopeless attempt to keep somewhere near up to date, and give away hundreds of old bulbs. As a garden investment, no other bulbs can equal the dividend-paying daffodils!

No other flower in the world is quite so universally and definitely associated with any one season, or so completely embodies in its characteristics the atmosphere and essence of a season. Nature has made the daffodil a perfect symbol of that time of year when all hearts feel the upsurge of new hopes and ambitions; when, as a poet has put it, "the hounds of spring are on winter's traces . . . and the hoofed heel of a satyr crushes the chestnut husk at the chestnut root." And—something to thank the Lord for—not all the hybridizers in the world have been able to so change the daffodil as to give it other forms or other seasons of bloom that would destroy this age-old association.

KNOW YOUR DAFFODILS

Yes, everyone knows the daffodil; but it is astonishing how few, even among gardeners of considerable experience, realize the wide range of types to be found in *Narcissus* species, or for how long a season they will flood the garden with cheerfulness if but given the chance to do so.

We are not referring now to named varieties (more correctly, cultivars, in modern parlance)—of which there is a plethora that threatens to submerge even the experts—but to those differences in flower form, in habit and especially in time of bloom that distinguish one type or class from another. Gain first some knowledge of types, and worry about varieties later.

This is not merely a matter of botanical interest. We all wish to enjoy daffodils as long as we can have them. At best they haste away too soon, and the last dancing blossoms have faded before "summer is y'cummin' in." And to have them for six weeks or more instead of the two or three which in most gardens cover their span of bloom, one must plant types other than the big trumpets and the large-cup varieties which get most of the display space in catalogues.

But it is not alone to have a longer-flowering season that you should be familiar with the several types. In addition to differences in season of bloom, there are differences in size, height and general habit of growth that are all-important when it comes to placing daffodils about your garden. The giant trumpet that makes such a bold display in the mixed border would be entirely out of character and out of scale in the rock garden, or in an intimate sheltered little nook of your terrace where one of the low-growing informal species or its hybrids might make, during its fairly long stay, the most delightful close-up in all your spring pictures. And, according to the types of varieties used, a naturalized planting may look really natural, or about as much so as a plastic Christmas tree. In height daffodils range from the 6 or 8 inches of several of the species (such as *Narcissus bulbocodium* and *N. triandrus albus*) to the 18-inch stems of some of the more robust new trumpets and large-cups; and flowers vary from thimble size, singly or in clusters, to blooms 5 to 6 inches in diameter.

Classification of Daffodils

The latest classification of daffodils is somewhat simpler than the previous one. For the average gardener, however, with no particular desire to grow daffodils for show purposes, the chief importance of any classification is to emphasize the fact that there exists such a remarkable range in size, form and (with the more recent introductions) even in color.

To make it easier to follow, the official classification is here put down in abbreviated form, presenting only the eleven main divisions.

DIVISION 1—*Trumpet:* the trumpet (or corona) as long or longer than the perianth (outer petal) segments; one flower to a stem.

DIVISION 2—*Large-cupped:* cup (or corona) more than one-third, but less than equal to, the length of the perianth segments; one flower to a stem.

DIVISION 3—*Small-cupped:* cup (or corona) not more than one-third the length of the perianth segments; one flower to a stem.

DIVISION 4—*Double:* double flowers. (*See comments below.*)

DIVISION 5—*Triandrus:* hybrids with *N. triandrus* characteristics clearly evident.

DIVISION 6—*Cyclamineüs:* hybrids with *N. cyclamineus* characteristics clearly evident.

DIVISION 7—*Jonquilla:* hybrids with any of the characteristics of the *N. jonquilla* group clearly evident.

DIVISION 8—*Tazetta:* hybrids with characteristics of any of the *N. tazetta,* without admixture of any other.

DIVISION 9—*Poeticus:* hybrids with characteristics of *N. poeticus,* without admixture of any other.

DIVISION 10—*Species and Wild Forms:* all species and wild, or reputedly wild, forms and hybrids.

DIVISION 11—*Split-coronas:* corona split for at least one-third its length.

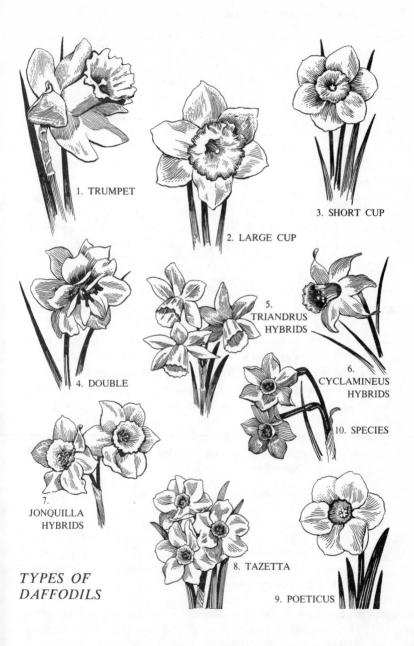

1. TRUMPET

2. LARGE CUP

3. SHORT CUP

4. DOUBLE

5. TRIANDRUS HYBRIDS

6. CYCLAMINEUS HYBRIDS

7. JONQUILLA HYBRIDS

8. TAZETTA

9. POETICUS

10. SPECIES

TYPES OF DAFFODILS

DIVISION 12—*Miscellaneous:* narcissi not falling into any of the foregoing divisions.

Comments: In Divisions 1, 2, 3, 5, 6, and 7 there are subclasses, based on color or on the length of the corona. Thus Division 1-a includes the yellow trumpets; 1-b, the bicolor trumpets; Division 5-a, triandrus hybrids with "the cup not less than two-thirds as long as the perianth segments"; etc., etc. These subdivisions are of importance chiefly in classifying varieties for exhibition purposes, where one must "go by the book."

Divisions 2 and 3, it seems to us, might better have been called "long-cups" and "short-cups" instead of "large" and "small." The classification is based on *length* of the cup, not on its size; and some of the short-cups ('Diana Kasner', for instance) certainly do not have *small* cups.

Division 4 (double) is somewhat ambiguous. Some of the bunch-flowered varieties have double flowers. In the official list of the Royal Horticultural Society, 'Elvira' is put in Division 8 (tazetta or bunch-flowered), while its double form, the delightful 'Cheerfulness,' is placed in Division 4 (double). Some authoritative catalogues list it in Division 8, where, it seems to us, it properly belongs. But the argument is immaterial—plant a few, and you'll always be glad you did it. Characteristics of the species and species groups which have lent their names to Divisions 5 to 9 are as follows:

N. triandrus (DIVISION 5)—rush-like leaves to 1 foot. Flowers per stem, 1–6 pure white and with cup-like corona half the length of perianth segments.

N. cyclamineus (DIVISION 6)—single flowers, drooping or nodding. Perianth, yellow; segments reflexed. Corona orange-yellow, narrow, wavy-edged, the length of the perianth segments.

N. jonquilla (group) (DIVISION 7)—leaves rush-like to 1½ feet. Yellow, fragrant flowers, 2–6 per stem. Corona less than half the length of the perianth segments, and wavy-edged.

N. tazetta (group) (DIVISION 8)—fragrant white flowers, 4–8 per stem, with light yellow coronas much shorter than the obovate perianth segments. Also pure white (Paperwhite Narcissus).

N. poeticus (DIVISION 9)—flowers usually solitary, white, fragrant, with *red-edged,* flat, waved yellow corona, much shorter than perianth segments.

This brief survey will give you a working idea of the classification of the various types and how to identify them. Our chief concern, however, is how they fit into the garden.

WHERE AND WHAT TO PLANT

Daffodils are not big plants, nor are they garbed with the brilliant colors which enable many of the other spring bulbs to dominate their surroundings. They offer a challenge to the imagination and craftsmanship of the gardener: *Here we are; see what you can do with us; if you use us skillfully, we can make your garden a springtime Eden at which every beholder will marvel, taking us for children of the rain and the hoyden wind.*

To accept the challenge successfully, you must use your head. Fortunately you will be working on a canvas where no brush stroke is final, for daffodils can be shifted about with the greatest of ease and with no danger of loss; and each paint tube will contain more pigment every time you go back to it!

In planning your daffodil plantings (the plural is used advisedly, for you will want several) keep in mind first of all that they will be for a spring exhibition. So a good way to start is to gaze out of your view window, unless the "view"—as in so many modern houses—is merely the street in front. Looking at your garden from indoors, you can readily pick out spots where, on a drizzly or too windy day in late March or April, there will be emerging from the dreariness of retreating winter the browns and reds and delicate greens of trees and shrubs coming back to life. Among these you can readily visualize settings where a group of daffodils, large or small, will add just the touch needed to complete a perfect spring picture: perhaps merely a miniature to be enjoyed at close range through a window; perhaps a spreading vista that invites you to dare inclement weather for a brief stroll where you can observe those day-to-day changes that make even a moderate-sized collection of daffodils, as one variety after another opens, such an exciting experience.

Daffodils lend themselves, in the various types available, to about every sort of use the gardener can think of. They are *par excellence* the flower for naturalizing—and for informal landscape groups of half a dozen plants or a hundred.

In small groups in the mixed hardy border they "stay put" without crowding in on their neighbors and, after staging their own act, gracefully retire from the limelight, requiring no further care, except possibly a tucking in of their green leaves, until other plants cover the drying foliage.

For use among rocks, either in the rock garden or more or less haphazardly on a stony bank or about individual boulders, you will seek far and wide indeed to find anything to equal the various daffodil species and their hybrids. For this type of planting they have two advantages: their inherent affinity for rocks and their ability to hold their own with such other rock plants or ground covers as may overrun them. At the same time they do not increase so rapidly as to require constant replanting.

Frequently daffodils are put to one use for which they are not well suited—narrow border plantings along paths, walls, or driveways. So used, during the few weeks they are in bloom they make a fine show; but following this the foliage, after maturing, gradually dies down, and for the latter part of the season the ground is left bare. If it is desired to make use of them for a planting of this sort, they should be interspersed with a few reliably vigorous perennials so that at least intermittent bloom may be had throughout the season. A good combination is daffodils for early spring, irises for late spring, phlox and day-lilies for midsummer, and low-growing chrysanthemums for autumn. Or sufficient space may be left between the daffodil clumps, even in a narrow ribbon border, to set in pot-grown or seedling plants of such long-flowering annuals as petunias, marigolds, dwarf nasturtiums, dwarf zinnias, dwarf dahlias, portulaca and *Phlox drummondii*.

Plan definitely, too, to enjoy daffodils indoors as well as in the garden. You can, of course, cut them from here and there about the garden, but unless you have many it will be well worthwhile to have a few short rows tucked away somewhere—the vegetable garden makes a good location—especially for cutting.

To be at their best indoors, blooms should be cut with long stems just as they are about half open. Then, if at once placed in deep

Another natural setting for daffodils is provided by a field. Home gardeners, who lack such space, can plant daffodils in the lawn but the grass can't be mowed until the daffodil foliage has ripened.

One of the most effective ways to enjoy daffodils is in a natural setting, such as in a woodland among ferns and wild flowers. Gardeners fortunate enough to have both a brook and daffodils are twice blessed!

water and hardened for several hours in a cool place, they will remain fresh for days. In the garden one hesitates to cut them when first opening; and if open flowers are cut at random, many of the blooms are likely to be several days old and will not keep fresh very long. In the cutting rows, types and varieties may be mixed together indiscriminately, but to assure a long season there should be some extra-early and extra-late varieties. The inexpensive mixtures often sold for naturalizing—for which purpose they are not desirable—do provide good planting stock for flowers for cutting. Surplus bulbs of varieties in the garden which may especially appeal to you for decoration or arrangement indoors are, however, the very best source of bulbs for your cutting rows.

TYPICAL VARIETIES FOR VARIOUS USES

As a starter list, here are some varieties of daffodils or narcissi (both names are correct) that we have found very satisfactory for the uses indicated. They should be considered merely as typical examples, as there are many similar ones in each group. More complete descriptions may be found in any good catalogue.

For naturalizing

Narcissus poeticus recurvus (Old Pheasant's Eye)—fragrant; white
    perianth, yellow eye rimmed orange
'King Alfred'—yellow trumpet
'Mount Hood'—white trumpet
'Cantabile'—white perianth, green eye rimmed red (poeticus)
'Liberty Bells'—2–4 lemon-yellow flowers (triandrus)
'February Gold'—golden-yellow cyclamineus; very early
'Peeping Tom'—deep yellow, narrow trumpet cyclamineus; very
    early
'Carlton'—large cup, yellow
'W. P. Milner'—sulphur-yellow miniature trumpet; 9 inches

For beds and borders

'King Alfred'—see above
'Spellbinder'—large lime-yellow trumpet

'Mount Hood'—see above
'Golden Harvest'—deep yellow trumpet
'Kingscourt'—very large golden trumpet; imposing
'Empress of Ireland'—large white trumpet
'Spring Glory'—white and yellow trumpet; long-lasting
'Magnet'—white and yellow trumpet
'Festivity'—large cup with white perianth, yellow crown; magnificent
'Kilworth'—large cup with white perianth, orange-red crown
'Actaea'—white perianth, dark red eye (poeticus)
'Duke of Windsor'—large cup, white perianth, pale yellow cup
'Mrs. R. O. Backhouse'—pinkish crown—original "pink" daffodil
'Louise de Coligny'—fragrant; apricot-pink crown
'La Riante'—pure white perianth and small cup of crimson
'Cushendall'—late; small cup (moss green) and white perianth

For the terrace or patio areas and rock garden or wall

N. *cyclamineus*—early species; golden-yellow
N. *bulbocodium conspicuus*—quaint and intriguing; rich yellow cup
    with rush-like foliage; 6 inches
N. *triandrus albus*—small creamy-white flowers, cyclamen-like; 9
    inches
'Thalia'—2–4 white flowers; late
'Cherie'—1–3 dainty flowers; ivory perianth with pale pink cup
'Rip Van Winkle'—small double yellow; different
'W. P. Milner'—see above
'Tete-a-Tete'—miniature trumpet
'Peeping Tom'—see above; excellent for terrace because it is so
    early and long-lasting

CULTURE

Daffodils have long suffered the fate of all "easy" plants. They
will survive with so little care—or perhaps it might be more accurate
to say under such extreme neglect—that in the great majority of home
gardens, once planted, they are left to shift for themselves like iris,
phlox, day-lilies, and a few other stand-bys which will continue to

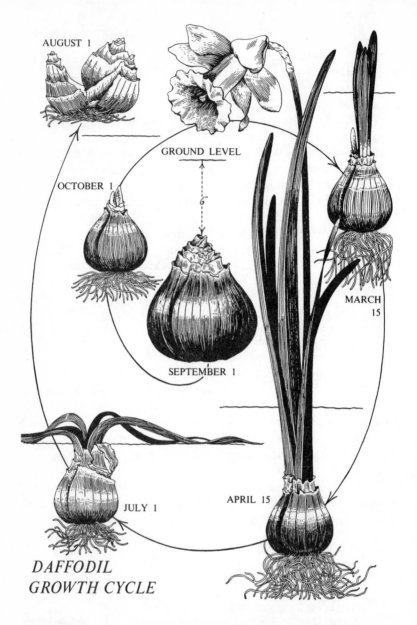

AUGUST 1

GROUND LEVEL

OCTOBER 1

6"

MARCH 15

SEPTEMBER 1

JULY 1

APRIL 15

DAFFODIL GROWTH CYCLE

come smilin' through no matter how abandoned to their fates. They get practically no attention from one end of the year to the other, while roses or dahlias or some other temperamental sisters are cuddled and coddled all season long. But while such neglected daffodils may continue to bloom spring after spring, they do not give such large flowers nor produce them as freely as they might; nor do they increase in number as rapidly as they are capable of doing, with a resultant extension of the original planting, or the production of surplus bulbs which may be given to gardening friends.

To produce really fine daffodils, the gardener should have some knowledge of how the plant grows—of its growth cycle around the year. This has been covered in a general way in Chapter 5. To be a little more specific, let us take a daffodil bulb of the type usually delivered to the home grower in September or October and follow it through a year's development under garden conditions.

When received from the seed store, the bulb, so far as appearances go, is completely dormant. It should be plump, solid and heavy if it has been properly handled; and within it already exists, completely formed, the flower or flowers which will appear the following spring. Changes which have taken place within the bulb during the storage or dormant period have prepared it for quick action once it is planted. As soon as it is placed in the soil, new roots begin to push out from all around the base. These grow rapidly and within two or three weeks have taken such a firm hold that the bulb cannot be raised without lifting a mass of soil with it. This root development continues until the soil freezes solid for the winter.

In the meantime the new leaves will have pushed up to or slightly through the apex of the bulb. Here, however, under normal conditions, they stop, and do not appear aboveground until the following spring. If the autumn is late and unseasonably warm, leaves may push up above the surface of the soil, but this is an abnormal condition. Usually at this time of year, as the nights grow colder, the soil temperature is considerably above that of the atmosphere. This, of course, tends to hold the top growth in check while at the same time giving the roots an opportunity to develop.

During the winter, in cold sections, the bulbs, with their mass of new roots, freeze solid in the soil and the processes of growth are suspended. If proper rooting has taken place, the fleshy bulb tissue is in no way injured by such freezing, although unrooted bulbs under the same conditions would be destroyed.

With the return of warmer days and the first thawing of the soil in spring, growth is renewed. The root system, already thoroughly established, supplements the plant food stored within the bulb, making possible an extremely rapid growth of foliage and flower stems.

The flower stems reach full development and the blossoms open and fade long before the foliage reaches maturity. During the period of early spring growth, the energies of the plant are devoted to the production of flowers and of the new bulbs; the old bulbs at this time are flabbier and lighter in weight than when they were planted in the fall.

After flowering, there follows a phase of the cycle of growth, several weeks long, during which the foliage reaches its maximum development. The size, weight and flowering capacity of the new crops of bulbs, whether they are to be left in the ground or taken up, *are determined by the growth made during this period*. This is the secret of successful daffodil culture.

The duration of the period of top growth after the flowers fade depends largely upon local conditions. Cool weather, plenty of moisture in the soil and an adequate supply of plant food tend to prolong the season of top growth to its full, normal extent. Poor soil, dry soil and high temperatures after flowering tend to cut it short. While it is not true that the biggest and heaviest bulbs (of any particular variety) always produce the best or the most flowers, as a general rule they do. Certain types of soil or an oversupply of nitrogen in the plant-food supply, especially late in the season, may produce heavy, soft bulbs which will not cure properly and are poor in quality. Such conditions are not likely to be encountered under garden culture.

Some varieties seed freely. The majority do not. In either case, the flower stalks and the foliage remain green until, in the bulb's annual cycle of growth, the time for the dormant or resting period arrives. Then the tops gradually wither, dry back to the ground and eventually slough off at the apex of the bulb under the soil. The roots also shrivel and dry, somewhat more slowly, and are often still firmly attached to the bulb at digging time.

Although the several weeks which follow are usually spoken of as the dormant period, this is—as we have already seen—a decidedly inaccurate use of the term, for growth changes within the bulb continue on.

A survey of this annual life cycle shows that there are three periods of active growth: first, immediately after the bulbs are planted, when the root system develops rapidly; second, early in the spring, when the foliage and flowers are being produced; third, a considerable period after flowering, while the foliage is being matured, before it begins to ripen off. Then follows the period when the bulb, *whether left in the soil or kept in storage,* undergoes its rest-period changes. Our system of culture should be built upon these facts.

Soil

In growing daffodils in the garden, there is not likely to be any very wide choice of soil. Most daffodils, fortunately, thrive in a wide range of soil types. We have had them do well in extremely light sandy soil within a stone's throw of the seashore and also in heavy clay loam inland. The ideal soil is a deep, rich clay loam containing enough sand to work nicely and be thoroughly friable.

In the matter of drainage, the home gardener is not apt to have much choice. From our own experience it seems that the question of drainage has been rather overemphasized in daffodil literature insofar as garden culture is concerned. While the roots are active—after planting in the fall and during the spring—most types of daffodils will in no wise suffer from a high degree of soil moisture. Probably it is for this reason that the poeticus type—which is the last to cease growth and the first to start it again in the fall, having practically no real rest period—will thrive in low moist ground unsuited to many other types. It is drainage during the summer rest period which should cause concern—a point which most writers have consistently overlooked. On several occasions we have known daffodils to grow normally and flower perfectly on soil quite saturated with water during several weeks in early spring. On two occasions we have had several lots of daffodils grown in bulb pans for forcing which—owing in one case to an early fall freeze and in the other to a burst water pipe—were literally under 6 inches of water, alternating with solid freezing, in the trenches in which they had been placed for the winter; and they grew and flowered normally after they were brought in. This despite the fact that an undue top growth had been made before they were subjected to this unplanned but convincing experiment.

Where drainage is not good, any of the usual methods of improving it, as suggested in Chapter 6, may be followed. For bulbs in moderate numbers, the simplest plan is to form raised beds 6 or 8 inches above the soil level and held in place by stone or sod borders. Even

Group of daffodil 'E. H. Wilson'—*from six bulbs planted two years previously.*

if this is not done for the entire planting, it may be desirable for the rarer and more difficult varieties, particularly for the light-colored trumpets.

In selecting an exposure for planting, the gardener may have somewhat more latitude. A slight slope to the south or to the east is to be preferred if it is available. A slope not only assures better drainage, but daffodils, particularly if they are to be planted in considerable numbers, are infinitely more charming on sloping ground than on a level plot.

Shelter, too, is important. If some of the extra-early varieties, such as certain of the species and their hybrids ('February Gold', 'Peeping Tom' and 'March Sunshine', for instance), can be placed in a sequestered spot, it may mean a matter of a week or so—in some seasons considerably more—in the time of their first flowering. With many plants, too warm and sheltered a pocket promoting early growth is distinctly a disadvantage, but that is not the case with these dainty but frostproof harbingers of spring.

For the later types, protection from driving winds by a hedge, a shrubbery border, or a wall often preserves the blossoms from being badly battered. Such protection is doubly important when flowers are to be grown for exhibition purposes, or even for cutting for indoor decoration.

Planting

With the ground once thoroughly prepared (see Chapter 7) the work of planting is at least 80 per cent done. Another 10 per cent of the work which remains can be accomplished at one's leisure. It consists of making out labels and setting out the bulbs in the order in which they are to be planted, so everything will be in readiness for the final rite of actually placing the bulbs in the soil. The rest is not only easy but one of those garden tasks which is almost an unadulterated pleasure.

Just what is the best time to plant daffodils?

In theory, it is just before the bulbs, having completed ripening and maturing processes which take place during the period of dormancy, are ready to send out new roots. This state will vary somewhat with different types and even with individual varieties, and also with local conditions. On an average, in the northern United States it would be in late August or very early September.

As a matter of practice, the planting date—at least for bulbs which must be purchased—is determined not by a theoretical ideal time, but by when the bulbs can be procured. But the planter can adopt as a guiding rule the principle of the earlier the better. Daffodil bulbs may be, and frequently are, planted in October or November, and even into December; but late planting is to be avoided if possible. If planting is very late, a heavy mulch, to postpone hard freezing of the ground, will provide a longer period for root development.

Do not let anyone persuade you that early planting is a matter of no importance. While late planting will by no means spell complete failure—and though it is of course infinitely better than not planting at all!—it does result in giving the bulbs a poorer start, and in all probability less perfect flowers for the first season. Some years ago we had occasion to plant, on a commercial scale, several varieties quite late in the season. They were put in the same field, under exactly the same conditions, as other lots of the same varieties planted some three weeks earlier. The result was certainly convincing proof of the advantage of earlier planting. These late-set bulbs produced barely half the volume of foliage made by those in the earlier planting. The flowers were smaller and the flower stalks little more than half as high. All the bulbs had come from the same source, and if there was any difference in quality, it was in favor of those which had to be planted late.

With many varieties there is another distinct advantage in early planting. Some sorts are decidedly poor keepers and are likely to begin to get soft or even to decay if held long beyond the time when they should be back in the ground. This is especially true of the white and light-flowered trumpets as a class.

So far as preference in time may be given, poeticus varieties and extremely early-flowering species and their hybrids should be planted first.

The depth of planting for daffodil bulbs—like the period during which they may be planted—is a matter of considerable elasticity. For the beginner it would almost be safe to suggest "the deeper the better." The instructions usually given to plant the bulbs deep enough so there will be 4 or 5 inches of soil above the top of the bulb are correct for most varieties and usual conditions. It might be more accurate to say the "shoulder" of the bulb rather than the top, as some bulbs have long tapering necks. We have found that beginners, however, often think they have covered the bulb 4 or 5 inches deep, when actual measurement with a ruler would reveal that it was little over half that depth. In light sandy soil it is advisable to increase the depth of planting by an inch or so.

The distance apart at which the bulbs are to be placed depends upon a number of factors. Large bulbs in groups in the border may be placed 6 to 8 inches apart each way. This is close enough to avoid a spotty effect the first season and yet leaves room enough for two or three years' increase before the group will become overcrowded. This is for strong-growing types, such as practically all the trumpets, and certain vigorous large-cups and small-cups. Bulbs of less robust growth—the true poets, many of the poeticus-like crosses, the jonquil and triandrus hybrids—may well be placed as close as 4 or 5 inches apart.

In naturalized planting, anything like a regular spacing of the bulbs must be studiously avoided or the desired effect will be spoiled. A method often employed is to take a basketful or pailful of bulbs and throw them out on the ground with a swinging motion, so that while the bulk of them fall fairly close together, others will be scattered to a considerable distance, with much more space between the individual bulbs. A few practice attempts usually enable the planter to secure a desirable distribution, and the bulbs may then be planted as they have fallen, with the removal of some where they happen to be too thick.

Even in the border, much more pleasing effects result if straight rows, rectangles and too regular spacing are avoided in planting. Nothing approaching the abandon of a really naturalized planting can be attempted under garden conditions, but an effect between this extreme on the one hand and studied formality on the other may be obtained. Mark off the soil in the border—after it has been prepared and raked smooth—into somewhat irregular circles and oblongs, each of a size which will accommodate the number of bulbs of the variety to be planted within it. The bulbs are then placed, somewhat irregularly, conforming to the outline which has been made. The effect of such a group, even the first season, will be that of a colony that has developed naturally by itself. If other planting is to be done, either at the same time or the following spring, the location of each group of bulbs can be marked by outlining it with a narrow ribbon of ground limestone or sand applied with a watering can, with sprinkler removed.

Watering immediately after planting, unless nature provides a good soaking, is always desirable. Without plenty of moisture in the soil, the new root growth will be delayed or start slowly and irregularly. In moist soil the roots make a quick strong start and within ten days or so will have taken firm hold and be in condition to forage successfully for themselves even if the soil remains comparatively dry for some time after planting.

As the soil will have become more or less packed down in the process of planting, it is advisable to loosen thoroughly and pulverize it to the depth of a couple of inches after the bulbs have been put in. This is especially important in rather heavy soil with a tendency to pack hard. Unless loosened up comparatively soon after planting, such soil will go through the winter with hard spots that may interfere considerably with the pushing up of the foliage in the spring. If left until spring, it cannot readily be cultivated without danger of cutting or breaking the growing foliage shoots just beneath the surface.

Mulching for the first season after planting is sometimes advisable, but many authorities consider it unnecessary. We have never known varieties of the really hardy types, *if* planted early enough to make strong root growth before the ground froze, to be injured for lack of winter mulching. In severe climates a mulch for new plantings of valuable varieties is worthwhile as an extra precaution. Varieties of the semi-hardy types, such as 'Paperwhite' and 'Soleil d'Or', if planted near the northern limit of where they may safely be grown out of doors, decidedly will be benefited by winter mulching.

In applying a winter mulch, do not put it on until about the time the surface of the soil begins to freeze. Wheat or rye straw and meadow or salt hay are the materials most often employed for mulching. Peat moss has the advantage, especially for the home garden, of not being unsightly during the winter and in the spring can be worked into the soil instead of having to be removed. Our favorite mulches are pine needles or short evergreen boughs applied just after the soil has frozen, and preferably over snow.

Spring Care

The first spring job in the daffodil border, if a winter mulch has been put on, is to remove this carefully before growth starts. Watch for any foliage which may be pushing up, as some varieties begin growth much earlier than others.

An application of plant food is in order at this time. As the annual cycle of growth of the daffodil plant makes plain (see page 136), there is now renewed activity of the root growth and a very rapid and vigorous development of both foliage and flowers. The fertilizer supplied should contain plenty of available nitrogen. One of the quick-acting, complete chemical plant foods put out under various trade names will answer. If bone meal is used, at least half of it should be in the form of bone flour. A supplementary dressing of nitrate of soda or sulphate of ammonia may be desirable, particularly if the spring is very cold and backward. Needless to say, all fertilizer materials should be applied carefully in accordance with the directions accompanying them. The fertilizers need be only lightly scratched in, as spring rains quickly carry them down to the roots.

Plate 9

ABOVE: *Daffodils and birch trees go together like peaches and cream. A dozen or two bulbs, in two or three years, will give an effect like this.* BELOW: *Double early tulips are long lasting and wind resistant. The varieties are fuchsia-colored 'Rossinant', its petals slightly green-tipped, and the deep yellow 'Aga Khan', which changes to dark orange.*

Plate 10

Plate 11

A water background enhances any spring bulb planting, whether it's an elaborate pond or stream or a modest reflecting pool that can be added to a terrace or backyard garden. Shown here are tulips 'Mr. Van der Hoef', blue grape hyacinths and tulips 'Peach Blossom'.

Plate 12

ABOVE: *With tulips, as with daffodils, differences in size and form are much greater than most gardeners realize. Shown are 'Red Emperor' and diminutive* Tulipa biflora. BELOW: *Fantastic in form, and now available in many dramatic color combinations, are the fringed and feathered parrot tulips.*

Plate 13

Plate 14

ABOVE: *Thumbing their chilled noses at frosty nights and late snows, bright* Tulipa kaufmanniana *varieties ('Gaiety', right, 'Gluck', left) last an incredibly long time.* BELOW: *A path bordered by tulips 'Golden Oxford', 'Red Matador', 'Orange Nassau', 'Gudoshnik', 'Jewel of Spring'. Violas and wallflowers are the interplanting.*

Plate 15

Fertilizers high in nitrogen should be applied only very early in the season. If used after the buds begin to develop, they are likely to result in soft flowers which stand up poorly, particularly if wanted for exhibition purposes.

For daffodils being grown in the garden, no further care, except to keep them clear of any weeds which may start, will be required after flowering. Where flowers are grown for exhibition purposes, protection and support may be required.

After Flowering

All too often, as the golden chalices or the gleaming white perianths of the daffodil blooms fade, the grower's interest fades with them. This is both the most universal and the most serious mistake in the culture of daffodils in the home garden. While the flowers may be gone, the daffodil plant is just midway in its most important period of growth. The gardener's aim from this point on should be to keep it growing as long and as vigorously as possible.

A second application of fertilizer, similar to that which was put on when the beds were prepared in the fall, may well be made at this time. In rich soil this may not be needed, but as a rule it is advisable, particularly in the border where the daffodils must compete with other annuals and perennials for the balance of the season.

A stirring of the soil between the clumps or groups of daffodils is important if the surface about them has become packed hard. Some varieties making strong luxuriant foliage growth, such as 'King Alfred' and others of similar habit, may be tied up with the green raffia or Twist-ems to prevent their sprawling over other nearby plants as the foliage begins to break down, and to facilitate cultivation around them. This is mainly only a necessity in small gardens or in terrace plantings. Nothing must be done to prevent the foliage from ripening naturally.

Watering, too, must not be neglected during this period of growth if best results for another year are to be expected. Very often, particularly in the Northeast and the Midwest, an early period of dry weather, even if it does not assume the proportions of a drought, follows close upon the heels of the season of daffodil bloom. Such weather, especially when supplemented by strong drying winds, will rob the daffodils of soil moisture just when they need it most. One or two thorough soakings under such conditions greatly benefit the plants. Allow water to run freely from the open end of the hose into the bed until the soil will absorb no more.

Although summer mulches are seldom recommended for daffodils, they are highly desirable in sections where excessive heat and dry weather are likely to be encountered. Not only do they aid in keeping the tops in a growing condition longer, but, where the bulbs are to be left in the soil, the lower soil temperature resulting from the mulch is beneficial, particularly to varieties which make sparse foliage, and in borders where there are not plenty of other plants interspersed with the daffodils to keep the soil shaded. Where annuals are used to follow the daffodils, they serve this purpose.

Fall Care

The old saying, "Out of sight, out of mind," is nowhere better exemplified in the garden than in the care—or rather the lack of care—provided hardy bulbs which are allowed to remain over from season to season without being disturbed.

In late summer—usually between mid-August and mid-September, but varying with varieties and with conditions—the new crop of roots, put out after the so-called dormant period, will be making vigorous growth. In order to do the job that is expected of them, they must have plenty of moisture and plenty of plant food. Often they lack both. After a dry period it takes more than a few refreshing showers to dampen the soil to a depth of 5 to 8 inches, where these new roots are lying. A little experimental digging in one's own garden will demonstrate this fact.

The gardener, therefore, should make it part of his routine to loosen up the surface of the soil in his daffodil border or over the daffodil clumps in the mixed border and, if the soil is dry, to give it at least one thorough soaking to provide more favorable conditions for growth until the usual fall rains take over the job. In order that this important chore may not be forgotten, it is well to fix in mind Labor Day as the approximate date on which it should be attended to.

It is well at this time also to make absolutely sure that there is no lack of plant food. A highly nitrogenous fertilizer is not necessary, but a few pounds of bone meal, supplemented perhaps by wood ashes or a high-potash fertilizer, will provide against any possibility of undernourishment.

A striking illustration of the importance of cultivation and fertilizing came to our attention recently. A large border which had remained undisturbed for several years, made over and refertilized in late summer, produced, the following spring, flowers from bulbs which the owner had thought lost or run out, while others which had been flowering each year were better than they had been since the first season after they were planted.

LIFTING AND REPLANTING

As a rule commercial bulb growers dig or lift daffodils every year. Occasionally, to provide planting stock (many small bulbs) or because of market conditions, lots of certain stocks may be allowed to remain down for two years, but not longer. Home gardeners will have occasion to lift bulbs only when they desire to increase some new or choice variety as rapidly as possible; when they wish to rearrange plantings; and when, as a result of multiplication and consequent overcrowding, the flowers produced are no longer up to par.

The time when lifting may be done covers a considerable period. The ideal time is when the tops have dried sufficiently to fall over and begin to dry up, but while they are still firmly attached to the bulbs, so that the latter may be readily located in the soil.

Commercial growers often dig while the tops are still quite green and before the roots have begun to shrivel. This is particularly true of late-maturing types, such as the poeticus, and in sections like the Northwest, where in moist spells or in moist seasons the new roots begin to form before the old have entirely disappeared. The only real disadvantage of digging early—this is after the tops have made their full growth but while they are still green—is that the bulbs will not have developed their maximum size. In the home garden this is of little consequence, although with the commercial grower it is, of course, a serious consideration. The chief objection to late digging—after the tops have completely withered and sloughed off of the bulb—is the increased difficulty of locating the bulbs and of getting them out of the ground without mechanical injury in digging.

In most soils a flat-tined digging fork will be found a safer implement to use than a spade and more efficient than a trowel, especially
if any considerable number of bulbs are to be taken up. Needless to
say, the greatest possible care should be exercised not to cut or spear
the bulbs, especially those of choice varieties. This can be accomplished by digging away the soil on one side to within an inch or two
of the clump before attempting to remove it from the soil.

If the bulbs come out clean and fairly dry, with few roots, they will
require little or no preliminary drying before being put into storage.
This is often the case when the bulbs are dug fairly late. If, however,
the tops and the roots are still firmly attached and considerable soil
adheres to the bulbs, they should be dried off for a period of from
one to several days before being stored. In any case, they should not
be exposed to a scorching midsummer sun, as this may result in
scalding them on one side. A place in partial shade, such as under a
tree where air currents can reach them freely, will usually accomplish
such drying as is needed almost as quickly as exposure to full sun.
For the home garden ordinary flats with cracks in the bottom make
convenient receptacles in which to place the bulbs for drying and
storing. Each variety, of course, should be carefully labeled as it is
taken up.

Unless there is some special reason for keeping the bulbs in summer storage until autumn, it is best to replant at once. In this event,
no preliminary drying is necessary. In fact, it is best to have the new
locations ready before digging and to shift the bulbs at once as one
would growing plants. If there is need to shift a planting without dividing the bulbs, they can be moved at any time after flowering if
dug with plenty of soil adhering to the roots and replanted at once.

However, if the grower wishes to obtain "splits" from which to
develop new round bulbs, a period of storage is necessary in order
that the offsets may be removed readily and without injury to the
parent bulb. Or it may be that replanting in a new location cannot
readily be done before fall. Then the question of providing the best
conditions for summer storage must be considered.

The two most important factors are a reasonably low temperature
and ample ventilation. Where only a few flats of bulbs are to be
cared for, a shelf arranged near a window or an air duct in a cellar
or basement may serve the purpose. A shed or loft, provided ample
ventilation may be given, will answer. We once had the ideal setup—

a small building under the shade of large trees, previously used for fancy poultry: it was equipped with trap-door openings along the sides, making possible quite complete control of ventilation.

The bulbs should be examined occasionally so that any which show signs of decay or disease may be immediately destroyed. After several weeks, when thoroughly dried and ripened, they may be gone over, cleaned, and graded, the larger bulbs being used for replanting in beds or borders or for forcing indoors, and the smaller ones for growing on.

Replanting

Such home-cured bulbs may be replanted at any time the ground is ready for them. If they can be put in before new varieties from commercial growers or seedsmen begin to come in, so much the better.

Small bulbs and splits are best handled by putting them in rows in a place by themselves, or in the vegetable or cutting garden, where they can be easily and thoroughly cared for. Our method is to open a furrow as deep as possible and plant the bulbs in the bottom of this, using a trowel to get them well down. They are set 1 to 3 inches apart, according to size and variety. Filling the furrow in level gives a good 4 inches of soil over the tops of the bulbs. A space of a foot or so is left between each variety and the one following it, and stout stake markers which will not be dislodged or broken in cultivating are used. Well in advance of freezing weather a moderate-sized ridge of soil is thrown over the row. This is leveled off early in the spring just before the tops begin to come through, leaving a mellow surface free from weeds for the early growth.

Even when one has acquired all the bulbs of a particular variety which can be accommodated in the garden, any surplus may be put to good use by planting in rows in the same way as suggested above, but somewhat deeper if they are full-sized bulbs, to furnish an abundance of bloom for cutting. There are few occasions throughout the year which afford the gardener more pleasure than having plenty of daffodils, especially if they are of the splendid newer varieties not yet too widely known, to present to appreciative friends. Then, too, full-sized bulbs from the cutting rows may be used for growing indoors for winter bloom. In this case summer storing and curing are not essential. Bulbs may be taken up in early fall, before they have made

Group of 'Moonshine' (*triandrus hybrid*) *from a stray bulb in soil filled in behind rocks.*

too much new root growth, and transferred to pots or bulb pans to be taken indoors later on, after they have made the usual preliminary root growth required for flowering indoors. (See Chapter 20.)

DAFFODIL TROUBLES

Having grown daffodils for many years and in many types of soil, and having never once had to dust, spray, or fumigate for any disease or insect pest, we do not burst out into goose pimples when we look through bulletins and articles devoted to narcissus troubles. The full extent of our treatment for these easily grown flowers has consisted in an occasional removal of a plant or the destruction of a bulb that looked "sick." On not more than a half dozen occasions, out of several hundred varieties, have we discarded all the bulbs of a weak-growing variety.

The narcissus, nevertheless, does have its troubles. Here are the half dozen or so most commonly encountered.

Diseases

Eelworm (nematode; *Ditylenchus dipsaci*) is commonly listed as a disease, although the eelworm is a worm so minute as to be invisible to the naked eye. Nematodes enter the foliage as it emerges in spring, causing it to become twisted and distorted as it grows, with characteristic swollen pimples ("spikkles") along the edges or at the center of the leaves. Later on the bulbs become affected and gradually rot, with brownish, disintegrating layers between normal firm healthy ones.

Control includes: (1) destroying infected bulbs by burning; (2) treating bulbs which *may* be infected with hot water and formaldehyde added (1 pint to 25 gallons), soaking for 4 hours at a temperature of 110–112 degrees and replanting at once; (3) disinfecting all equipment by dipping in water with formaldehyde added (1 part to 9 of water); (4) sterilizing soil with DD mixture, a soil fumigant.

Basal rot attacks basal plate of bulb, causing a chocolate or reddish-brown decay which spreads into the bulb itself. Secondary symptom is a pinkish-white fungus around base of bulb. Spreads through bulbs in storage; most serious in warm climates and on bicolor varieties.

Control: (1) destroy infected bulbs; (2) avoid cutting or bruising bulbs when lifting, and dry off as quickly as possible; (3) after bulbs are dug, treat with benomyl or thiabendazole as soon as possible; (4) store bulbs in thin layers and keep well ventilated, *and examine frequently.*

Mosaic (gray disease), a virus causing stunted plants, with foliage showing grayish, yellowish, or brown stripes, especially in upper two-thirds of leaves, and small streaks or blotches on blooms.

Control: (1) as symptoms appear early in growth, destroy diseased plants and keep plants free of aphids, which carry disease.

Narcissus fire (botrytis) is a disease (similar to the well-known tulip fire) which affects narcissus on the Pacific Coast only. The tazetta species and hybrids, particularly, throw spotted blooms. After withering, these diseased flowers produce spores which cause an infection on the foliage later in the season.

Control: (1) destroy all spotted flowers and blighted leaves as soon as noticed; (2) spray growing plants in spring with Bordeaux mixture, ferbam or zineb. Similar measures are used against gray mold blight. (See Chapter 10.)

Narcissus smoulder causes decay of bulbs in storage as well as in garden beds where the flowers and foliage rot. Cold, wet weather conditions foster the disease. Slightly affected bulbs produce malformed shoots which turn yellow and later are covered with gray spore masses. Destroy affected bulbs promptly. For Southern Blight and Leaf Scorch, see Chapter 10.

Insects

The two most commonly encountered insect pests of daffodils are the large bulb fly (*Merodon equestris*) and the lesser bulb fly (*Eumerus tuberculatus*), the grubs of both of which destroy bulbs in much the same way as the familiar onion maggot destroys that succulent occupant of the vegetable patch.

The large bulb fly is quite large, in general appearance not unlike a bumblebee, and variously colored, brown, black, or banded. Eggs are deposited singly, usually as foliage is dying down, at the base of the stems. The egg hatches in a few days and the grub spends the rest of the season and the winter eating its way through the bulb, which is completely destroyed.

The lesser bulb fly resembles an ordinary house fly. It lays its eggs in clusters, somewhat earlier than the larger fly, and several larvae find their way into a bulb—two or three to ten times that number. This first brood, leaving the bulb a decaying mass, matures about July, to generate a second brood.

Controls: when planting, never use a soft "squashy" bulb unless certain it has been given the hot-water treatment or fumigated.

Bulb mite is the same pest which attacks lilies. For description and control, see Chapter 10.

If the daffodil claims as its own that tumultuous season between melting snows and barren boughs, and the time when bursting buds and the green flames of new grass spread through brown meadows, then no less does the tulip reign supreme when spring has definitely arrived and settled down to stay. The daffodils have little competition; the season's setting is a perfect foil for their airy and delicate colorings. The tulips find plenty of competition, but their more massive blooms and brilliant hues make them equal to the task of holding the garden spotlight through the year's most colorful period.

It is difficult to think of a spring garden without visualizing the picture largely in terms of tulips. Of all flowers, they present the garden maker with the widest range of colors from which to make selections for the effects he may wish to achieve.

If the designer wants strong hues rivaling those of the spectrum in intensity and clarity, they are to be found on the tulip palette; if he prefers somber shades or the most delicate tints, these, too, are available. Hues in the tulip world include nearly a full two-thirds of the color circle, ranging from violet-blue through reds, oranges and yellows to green-yellow and white.

Moreover, you can be certain (at least to the extent that one can be certain of anything in gardening) that colors will come out as you planned them, and when they are needed; for tulips, if one secures good bulbs, are remarkably dependable in their performance.

While most gardeners think of tulips as being colorful, comparatively few have any idea of the wide range in form, size and season of bloom that is to be found among them. Not one gardener in a hundred will name you a *fragrant* tulip, though there are a fair number of varieties that on this score vie with any rose.

Or take the matter of season bloom, which is of the utmost importance if you wish tulips to contribute all they are capable of contributing to the beauty of your spring garden.

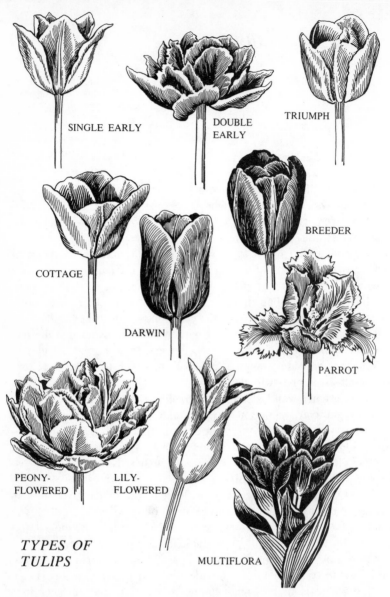

SINGLE EARLY

DOUBLE EARLY

TRIUMPH

COTTAGE

DARWIN

BREEDER

PARROT

PEONY-FLOWERED

LILY-FLOWERED

MULTIFLORA

TYPES OF TULIPS

The three types of tulips that are probably best known to gardeners are the cottage or May-flowering, the Darwins and the lily-flowered. But also well-known are the parrots with their large, distinctive laciniated petals which bloom a little later than the preceding. With a careful selection of early-, medium- and late-flowering varieties, you will get three to four weeks of bloom. If you are wise enough to include in your plantings some of the tulip species (and their hybrids and selections), and some of the really early-flowering garden types, such as the single and double earlies and the triumphs, you can enjoy an additional three to four weeks of tulip gaiety.

Nor need you have an estate in order to do this; a few groups of them—a dozen or even a half dozen of a kind tucked in here and there—will give a breath-taking lift and brightness to your spring flower border or terrace planting, to a garden of naturalized bulbs, or to the rock garden.

THE CLASSIFICATION OF TULIPS

Early Flowering

1. SINGLE EARLY TULIPS

2. DOUBLE EARLY TULIPS

Mid-Season Flowering

3. MENDEL TULIPS

Chiefly the result of crosses between the old Duc van Tol and Darwin tulips and which generally do not have the habit of triumph tulips.

4. TRIUMPH TULIPS

Chiefly the result of crosses between single early and late (May-flowering) tulips; plants of stouter habit than Mendel tulips.

5. DARWIN HYBRID TULIPS

Chiefly the result of crosses between Darwin tulips with *Tulipa fosteriana* and the result of crosses between other tulips and botanical tulips, which have the same habit and in which the wild plant is not evident.

Late-Flowering

6. DARWIN TULIPS

Lower part of flower usually rectangular in outline; segments of good substance; stems tall and strong.

7. LILY-FLOWERED TULIPS
Flowers with pointed reflexed petals.

8. COTTAGE TULIPS (SINGLE LATE TULIPS)
Flowers oval, which do not belong to division 6 or 7.

9. REMBRANDT TULIPS
Broken tulips, striped or marked brown, bronze, black, red, pink or purple on red, white or yellow ground.

10. PARROT TULIPS
Tulips with laciniate flowers, generally late-flowering.

11. DOUBLE LATE TULIPS (PEONY-FLOWERED TULIPS)

Species
(Wild plants and hybrids in which the wild plant is evident)

12. KAUFMANNIANA, varieties and hybrids.
Very early flowering, sometimes with mottled foliage.

13. FOSTERIANA, varieties and hybrids.
Large, early flowering, some cultivars with mottled or striped foliage.

14. GREIGII, varieties and hybrids.
Always with mottled or striped foliage, flowering later than kaufmanniana.

15. OTHER SPECIES and their varieties and hybrids.

SIZE AND FORM

While we're rounding out the tulip picture, let's take a glance at some other differences in this versatile genus that are too little recognized, for the simple reason that the cottage, Darwin and other big tulips get all the breaks in color display in most catalogues. Admittedly, a huge 5- or 6-inch cup on a 36-inch stem is more impressive to most people than a much smaller flower held 6 to 20 inches above the ground. But the latter may fit quite as well into a particular garden picture. In fact, these earlier, smaller tulips are often much easier to use effectively with groups of other flowers than are their giant cousins, with all their regal splendor. There are many shapes and color designs, too, in these little ones that are not to be found in the more popular types; rounded or star-shaped blooms; tapering, twisted petals that are almost fantastic; others having two, three, or four flowers to a stem; gracefully waved and mottled foliage—in all, a fascinating and intriguing group to discover.

FOR WEEKS OF BLOOM

To get an idea of how to use the various types to best advantage, let's follow the tulip trail from one end to the other. We can take them in the order in which they bloom—almost from melting snows to early summer!

Species and Hybrids: Although arranged last in the revised Classification of Tulips (classes 12, 13, 14, 15), here is a whole group of tulips that bloom ahead of or with your early daffodils! They are short-stemmed, but so gaily colored, so resistant to injury from storms or cold and so long-lasting that they are quite as rewarding as the larger ones that flower a month later. Moreover, they remain much longer without "running out," and therefore are really valuable for naturalizing.

A few of the species bloom late, but the group of *Tulipa kaufmanniana* varieties and hybrids are the earliest of all generally available tulips, and most of the species bloom well in advance of the popular garden sorts. As if to make certain of giving you your money's worth, many of them put on a double-feature billing, with brilliantly striped, pointed, closed flowers in the morning and evening and on cloudy days, and entirely different, widely expanded blooms when a few sunny hours cause them to open.

The uses to which the various tulip species can be put are manifold. They will thrive in soil less well supplied with plant foods than that required for the large garden varieties, and they rather like a pretty thorough baking during the summer. They are ideal for planting among or around rocks or along a path with a stone edging. In selecting a location, keep in mind the height of the particular kind being planted, as they vary from 6 to 10 inches, with a few going to 15 or more. The bulbs of most of the species are quite small, but do not overcrowd them when planting; a spacing of 5 to 6 inches is none too much.

The Single Early Tulips come next in time of flowering. In this group there have been few new varieties introduced recently, but most catalogues list several varieties. Don't overlook them when making up your bulb order. For growing indoors, too, they rank at the top of the list, especially as many of them are delightfully fragrant.

The single earlies, formerly used extensively for bedding, should not be discarded because that particular type of planting has gone out of favor. Of modern height—10 to 16 inches—they withstand more hard weather than the Darwins and cottage types and hence are better for exposed positions. In the mixed border they should be toward the front.

The Double Earlies are similar to the single forms, but the flowers are much longer-lasting, both in the garden and when cut. They are equally desirable for forcing.

Triumphs and Mendels and the Darwin Hybrids: These first two groups fill in the gap, in time of flowering, that formerly existed between the single earlies and the cottage and Darwin groups and are classified as mid-season flowering. They were developed by crossing single early with Darwin varieties, with the result that they are about ten days earlier than the latter and much larger-flowered and taller than the former, averaging in height from 20 to 24 inches. They are excellent for forcing, having the advantage over the single early of stiffer, more upright stems and longer-lasting blooms.

The third group of mid-season flowering tulips is composed of Darwin hybrids. These comparatively new tulips can truly be described as sensational. The results of crosses between Darwin tulips and *Tulip fosteriana,* they possess exceptional qualities—brilliant colors, great size and imposing stature. We know of no gardeners who have not been impressed by these beauties.

Late-flowering

The species and early sorts take us through three to four weeks of tulip enchantment, but we still have ahead of us the really big show: the May-flowering cottage, Darwin, lily-flowered and parrot groups, which completely dominate the garden scene during their season of bloom. As these are so well known, we give them little space here, except to point out a few differences that still exist to some degree, although interbreeding has been carried on to such an extent that the lines of distinction are rapidly disappearing. Few May-flowering tulips are adapted to forcing.

Cottage: These are characterized by long, flexible stems; flowers with rather long, pointed petals and clear, brilliant colors, often blending. Many tones and tints of yellow and orange, but no purples, lavenders, or bronzes are found in this group. The so-called "green" tulips, such as 'Artist' and 'Greenland', belong here.

Darwin: Long, slender stems support huge, globular flowers in a wide range of color from pure white through deep shades to near black; often with strongly contrasting centers.

Breeder: This class has been eliminated and all varieties formerly classified as breeders have been placed in other classes.

Rembrandt: This class now includes all "broken" tulips, those that are striped or marked.

Parrots and Lily-flowered: These two interesting groups are really strays, with distinctive flower forms, from other classes. Most of the parrots are sports from well-known garden varieties ('Fantasy' from 'Clara Butt') which have laciniated and more or less twisted petals, often with green markings. Even the stems tend to assume informal curves. The lily-flowered tulips have long, pointed, recurving petals. 'White Triumphator' and 'Red Shine' are known to many.

Both the parrots and the lily-flowered tulips are exceptionally useful as cut flowers, alone or with other plant material.

Double Late (*Peony-flowered*): These tulips with their large, peony-like blooms come into bloom with the earlier Darwins. While making very effective and long-lasting color groups in the border, they are likely to be bowed down in rainy weather.

While bulb catalogues give a good idea of the tulips available for your garden, especially the May-flowering sorts, the only sure-fire way of getting precisely what will please you best is to make selections where you can actually see them in bloom. Extensive collections are to be found at botanic gardens, many public parks and at the trial grounds of nurserymen and seedsmen. Why not treat yourself to a "Tulip Day" so you'll know exactly what you'll want to order for next fall's planting?

USES

Despite their brilliant and varied coloring, tulips are much more limited than daffodils in the uses to which they can be put in garden making. The horticultural varieties require rich soil and careful culture if they are to be kept flowering for more than a season or two; hence they are of little use for naturalizing, even quite aside from the fact that in northern latitudes they just do not fit into naturalistic settings.

Some of the species, such as *Tulipa kaufmanniana* and *T. dasystemon* and *T. marjolettii,* self-seed freely and in congenial surroundings form spreading colonies. Even the species, however, are by no means as sure-fire as daffodils for naturalizing, nor adaptable to so wide a range of soils and drainage conditions. Most of them should have particularly good drainage and like rather sandy soil and a real sun baking during the summer months. Their ideal home is a rocky slope or bank, or in the rock garden.

The large-flowered horticultural varieties of tulips, from the single earlies to the latest parrots, are at their best in mixed borders or in a special tulip border. Such a border can be in the foreground of a shrubbery planting where the tulips can be planted in drifts, more or less following the informal lines of the shrubs. In either case, height, color and flowering time should be carefully considered in ordering bulbs and in making up the planting plan; otherwise there will be gaps in the season of bloom. In making out an order list for tulips, it is advisable to put down first the types you would like to grow and then to select varieties under these headings that will fit your available space. By so doing you can keep your plantings balanced and be assured of a long season of bloom.

In former days tulips were considered the ideal flower for "design" beds, or for uniform blocks of color in large, formal landscape designs. They are still occasionally so used, and there has been a trend back to this type of planting, but with the passing of big estates (and the imported-professional-gardener school of landscaping that accompanied them), and with the more informal treatment of public buildings and grounds now in vogue, this use of tulips has almost disappeared.

As a general rule tulips should not be planted in mixtures. (This does not apply to the cutting garden, to which odds and ends and

When planning or building a terrace, some room should be left for spring bulbs. This terrace is decorated by a generous-sized planting of greigii tulip varieties and pots of daffodils.

surplus bulbs from replantings may well be consigned.) Like all general rules, however, this one is sometimes broken to advantage. We recall one place where, each fall, the gardener placed a few stray bulbs of tall tulips in the edge of a planting of broad-leaved evergreens. Coming out a few at a time, their unexpected appearance in such a setting carried with it a certain elfin charm, as though the pixies had been at work when the gardener's back was turned.

We once had a somewhat similar result. We used a truckload of soil from an old tulip border in mixing compost for a new rock garden. Some of the bulbs that came along with this soil must have been covered at least 18 inches deep, but they all found their way up the following spring, from under stones and through spreading rock plants, to provide bursting stars of color over a period of several weeks. The flowers were much smaller than normal for the varieties —a fact that contributed largely to the artistic effect. Our clients were highly pleased and free with compliments, but in all honesty we had to confess that the whole thing was purely an accident.

CULTURE

The need of securing top-quality bulbs has already been empha-sized, but with tulips special care in this respect is of vital impor-tance. With daffodils and most of the other hardy spring bloomers, a small bulb or even an injured one may improve during the following season or two. Unless you can provide them with exceptionally good care and have a soil to their liking, *the flowers from your tulips will be better the first spring after planting than they will ever be again.*

When to Plant

It has long been taken for granted that tulips should not be planted until October or early November. The argument is advanced that earlier planting is likely to result in premature top growth, especially during a late, mild fall. A considerable amount of research through tulip literature has failed to reveal an account of any experiments or tests to prove or disprove this assumption. It seems to be another of those taken-for-granted statements handed down, without being challenged, from one generation of gardeners to the next.

In England, where in many sections there is little or no deep freez-ing of the soil, and in our own southern states, late planting may be desirable, but for the rest of the country there doesn't seem to be any advantage in it. In plantings we have made in various types of soil from Massachusetts as far south as the District of Columbia, we have never had any injury from early planting; nor have we ever heard of an authentic case of such injury. In southern New Jersey, where for several years we had charge of commercial plantings of forty acres or more, we had to begin planting—to get them all in—as soon as the bulbs were received (earlier than they usually can be obtained from seed stores); and even in that comparatively mild climate there was never any serious premature fall growth.

Again, what happens to tulips that remain in the ground from one season to the next? Surely these have every opportunity to make pre-mature top growth. But they decline to do so and, while making vig-orous roots, keep their tightly rolled little white caps safely under-ground until spring. Today, January 20, we dug one up from a sheltered spot, mulched by nature with fallen leaves so the ground had not frozen. The top growth was still three inches below the sur-face. Bulbs, like seeds, have built-in automatic controls that usually

Tulips grouped against stone wall. Use of white makes good contrast.

work under normal conditions. (Ever have a cluster of self-sown to-
mato or squash seed come up in your garden? Didn't they wait until
danger of late frosts was over, no matter how warm the weather had
been earlier in spring?)

The most substantial argument we have found against early planting is given by Sir Daniel Hall in his *Book of the Tulip*. There he
makes the point that early-planted bulbs may emerge in January or
early February, and that "the tips of the shoots may easily be damaged by frost following wet, and so afford entrance for the botrytis
spores. The later the development of the shoot, the safer it is from
attack." But this is not at all the same thing as premature fall growth.
And in sections where there is any danger of growth starting too
early in the spring, winter mulching *after* the soil has frozen is a
more reliable method of delaying spring top growth. In our experience, the date of planting makes very little difference in the date of
emergence.

Many varieties of tulips, held long after being received before being planted, are likely to deteriorate, especially under makeshift storage conditions (far from an even 40 degrees temperature, which is the ideal). In addition to drying out, bruises invite infection, dry rots and molds. We consider *the dangers from long-delayed home storage much greater than those from early planting.*

On the other hand, if bulbs are not received until late, or if for any other reason planting must be delayed, the grower has nothing to worry about. If still in good sound condition, the bulbs may be planted as late as mid-December and still give perfectly good results. With such late plantings, however, mulching is desirable. (See Chapter 7.)

Depth of Planting. How deep should tulips be planted?

That is a question concerning which there is a deal of discussion these days. The tendency is toward deeper planting than has formerly been the general practice. The depth usually advised is 4 to 5 inches—without specifying whether this is to the top or the bottom of the bulb. The depth given should be to the *top* of the bulb, as otherwise the largest bulbs (some of which will be 2 inches or more in vertical diameter) will have the least covering, whereas, if any distinction is made, they should go deepest.

Tulips will grow and flower perfectly well, however, when planted 10 or 12 inches deep, and such deep planting, as often as not, is advisable. The tulips will be happy either way: it all depends upon the gardener's objectives.

Deep planting has several very definite advantages:

1. It discourages the multiplication of new bulbs; and as fewer are formed, they have a better opportunity to develop and consequently to produce better blooms the following year.

2. With a limited number of new bulbs produced, the necessity for lifting and separating is delayed. Under favorable conditions they may continue flowering satisfactorily for five years or more instead of the usual two or three. Many instances of continuous good bloom for six to ten years have been reliably reported. Individual varieties vary greatly in their capacity to survive.

3. Deep planting lessens the danger of injury from "fire" or botrytis blight (see page 168). In one set of experiments made in Eng-

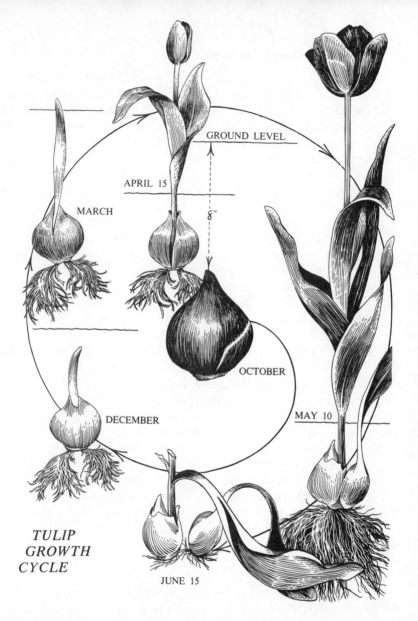

GROUND LEVEL

APRIL 15

MARCH

8"

OCTOBER

DECEMBER

MAY 10

*TULIP
GROWTH
CYCLE*

JUNE 15

land, two beds planted 14 inches deep showed 4 to 12 per cent infection; two planted 12 inches deep, 10 to 15 per cent; and those planted at the regulation depth of 5 inches, 50 to 65 per cent. The record was taken when the flowers were ready to cut, by which time the disease, starting with the shallow-planted beds, had had an opportunity to begin to spread to the others. One test doesn't prove a case, but other experiments have seemed to substantiate the assumption that deep planting definitely lessens the danger of botrytis. Deep planting also gets the bulbs down below the level of mole runs and the accompanying danger of fall injury from mice and voles, and also out of reach of chipmunks.

4. Deep planting makes it possible to cultivate and to grow annuals or tender bulbs near or even directly over the tulips without danger of injuring them. This is especially important where tulips are used in groups in a mixed flower border. Dwarf dahlias, cannas, montbretias, started in pots, or late-planted gladiolus are but a few of the many fill-in plants that make attractive succession plantings to conceal the maturing foliage of tulips and provide masses of late-season color in their place.

Despite all advantages, however, the gardener should be careful about going off the deep end on deep planting. It may well result in failure *if:* (a) drainage is poor, so that the bulbs would have soil water standing about them; (b) the soil is not prepared to a depth of 15 to 18 inches to provide congenial conditions for root growth below the bulbs; (c) or the soil is heavy clay, shutting out air and offering mechanical obstruction to emergence.

Again, if you wish to increase your stock of a favorite variety, if you wish to rearrange the planting of your border after a year or two, or if you are not certain that you have found exactly the right location for a group planting or for a particular variety, then you will do better to plant not more than 5 or 6 inches deep. In any event, it is advisable to try deep planting first on a small scale, to see if *your* conditions favor it. If the bulbs give satisfactory bloom the second year, you can feel safe in proceeding on a larger scale.

Planting

The general procedure for planting outlined in Chapter 7 applies to tulips. Extra precautions to protect them from injury from rodents may be necessary. The most effective protection from mice is to plant in wire baskets, bought ready-made or constructed from ½-inch mesh wire. Such baskets have a secondary use when it comes to taking up the bulbs—they can be "lifted" quite literally. Baskets are practical for a few groups but involve more expense and work than

Tulipa clusiana, *the candy-stick tulip; dainty, striking and a great favorite for cutting.*

most gardeners will wish to assume when any considerable number of bulbs are being planted. Some gardeners claim successful protection by using naphthalene flakes generously in the soil about the bulbs. Chopped-up tobacco stems are recommended by others; we have never tried them, but most animals dislike them, and at least they would add some organic matter and potash to the soil. Another control that has proven effective in some cases is powdered red lead —one pound to 50 bulbs. Place a few bulbs at a time in a tight container, and "powder" with the lead as a housewife sugars doughnuts; wear gloves to protect hands. Or coat the bulbs before planting with thiram. (For protection from rabbits, see Chapter 10.)

In the deep south, where the soil does not freeze after planting, many growers have had best success by pre-cooling the bulbs for three to five weeks, at a temperature of 35° to 40°, before placing them in the ground, which is done in December.

Cultivation

Tulips, more than most hardy bulbs, should be kept free from the competition of grass and weeds if they are to do well. When they first come up in the spring, the leaves are rolled together in tight spikes. At this season it is easy to work between them and loosen the surface soil with a hand weeder or small-bladed hoe. Later—often only a few days later—the broad, brittle leaves will have spread out, and any working about them is almost certain to result in cracks or bruises which invite the attack of botrytis blight and other diseases. If large weeds come in later, they should be removed by hand.

Fertilizing

The best time to apply fertilizers is also very early in the spring. Garden tulips (those of horticultural origin), more than any other hardy spring bulbs, are dependent upon a generous, well-balanced diet. Quick-acting, high-nitrogen fertilizers should be avoided, for there is no purpose in hastening early growth. In fact, it is better to hold it back. If only a complete fertilizer—such as 5–10–5—is available, it is well to supplement it with wood ashes and superphosphate.

Mulching

Where the bulbs are to be left in the ground, weeding during summer and autumn can be much reduced by the use of a mulch. It should be a material that will not remain wet and soggy after rains, and is best not applied until after the foliage has begun to ripen.

DISEASES

Only one tulip disease is likely to prove troublesome in the garden, and you may grow them for years without encountering it.

TULIP FIRE (*Botrytis tulipae*). Its appearance and spread depend largely upon weather conditions; it usually appears during a warm, wet, or muggy spell in spring, when the foliage is growing rapidly, up until the time flower petals are dropping. The first symptom is usually a yellowing and shriveling of the leaf tips, followed by spots near the edges which increase and run together. White spots appear on dark flowers and brown spots on white, followed by rotting and the development of a mushy gray mold. Under favorable conditions the

ABOVE: *Parrot tulip 'Fantasy', old-rose pink, and light blue* Phlox divaricata *make a pleasing combination.* BELOW: *Light and dark peony-flowered tulips against a protective background of evergreens.*

Home-grown tulip bulbs, cured and ready for replanting.

disease spreads so rapidly as to have earned it the common name of "fire."

If detected early enough, the disease can be checked to some extent by removing affected leaves, buds or flowers, and especially fallen petals, and spraying thoroughly with Bordeaux mixture or preferably with ferbam or zineb. Precautionary measures are: plant in soil where tulips have not been grown for three or four years or where there is free circulation of air and full sun; examine bulbs at planting time and discard any which show tiny hard black specks—the sclerotia that carry the disease over the winter—on or under the brown skins or on the basal plates.

PESTS

The most serious insect and animal pests of tulips are aphids, bulb flies, mites, nematodes, mice, and slugs, for all of which see Chapter 10.

Frequently injury from mice is not noticed until the flower buds are well developed or even beginning to open. Then a sudden withering of a plant shows that something is wrong, and the slightest pull will remove the stem from the ground, revealing that it has been eaten through just above the bulb, which may or may not be found intact. When generous numbers of bulbs have been planted in the fall, but fail to make an appearance in the spring except for a plant here and there, it can be assumed that mice feasted on the bulbs all winter. (Moles are carnivores and do not eat bulbs although mice may use their runways.)

Of all very early spring bulbs, crocuses are the most colorful and most widely grown. Often, despite extreme neglect, they persist for years, increasing by natural multiplication of the corms and by self-seeding.

Despite the popularity of the horticultural or garden varieties—the "Dutch" crocuses displayed in color in most catalogues—comparatively few gardeners know, and still fewer grow, any of the species and their varieties. These are immensely more interesting, and most of them are considerably earlier and remain longer in bloom.

To enjoy these intriguing, more graceful "wild" crocuses, it is by no means necessary to possess a rock garden, although they are ideal subjects for such a setting. Despite their small stature—they range in height from 3 to 6 inches—they will make a fine showing if they are planted where they will not be overcrowded by other plants, or overlooked. Since most of them bloom so early in the spring, one of the best ways to enjoy them is from the house. What better place for planting them then is the terrace or patio. Here they can be enjoyed from windows or through glass sliding doors—or, for closer observation, require only a few steps from the house. In the lee of individual rocks, around the bases of trees, at the edge of a small pool (but where the ground is not wet), they will make a brave showing.

Crocuses are often naturalized in lawns or other grass areas. No other flower defiantly thumbs its nose at the biting winds of March with quite the same irrepressible pertness. But if you want crocuses in a neatly kept lawn that must be cut early in the spring, it is best to figure on planting additional bulbs each fall. Unless the foliage can be left for several weeks after the flowers fade—even if it does not reach full maturity—the succeeding corms will be severely injured. Often, however, there are spots in corners, around trees and fronting shrubbery where they can be naturalized without any necessity

Crocus 'Remembrance', *a light lavender blue, naturalized by a pool.*

for shearing off the foliage too soon in the spring. We have a group of them in a semi-kempt terrace under birches that has been in for ten years and is still going strong. In fact, these crocuses seem to have a taste for adventuring and occasionally pop up in unexpected places —and with parental records that would not stand up well under too close questioning.

While in most home gardens crocuses are thought of as supplying a two to three weeks' show in spring, they may be enjoyed during three or four months of the year if one will take the trouble to include both the spring- *and* autumn-flowering species. And if you want to do a little specializing in crocuses and the crocus-like but not closely related colchicums (often catalogued as giant autumn-flowering crocuses), you can add another month or two to that! With very few exceptions, all the crocuses ordinarily obtainable are very inexpensive, and a few dollars will provide quite a collection of them to start off with.

CULTURE

Crocuses are exceptionally easy to grow and are seldom troubled by any insects or diseases. Unfortunately, however, the corms seem to be considered choice tidbits by mice, squirrels and chipmunks, and rabbits are equally delighted with the young foliage. Keep this in mind when making your plantings. We lost completely a very nice collection by planting them too far from the house, with no protection. Of recent years, with a cat and a dog, which serve as deterrents, we have experienced little trouble.

Crocuses, more particularly the species, have a liking for soil a bit on the sandy side. In heavy soil it is advisable to dig in a shovelful or two of sand or cinders where each group is to go. If the drainage is known to be poor, sand can't solve the problem. Better to raise the planting area or bed a few inches above the surrounding soil. But the species will do on a rather meager diet; if fertilizer is used, apply only about half the usual amount.

As to exposure, crocuses like full sun—the more the merrier. Light high shade, after the flowering season, will do no harm. *Effective shelter from prevailing spring winds will often make a difference of two weeks or more in the opening of the first flowers.* The bloom period can readily be nearly doubled by making two plantings of a variety in different exposures.

Planting

Plant as soon as you can secure the corms—early in September if they are available. *This is especially important with autumn-flowering kinds.* If they are planted late, after growth starts—which it will, even if the corms are stored dry in paper bags!—your first crop of flowers may be curtailed or sacrificed entirely. In ordering, it is advisable to request that autumn crocuses (and colchicums) be shipped in advance of the rest of your other bulbs.

For planting crocus corms, the depth given in most articles and bulb-planting charts is 2 inches. We plant them considerably deeper —a good 4 inches to the tops of the corms, which are spaced 2 to 4 inches apart. For this deeper planting there are three reasons: they come up just as well and, apparently, just as early; they are less likely to be found by mice or squirrels; and the corms are in less danger of working up close to the surface. It is possible, too, that they multiply less rapidly, though we have no evidence of our own —nor have we found it elsewhere—to prove this.

In speaking of the "working up" of the corms, we touch upon one of the interesting points in the crocus growth cycle. As with the

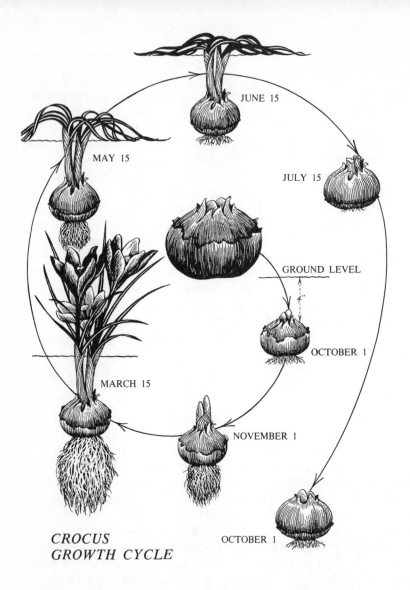

JUNE 15

MAY 15

JULY 15

GROUND LEVEL

4"

OCTOBER 1

MARCH 15

NOVEMBER 1

OCTOBER 1

*CROCUS
GROWTH CYCLE*

gladiolus, new corms are formed on top of the old one, which withers away. When crocus corms get too near the surface, long fleshy roots penetrate deep into the ground and, after becoming firmly established, exert a contractile force which, unless the soil is unduly dry and hard, will pull the corms deeper down into it.

Any ground cover used over crocuses should be low-growing and not too dense. Creeping phlox (*Phlox subulata*), moss sandwort

(*Arenaria verna caespitosa*) and various creeping dianthus, *Vinca minor* (which has not become too dense) and primroses are a few that do nicely. Started seedlings of the lighter growing annuals, such as candytuft or pansies, may be set in among groups of crocuses to provide a flowering cover for the dying foliage. Crocuses may be used, too, as an edging for beds of later spring bulbs, such as daffodils or tulips, their curving foliage—which Louise Beebe Wilder has described as the most graceful line in nature—making a pleasing finish.

Like most other hardy bulbs, the crocuses will eventually become too crowded to continue a good display of flowers. When that point is reached, they should be taken up as the foliage begins to die down, sorted and immediately replanted. The very small corms can be saved for growing on, or placed in new colonies where, after a year or two, they will reach full flowering stage.

For Indoor Bloom

No bulbs are more easily grown for flowering indoors than the crocuses, nor more charming in the peculiarly cheerful uplift they can give to a room during the frequently dull and dark days of January, February and early March. For window-sill culture, their dwarf stature, as compared with that of many other bulbs used for forcing, is a distinct advantage. We have found, too, that they may be transplanted with the greatest of ease even when the buds are well developed, and therefore are ideal material for use in dish gardens or for inserting in pots of taller-growing bulbs; the foliage remains attractive even after the blooms have faded and been cut off.

The term "forcing," which we have elsewhere referred to in its connection with spring-flowering bulbs (page 269), is even less applicable to crocuses than to daffodils, tulips, and others. The crocuses should not be forced in the slightest degree. After they have made root growth in bulb pans or flats, any temperature above freezing, combined with plenty of sunshine, will bring them into bloom. This makes possible a "have your cake and eat it too" proposition insofar as crocuses are concerned. If the foliage is kept growing until they can be planted out in open ground, they will usually give a full crop of flowers the succeeding spring, without skipping a season as is the case with many forced bulbs.

Planting for indoor bloom should be done early. A 5-inch pot or bulb pan will accommodate eight to ten corms of average size; a 6-inch pot, however, requires little more space and will make considerably more of a showing owing to the increased number of blooms obtainable. An ordinary flat with the corms spaced 2 to 2½ inches each way will provide four or five dozen plants for transplanting as suggested above.

Except for the advisability of extra-early planting and the necessity of keeping them very cold—frozen if possible—after the roots have formed until it is desirable to bring them indoors for February or March bloom, the details of planting are the same as those suggested in Chapter 20.

THE MORE IMPORTANT CROCUS SPECIES

The spring-flowering crocus species are very different from the popular horticultural or "Dutch" varieties, for they bloom earlier and are more persistent. Leading the procession is the dull lilac *Crocus imperati* in early March, followed by blue *C. sieberi* and golden *C. susianus* (cloth-of-gold). *C. tomasinianus,* pale lavender, is especially free-flowering and good for naturalizing, as is *C. biflorus,* the old favorite Scotch crocus. *C. korolkowii,* golden orange, is popular for rock gardens; *C. aureus* (*moesicus*) is orange-yellow; *C. aureus* 'Sulphureus Concolor', a pale yellow.

There are autumn-blooming crocus species, too, which give a peculiar charm to the fall garden. Dutch catalogues list many species and varieties, and in garden books you can find mention of still more. Of the half dozen to a dozen generally listed in American catalogues, the best known are *C. zonatus, C. speciosus* and *C. sativus,* though the latter is sometimes unreliable and may well be omitted if only a few kinds are to be planted. Its red-violet flowers are less attractive to most persons than those of other species. *C. speciosus,* with light blue flowers and brilliant orange stigmas, is one of the most reliable as well as one of the most beautiful; normally it begins flowering in late September. Of this there are some half dozen sub-species and varieties. *C. speciosus aitschisonii* is a very pale blue and the largest of the wild forms; and *C. speciosus albus* is white with a rose tint on the outer petals. *C. zonatus* blooms a little later

ABOVE: *Autumn-flowering* Crocus speciosus 'Aitschisonii'. BELOW: *Colchicum or meadow saffron (sometimes listed as autumn crocus) brings a sudden and unexpected renaissance of spring to the late garden.*

than *C. speciosus,* its pale lilac, yellow-throated flowers usually carrying into October.

C. medius is perhaps the showiest of all the species, with scarlet stigmas contrasting with its deep lilac petals. It is also very free-flowering and a vigorous propagator. *C. asturicus* produces dark violet blooms in mid-October; *C. cancellatus albus,* late September, is a pure white that contrasts nicely with the other varieties and has fragrance to add to its charm. Other whites are *C. pulchellus* 'Zephyr' and *C. ochroleucus,* small-flowered and exceptionally dainty. Latest to flower—often into December—is *C. laevigatus,* white flushed with pearl, and fragrant.

CHAPTER *14. The "Minor" Bulbs*

There is a group of spring-flowering bulbous plants usually referred to in the trade and in garden literature as the "minor bulbs." The gardener thinks of them as minor because most of them are diminutive in stature; the dealer, perhaps because of the small part they play in the total of his bulb sales—and certainly in most instances he gives them a very minor display in making up his annual catalogue.

But in the pleasure they afford and in the touches of exquisite, delicate beauty they can bring to the garden, these less well-known bulbs are by no means minor! Of all the plants we grow, there are none to whose reappearance each spring we look forward with keener anticipation. And there are none with which visitors are more delightfully surprised, or concerning which they seem more amazed when informed that most of them could be enjoyed about their own grounds with little or no more care—and in many instances with less —than they bestow on the things they do grow.

The species to be discussed in this chapter, because they merit somewhat more extended treatment than others listed in Part Three of this book, include the following:

Camassia (Camas)
Chionodoxa (Glory-of-the-snow)
Endymion (Wood-
   hyacinth and
   English Bluebell)
Eranthis (Winter-aconite)
Fritillaria (Guinea-hen Flower and
   Crown Imperial)

Galanthus (Snowdrop)
Hyacinth
Leucojum (Snowflake)
Muscari (Grape-hyacinth)
Scilla (Squill)

EARLY SPRING GROUP

Always, in late July or early August, there comes a day when, walking about the garden at dusk, we become conscious of that touch of sudden, peculiar coolness in the air which so definitely presages autumn. The first unkind foreboding of impending change usually projects on the screen of imagination the melancholy picture in Bridges' lines:

> The wood is bare; a river mist is steeping
> The trees that winter's chill of life bereaves;
> Only the stiffened boughs break silence, weeping
> Over their fallen leaves,
> That lie upon the dank earth, brown and rotten
> Miry and matted in the soaking wet,
> Forgotten with the spring that is forgotten
> By them that can forget.

But even this rather dismal preview of onrushing darker days and driving rains leaves us, we confess, with no sense of sadness. Our thoughts turn, rather, to what will be happening then down in the ground, deep under the matted and miring leaves. For there, we know, will be stirring into life the hundreds of tiny bulbs that have been sleeping comfortably all summer long—the little ones that give us a full extra month of amazing and vibrant color just at the season when we feel most in need of it and when other gardens about us are still brown and barren.

In the mixed borders, against clumps of birches or a dogwood, with their backs against great boulders acting as warming pans for their cold beds, and especially in the nooks and crannies and along the twisting narrow footways in the rock garden, they will be drinking in the autumn rains, pushing out greedy roots, and thrusting their pointed noses up—but not too far!—getting ready to respond to the magic of March sunshine with a burst of pre-spring glory.

Natives of many climes, these little bulbs—from the high Alps and low Mediterranean shores and the forbidding vasts of Russia—as yet little "improved" by the hand of man; immigrants gathered together here in a happy band, asking little but the opportunity to find a foothold, and welcome the first staggering, half-frozen bees to the gaily decked feasts they spread in such abundance.

Do you know them? Do you *grow* them? If not, we can think of no greater garden service we can perform for you than to urge that you make their acquaintance. By all means give them an invitation to *your* garden and enjoy a real pre-spring show.

Major Roles for Minors

Quite as intriguing as the many and varied forms and colors to be found in the little spring bulbs are the things you can do with them in the way of getting unusual garden pictures. Used in quantity—the "drifts" that garden writers like to talk about—they produce spreading, low masses of color in early spring that are most charming.

Fortunate is the gardener who possesses a stony bank, a rock ledge, or the means of creating even the most elementary sort of rock garden. If you are so fortunate you can give these small-scale beauties just the kind of setting that suits them best. But don't be discouraged if such an ideal setting cannot readily be provided. Unusual indeed is the place where some nook or corner cannot be found that will serve to accommodate at least a moderate number of these enchanting couriers of spring.

The smallest of the minor bulbs are best placed where they are elevated somewhat above the general ground level. Such a location makes it possible to see them in detail. It also provides protection from chance accidents, and assures that extra-thorough drainage which, with few exceptions, is an essential factor in their continued happiness. Permanent labels are extremely important. Even if you can trust to memory for names, or just don't care what they are so long as you have the flowers, the labels serve as added protection, for these little bulbs spend much of their lives underground and in the course of the year's operations are quite likely to be dug up, overplanted, or otherwise maltreated or lost track of unless their locations are plainly marked. Such labels need not be conspicuous, but they should be sufficiently substantial to resist heaving and chance dislocation.

One thing to keep in mind in planting these little bulbs is that, with a few exceptions, the flowers are borne on comparatively short stems. This, combined with the fact that they bloom in early spring, when frequent driving rains occur, results in their becoming so mud-spattered that much of their beauty is lost unless they are so placed that this cannot happen. Do *not* plant in such locations as the front of a bare-soil perennial border or in rows or groups in any open soil. They are well suited to most terrace and patio areas—especially in soil pockets of the paving or in between flagstones.

Both for artistic effect and for their comfort and good growth, the little bulbs are best planted in sheltered nooks and crannies. They associate particularly well with rocks, where they get good drainage, protection from wind and the full benefit of the earliest spring sunshine. They are good for naturalizing, either in quantity or in "spots" under deciduous trees, because they are through blooming by the time the shade becomes dense. Another desirable planting place is the southern side of evergreens, where the spring sun can reach them under the lower branches.

The common characteristic of all these little bulbs is their informality. Give them a setting where this will be enhanced by their surroundings. Try planting several different kinds of bulbs with blue or purple flowers under or in the foreground of a spring-blooming shrub such as forsythia or cornelian-cherry. We tried this—with delightful results.

The range of colors in the early spring group includes a wide spread of blues, from deep grape-purples to delicate azures and lavenders and some good pure yellows. Reds are lacking, and the pink varieties, on the whole, are not too pleasing. The pure and glistening whites, however, at this season of the year are quite as effective as strong colors.

CHIONODOXA. If we had to be restricted to one of the half dozen species mentioned at the beginning of this chapter, our choice would be the *Chionodoxa*. Best known, perhaps, is *C. luciliae,* with informal starry flowers of delphinium blue shading to white centers, borne eight or more on a stem. There are white and pink varieties of this. *C. sardensis* has deeper, gentian-blue flowers. 'Gigantea' has larger flowers of light blue. Chionodoxas and the widely naturalized coltsfoot (*Tussilago farfara*), with its golden dandelion-like flowers, make a charming combination. Chionodoxas are especially lovely, too, as cut flowers.

CROCUS. Though all the choice types and varieties of this well-known harbinger of spring are discussed at length in Chapter 13, they rightfully belong among the minor bulbs. They have so much to offer the gardener that we have devoted a separate chapter to them.

ERANTHIS HYEMALIS. The winter-aconite appeals to gardeners in northern sections because it is usually the first bulbous flower to put in an appearance, running neck and neck with the snowdrop. Its bright yellow blossoms, like miniature marsh-marigolds, are borne on 2- or 3-inch stems above decorative foliage reminiscent of that of an anemone. Plant the little shriveled-up-looking tubers as soon as they

Winter-aconite—first gold in the spring garden. Variety is Eranthis tubergeni; *photographed March 30, Hyde Park, N.Y.*

are delivered. If they seem very dried out, plump them up in moist peat moss before planting. Place them in a raised bed in the rock garden or at the top of a wall where they can be seen readily without stooping. Semi-shade during midsummer is desirable.

FRITILLARIA. There are some seventy species of *Fritillaria* hailing from temperate zones in all parts of the world, but only a few of these are generally available. Most appealing is *F. meleagris,* the so-called Guinea-hen flower, which takes its name from the mixed reddish-brown and purple coloring of its nodding bells. There is also a white form.

Blooming early in April on 12-inch wiry stems, this modest little bulb has an appeal all its own. Plant the bulbs as soon as they are received, 3 inches deep in light shade in a spot in the rock garden which will not dry out completely during hot weather. The fritillarias native to our own West are commonly called mission bells. They are somewhat taller than the Guinea-hen flower, except for *F. pudica,* a dwarf of 6 inches, each short stem bearing a single, clear yellow, bell-like bloom. This species likes full sun and a typical well-drained, sandy rock-garden soil; as does also *F. pluriflora,* another low-growing sort with racemes of pink-purple flowers of four to a dozen blooms in each cluster, each 1¼ inches long. For naturalizing in open, rather dry woods, try *F. lanceolata,* 18 to 24 inches, flowers mottled brown and green, and *F. recurva,* of similar height but with bright orange-scarlet flowers resembling a true lily.

GALANTHUS. The snowdrops are beloved of all gardeners because of their quaint nodding blooms that, despite their frail appearance, defy the last desperate onslaughts of frost, snow and ice. Outside our kitchen window is a clump that frequently is snowed under for one to three weeks *after the flowers have opened,* yet they always come out smiling to provide their good cheer for a long period.

The snowdrop most commonly grown is *G. nivalis.* It has a double form known as 'Flore pleno'. *G. elwesii* has larger flowers. Snowdrops prefer a rather heavy soil and do well in considerable shade, spreading slowly by self-seeding.

HYACINTH. Here is another good flower which has suffered from association of ideas. The hyacinth has so long been used for mass bedding effects, especially when "design" flower beds were in vogue, that few persons ever stop to consider the possibility of planting it in any other way. The giant exhibition hyacinths displayed at flower shows, with their huge, stiff, almost club-like stalks of bloom, certainly do not tend to suggest that the hyacinth should be given a place in modern informal home-garden landscaping.

Discard your prejudices and try a few hyacinths, either in small, irregular groups at the front of the mixed border, against shrubs, or in a grassy spot in sun or semi-shade that does not have to be cut close in spring; or a few groups at the edge of the foundation planting if your house is on a small plot. Better yet, add a few clumps to the terrace area so on a sunny spring day you can revel in the exquisite, heady fragrance of the flowers—reason enough for growing hyacinths. And they are especially charming near a small pool.

Many gardeners, we find, have a feeling that hyacinths are not reliably hardy. With the exception of the less hardy Roman hyacinths, we have found them fully so. We have a large group of the pale yellow 'City of Haarlem', planted on a semi-shaded terrace twelve years ago, that is still a spot of beauty each returning spring. Other varieties, after having been grown indoors for winter bloom and then transferred to the open, have readily established themselves and gone on for years.

The quaint and decorative checkered-lily or Guinea-hen flower—Fritillaria meleagris.

Grades of bulbs: Bulbs of hyacinths, which are comparatively expensive, are listed in catalogues as top size (exhibition), 19 cm. or over; first size, 18–19 cm.; second size, 17–18 cm.; third size (bedding), 15–16 cm.; and miniature (Dutch Roman or Cynthella), 14–15 cm. Most retail catalogues today limit their bulb-size offerings to exhibition or first size and bedding—choice enough for most home gardeners. There are also "prepared" or "treated" hyacinths—higher-priced and used especially for early forcing. The *varieties* in all these grades are identical, but the smaller sizes throw up rather loose graceful spikes, very different in appearance from the formal, stiff blooms from big bulbs. The Roman hyacinths (*Hyacinthus orientalis* 'Albulus'), however, are quite distinct from the Dutch hyacinths. They flower earlier and are not as hardy. The individual florets are smaller, and several spikes are produced in succession. If attempted out of doors, they should be well mulched.

Culture: Extra-good drainage is probably the most important requirement in hyacinth culture, for they cannot stand wet feet. In heavy soil or on low ground it is best to use a raised bed with gravel, small stones, or other drainage material under it. Hyacinths also demand full sun, but for perfect blooms a sunny location should be provided, with natural shelter against storms, as in an exposed position the heavy heads of bloom are easily beaten down.

A rather light soil is best for hyacinths. Clay or heavy loam should be lightened with sand or the planting area actually raised by the addition of added soil if drainage is known to be poor. If large bulbs are being planted in a formal bed where masses of bloom are desired, the bed should be well enriched with cow manure, either well rotted or the commercially dried compost. For a formal bed dig out a foot of soil where the bed is being made, and then mix the manure and bone meal into the soil below, which should be thoroughly turned and broken up. Set the bulbs in place on this, and fill in with the soil which you removed, well pulverized and mixed with peat moss. Cover the bulbs 4, 5, or 6 inches deep, depending on the size. After planting—which should be in late September or early October—give a good watering if the weather is dry. Moisture is needed all through the late autumn to help the bulbs develop a strong root system before hard freezing. After the soil freezes during the year of planting, mulch with leaves or salt marsh hay. Thereafter no winter mulch will be necessary.

When planted in formal beds, hyacinths are usually lifted after bloom to make room for other flowers. They are carefully heeled in to ripen, or lifted with a fork *after the foliage has turned yellow,* and stored like other hardy bulbs, or covered with *dry* soil in a frame with the sash on but partly open for ventilation, until they have cured. If hyacinths are informally planted in groups in the foreground of shrubs or in the mixed border, there is no need whatever to lift them until they become so crowded that bloom ceases. We have found that this does not occur for from six to eight years when the bulbs are planted deep and far enough apart—6 to 8 inches—to allow for increase.

One that really blooms in the snow—and continues in bloom for a month or more: the common snowdrop, Galanthus nivalis.

Varieties: There are many varieties, in good clear colors, from which to select. It is also possible to choose varieties with blooming heads of different shapes. All are not heavy and club-like. Recommended varieties are: *Early:* 'L'Innocence', white; 'Anna Marie', 'Pink Pearl', pink; 'Jan Bos', 'Victory Day', red; 'Delft Blue', 'Dr. Lieber', light blue; 'Ostara', dark blue; 'Gypsy Queen', 'Yellow Hammer', yellow and orange. *Medium:* 'Edelweiss', white; 'Princess Margaret', 'Lady Derby', 'Marconi', pink; 'Garibaldi', 'La Victoire', red; 'Myosotis', 'Perle Brillante', light blue; 'Mary', dark blue; 'Orange Boven' ('Salmonetta'), orange. *Late:* 'Carnegie', white; 'Queen of Pinks', pink; 'Cyclops', red; 'Queen of the Blues', light blue; 'Ivanhoe', 'King of Blues', dark blue; 'City of Haarlem', yellow.

LEUCOJUM. To follow the snowdrops in bloom there should be a planting of snowflakes (*Leucojum*), which are somewhat similar but later-flowering, larger and taller. The spring snowflake (*L. vernum*) has drooping, bell-like flowers tipped with green. The form 'Gravetye' is even more robust. The summer snowflake (*L. aestivum*), attaining a height of 12 to 18 inches, blooms in May.

MUSCARI. Grape-hyacinths are the most commonly encountered of the little bulbs, probably because of their extreme long-lastingness and the freedom with which they self-sow. We have come across their upstanding, tapering little spires of scented, cobalt-blue bells around old homesites where no gardener's foot had trod for years. *M. azureum* (strictly, *Hyacinthus ciliatus*), in a sheltered spot, will flower in February or early March. *M. armeniacum* 'Early Giant' is the variety to get if you want but one. It is larger and a clearer blue than 'Heavenly Blue', and fragrant; an excellent companion for daffodils. *M. armeniacum* 'Cantab' is a lighter blue and considerably later, and 'Blue Spike' is unique because of its double blue flowers. *M. botryoides* and its variety *album* both have more compact foliage and are good for small rock gardens. The grape-hyacinths thrive in almost any well-drained soil, in sun or light shade. Don't be alarmed if some of them form clumps of foliage in the fall!

SCILLA. Earliest of the squills to flower are *Scilla sibirica* and its white form, *alba*. 'Spring Beauty' is a more robust form, growing to 6–8 inches or so, nearly twice as high as *S. sibirica*. The color is a real singing blue—we know of no other flower that can add quite so much cheer to a dull spring day. *S. bifolia* is also early, but of a gentian-blue color. *S. pratensis,* deep blue, flowers in May. (*S. peru-*

viana has 6-inch cones of blue flowers and substantial strap-shape leaves. It is hardy only in mild climates and in the North is grown in a sunny window.) The broad, spreading foliage of the scillas affords some protection from mud spattering and makes them more suitable for use in borders or for edging, especially if allowed to form thick groups.

FOR LATE SPRING

Entirely different from the early-flowering scillas are wood-hyacinth (long known as *Scilla campanulata* but now placed in its own genus, *Endymion,* its correct full name being *Endymion hispanicus*) and the beloved English bluebell (formerly known as *Scilla nutans* or *nonscripta,* now correctly *Endymion nonscriptus*). These bloom much later—about the same time as the late tulips—and are much taller, often up to 18 inches. Unlike most of the early spring bulbs, they prefer partial shade (though they will take full sun) and are therefore good for naturalizing in open woods or planting under trees—even pine and hemlock—and under shrubs. The foliage is heavy and coarse and should be left uncut—a fact to be considered when selecting a location for planting. The several varieties of *E. hispanicus* include light and dark blue-purples, pink, and white.

The so-called feather-hyacinth or plume-hyacinth (*Muscari comosum monstrosum* or *plumosum*) is a very interesting frilled or laciniated, almost freakish, violet-flowered species which blooms in late May. Lasting unusually long, it is good for cutting and will prove to be arresting in an arrangement at your local flower show.

A May-blooming member of the *Fritillaria* genus which is as showy as the Guinea-hen flower is modest is *Fritillaria imperialis,* or crown imperial. This traditional bulbous flower may be seen blooming in many old-fashioned gardens, where it throws up 3- to 4-foot blossom stems which bear red, yellow, or orange umbels of drooping bell-shaped flowers in a crown-like cluster under a whorl of leaves. Once established, it should not be disturbed. Plant 4 inches deep in rich, partly shaded ground as soon as the bulbs are delivered. Its one undesirable feature is a characteristic skunk-cabbage-like smell but to us this has never been so overpowering as to be offensive.

CAMASSIA: Lovely flowers, far too little known, that are easily satisfied and hardy without protection. Their first delicate racemes of tall, lacy florets appear with the daffodils, while other species bloom one to three weeks later. Unlike some other natives of our West, camassias are of easy culture and seem to acclimate themselves readily to northeastern conditions. *Camassia scilloides,* known as wild-hyacinth, is, in fact, native to Pennsylvania, Minnesota, Georgia, and Texas. These bulbs are showy enough to be a very real addition to the border or large rock garden. In our own rock garden they have thrived for several years in considerable shade, among rocks where their delicately colored, starry, deep or China-blue spikes of bloom attract attention from a considerable distance.

Well-worth growing are these camassia species:

cusickii—3 feet, with pale blue flowers
leichtlinii—2 feet, varying from dark blue through China-blue to creamy white
scilloides (syn. *esculenta*)—2 feet, blue or pale violet to white

Planted in rich, loamy soil in sun or semi-shade, 9 inches apart and 4 inches deep, the bulbs of this member of the lily family should thrive untended for years. (Though most authorities stipulate 3 to 4 inches between bulbs, having grown camassias for some years, we know that the basal foliage soon covers almost a foot of soil.) If you are lucky, they will increase slowly by self-sown seeds.

CULTURE

In general the culture required by these less well-known bulbs is the same as that suggested for crocus.

As few of the minor bulbs have been developed into horticultural varieties far removed from the original species (many of them are untamed species or selections from them), there is little to be gained by intense feeding; in fact, it is more likely to be harmful than beneficial. Most of them we plant with no additional fertilizer, in fairly good soil that has had a considerable amount of sand or gravel or fine crushed stone dug into it because our soil is heavy clay. Sharp crushed stone—pieces ¼ to 1 inch—may discourage the foraging of mice and chipmunks, two of the worst enemies of most small bulbs.

Many of the minor bulbs are quickies, as far as their vegetative growth aboveground is concerned. Their flowers appear almost as soon as the foliage starts growth; and from the time the foliage dies down, they are out of sight until the following spring. Seedling plants of shallow-rooted annuals—sweet-alyssum, ageratum, dwarf spreading zinnias such as *Z. linearis,* or the zinnia-like *Sanvitalia procumbens*—may be transplanted to take their place, or the seeds can be scattered over the soil. Our favorite succession crops are sweet-alyssum and portulaca, the seed being sown as the bulb foliage withers. Both of these self-sow but never become really troublesome.

CHAPTER *15.* *Lilies*

With the fading of the last of the tulips there is a temporary lull in the show made by hardy bulbs in the garden. Such non-bulbous, perennial garden flowers as Oriental poppies, irises and peonies take over; but before these have passed, the bulbs are staging a comeback, with lilies playing the leading role.

We have had the earlier umbellatum lilies, such as Golden Chalice and Rainbow Hybrids, open their spreading cups by the first week in June, with the madonna lily, *Lilium candidum,* and Bellingham Hybrids following in close succession; and from then on they supply a series of garden highlights until late in summer. No other group of plants is followed with greater interest or for so long a period.

In two respects the lilies stand quite apart and distinct from other hardy bulbs: they have, as a group, a very much longer period of bloom and they are tall, upright growers. The lily enthusiast with twenty-five or more species and varieties can enjoy a practically uninterrupted succession of flowers from mid-May until mid-September or later, and even the half dozen or so kinds which any small garden can accommodate will, if selected with regard to their flowering dates, provide a very satisfactory all-season effect.

Owing to their height, habit of growth and the distinct form of the flowers, almost any variety of lily, even if there be but a single stalk of it, is pretty sure to dominate its surroundings. This, coupled with the fact that some species or variety may be had in flower at any time except spring, makes them almost indispensable in the design of attractive gardens.

THE LILY REVOLUTION

Several things have happened to give impetus to the use of lilies in American gardens. There is the success achieved by our hybridizers in finally breaking through the traditional reluctance of *Lilium* species to intercross, thus providing a whole new race of hybrid strains and species. There is the fact that American-grown bulbs, reaching the gardener earlier and in better condition than imported bulbs, have greatly decreased failures that were formerly due to unseasonable planting, to dried-out, withered roots and bruised scales and to diseased bulbs. And there is the increasing knowledge on the part of home gardeners as to the proper culture of lilies. The American Lily Society undoubtedly exerts a tremendous influence in increasing still further the appreciation and use of this most important of summer-flowering bulbs.

The development of lily hybridizing and the commercial production of bulbs in America provide one of the most interesting chapters in our horticultural history, but we can here give it only a passing paragraph. While there were some American lily hobbyists in the early days, the credit for serious work, both in hybridizing and the commercial production of bulbs, belongs to the late Dr. David Griffiths, who, while internationally esteemed among professional horticulturists, was little known to the public. It is not generally recognized, for instance, that while E. H. Wilson brought us the regal lily from western China, it was Griffiths who interested American growers in its propagation and dissemination.

While American hybridizers achieved some success in developing new varieties, it was not until World War II practically terminated the importation of bulbs from Japan and Europe that commercial production of bulbs in this country was undertaken on a large scale.

Of greater interest to gardeners is the fact that American hybridizers have not only produced more than those of all other countries together, but have succeeded in crossbreeding original species never before successfully mated. The progeny of these crosses, for the most part, hybridized readily, so doors were opened for innumerable new creations. Many of these new lilies, with the usual character, vigor, and adaptability of hybrids, have proved to be more amenable to garden culture than are most of the species.

Before this revolution the commercial production of lily bulbs was almost entirely by asexual propagation—bulblets and scales. This procedure, which had been followed for a long time, established clones or stocks developed from a single plant.

The original plant used to establish a clone is a "selection"—that is, one picked as having the most desirable qualities from a group of plants of the same kind; a sub-species that differs in some way from its normal type; a sport (a natural mutation that differs from the normal type in some characteristic, such as color, size, or habit of growth); or a new variety resulting from a seed cross. Whatever the source of the individual plant that becomes the foundation of a clone, the process of propagation from it is, as compared with growing from seed, slow and expensive. The result is that bulbs so produced become available but slowly, and long remain quite high in price. Many of these are worth the cost, it is true, but the number of gardens to which they can find their way is limited.

Quite different from this method is the newer one of mass production from seed. Some species are very prolific seed producers and are readily grown from seed. Notable examples are the regal lily (*Lilium regale*) and *L. formosanum*. Bulbs of these have long been commercially grown from seed; that is why they have become so universally available at moderate prices.

There is some variation in the plants from such seed-grown bulbs but not enough to make them less desirable for garden use. In fact, in the garden, some range in height and time of flowering is often desirable. (For florists' use for forcing, it is a different story, since here it is very important to have a crop that is uniform, especially in the matter of date of flowering.)

In addition to this speedier and more economical production, another important advantage of seed-grown stock is that bulbs so produced are more vigorous and free from diseases, especially the dread mosaic (related to the cucumber virus disease), which is the one greatest scourge of amateur lily growers.

By growing from seed and transplanting the seedling stocks to fresh soil, in areas thoroughly isolated from old stocks, it is possible to produce bulbs that are 100 per cent free from mosaic, whereas bulbs produced from scales or offsets are sure to carry it if the parent stock is infected; and no lily plant once suffering from mosaic can ever be cured by any control yet discovered.

Those who favored propagation from seed felt that supplying vigorous disease-free bulbs was more important than obtaining such uniformity in flower form, color, or habit as may result from clone bulbs produced asexually. Fortunately most lily species, and many

Flat prepared for starting lily seeds. Three layers are placed as indicated. (Courtesy U.S.D.A.)

varieties, come reasonably true from seed. Seed-grown hybrids, of course, show more variation, but by continued selection and reselection they have been developed into strains that are sufficiently uniform.

Not only new lilies but new methods of producing the bulbs commercially were developed in the Northwest, principally at the Oregon Bulb Farms of Jan de Graaff.

IN THE GARDEN

There are three purposes for which lilies are especially suited: as accent plants in the mixed border, for landscape groups or massed plantings among shrubbery and for naturalizing. In the rock garden they play a very minor role, and that, unless the landscaping is on a fairly grand scale, is limited to two or three species.

Lily seedlings from a single lot of seeds, showing variation in germination and development. (Courtesy U.S.D.A.)

Because of their height, size and form lilies have the power to dominate any group of plants in which they appear. For this reason, as well as for their cultural requirements, the gardener should exercise particular care in placing them. They are not plants to be purchased in a moment of enthusiasm and then stuck into any corner that happens to be available. Like most tall and slender flowers, lilies are seen at their best when silhouetted against a suitable background, such as evergreens, shrubs, a wall, or the shadowy depths of open woodland.

Two other points to bear in mind are that lilies make much more beautiful displays when grown in groups or colonies, and also that they are *effective at a distance,* and therefore can well be used, especially in white or light-colored varieties, near the termini of vistas viewed from either indoors or outdoors.

When you have decided to add lilies to your garden, a good practical plan is to start out with an armful of bamboo stakes or other markers and place one or more in each location that seems particularly suitable for a group of lilies. If some of these spots are already occupied by other plants, don't be deterred by the necessity of transplanting them, for there are few indeed which will merit priority over the lily.

With your markers in place, check each location:

First, for good drainage; the primary requirement for their successful growth.

Second, for background—and with it, protection from strong winds.

Third, for garden effect as points of interest in the landscape scheme, or for their relation to surrounding plants if in a border.

Fourth, for sun and shade, a matter of much less import than commonly believed, because most species, and practically all the horticultural varieties, will tolerate either full sun or partial shade, provided other conditions—such as adequate mulch or moisture if they are in full sun—are favorable.

So far, each stake or group of stakes represents an X variety—one not yet decided upon. With the planting positions once determined—you can make the most intelligent selection of varieties that will give you what you want, for some lilies grow only 2 or 3 feet tall, others 5 to 7; some flower in June, others during July or August (when possibly you are away for the summer), or as late as October.

Beds of lily seedlings as they were grown in open at Oregon Bulb Farms when Jan de Graaff began his famous breeding programs. Sown in March; photographed in June; to be transplanted later in season.

But before we attempt to select individual species and varieties, let's consider conditions which lilies prefer, and their general culture.

CULTURE

We have already emphasized that *good drainage* is the primary requisite in growing lilies. At peril of becoming boresome, we reiterate it again here—annoyance sometimes becomes a successful barb in making a point stick in one's memory. Aside from drainage, the matter of soil is not nearly so vital a factor as many writers have indicated. Don't take our word for it. Dr. George Slate, a lily authority with extensive experience in growing many species under home-garden conditions, says, "Cultural requirements are easily met. Any good garden soil that is well drained and has demonstrated its suitability for a general assortment of vegetables and common annual and perennial flowers will do very well for lilies. If neutral or slightly acid in reaction, and well supplied with organic matter or humus, it will serve satisfactorily."

The above quotation from Dr. Slate mentions soil "neutral or slightly acid," and "well supplied with humus." The directions in Chapter 6 tell you how to provide these requirements. In soil that is likely to be too wet, drainage can be assured by one of the methods described on page 68. Most lilies have their roots well below the surface, so a *deep* soil—at least 12 inches and preferably 18—is desirable. Extra depth can often be provided more easily by making a raised bed than by excavating, and this method at the same time improves the drainage.

As lily bulbs often are not received until after hard frosts, *assure easy planting by preparing the soil well in advance and then covering it.* A layer of peat moss, straw, or leaves 4 or 5 inches deep, covered with scrap boards or pieces of old roofing paper, will keep ground open through December even in a severe climate.

Care on Receipt

The ideal time to plant a lily bulb is within fifteen minutes after it has been dug! Such planting, of course, is impossible except with bulbs dug in your own garden. So the best we can do in buying bulbs is to get those which have been out of the ground as short a time as possible.

Much of the food for the new growth of a lily bulb is stored in the persistent fleshy roots. The less these have become desiccated or bruised during the period they are out of the ground, the better. If they shrivel completely, the bulb is severely injured even though it may grow.

The scales of a bulb in good condition are plump, firm and securely attached to the basal plate. If soft, fleshy and easily dislodged, they indicate that the bulb has suffered in transit. Bruised scales invite disease, rots and molds that eventually destroy the bulb. Bulbs only moderately shriveled and otherwise in good condition can be plumped up by placing them, for a fortnight or so *only,* in moist peat moss or sand before planting. Injured bulbs can be salvaged by using them as a source of bulblets. (See Scaling, Chapter 9.)

Bulbs that must be held for a considerable period or kept over winter for spring planting are best stored in peat moss or sand. We use a mixture of both, as it is less likely either to dry out or to stay too moist. The mixture should be kept barely moist enough to prevent shriveling. Even better, however, if one has the facilities, is to pot the bulbs individually, keep them in a dark, cool, frostproof place until they can safely be transferred to a cold frame in spring, and plant them out after danger of severe frosts. We once carried through an assortment of late-arriving bulbs in this way without the loss of a single one, and with much better first-season results than if they had been kept in dormant storage.

Spring Planting

Many lilies, however, especially stem-rooting kinds, make a good showing the first season from bulbs planted in spring *if* the bulbs have been properly stored. If bulbs must be planted in spring, get them in as early as possible and, above all, plant immediately upon receiving them.

Planting

As a general rule for depth of planting, two to three times the thickness of the bulb (vertical diameter) will answer. The important point is that the roots should have moisture, but not be in wet soil. In light, sandy soil they may go 50 to 75 per cent deeper than in heavy soil. These depths are to the *top* of the bulb when planted.

Some lilies throw out roots from the stem growth just above the bulbs as well as from the bases of the bulbs. These are termed "stem-rooting" and are planted considerably deeper than those which root only at the base. Usually, base-rooting sorts should go 4 to 6 inches (to top of bulb) and stem-rooting kinds 8 to 10. It is better to plant too deep than too shallow. Planting depths for individual species and hybrids are given in the catalogues of some specialists.

American and English authorities seem to differ as to the advisability of placing sand under and around the bulbs when planting. Evidence in the form of direct comparative tests seems to be lacking, as it is in so many gardening rules that are handed down from one writer to another. Certainly sand is not needed where drainage is as good as it should be. We have used sand (or fine gravel) when planting in heavy soil in wet weather—on the theory that it might help and could do no harm. But ordinarily we never use it. Most American authorities agree that sand planting is wasted effort. The same holds true for setting bulbs over inverted flowerpots. Some growers plant thick-scaled bulbs (such as regal and martagon) on their sides, the theory being that surplus moisture will drain out. With bulbs taken up after a heavy rain, we have failed to find any difference resulting from this method of planting.

Two things that are helpful can be done in preparing the bulbs for planting. The first is to cut back the withered tips of fleshy roots and in general give them a trimming that will make them easier to handle in planting; the second is to dust them with a fungicide.

In planting, make a hole sufficiently large so that the bulb can be placed in it with the roots spread out and down, as they naturally grow. Holding the bulb with one hand, work fine soil under and around it to secure it in this position. We have seen so-called gardeners force the bulbs into small holes in such a way that the roots were actually turned up around them, crowded together and pointing skyward.

As the first year's performance, and to some extent the future life of a lily, will depend largely on vigorous new root growth before the soil freezes deep, the following precautions may be taken to attain this end. First: if the soil is really dry, water the bottoms of planting holes, repeating until the soil will not readily absorb more, then fill in a little dry soil and plant. Second: if planting must be done just before frosts, mulch to keep ground frost-free as long as possible. Third: make sure that surface soil does freeze later (removing mulch if necessary), and when it has frozen, mulch thoroughly (*over snow if possible*) to prevent the early emergence and consequent injury from any late frosts, especially if the planting has a sunny southern exposure.

The location of each bulb or group should be marked with a substantial, permanent label. Where there is a group planting, it may well be outlined for the first season with a barrel hoop or a ribbon of lime or white sand.

Spring Care

The sprouting stalks of lilies are about the most brittle things in

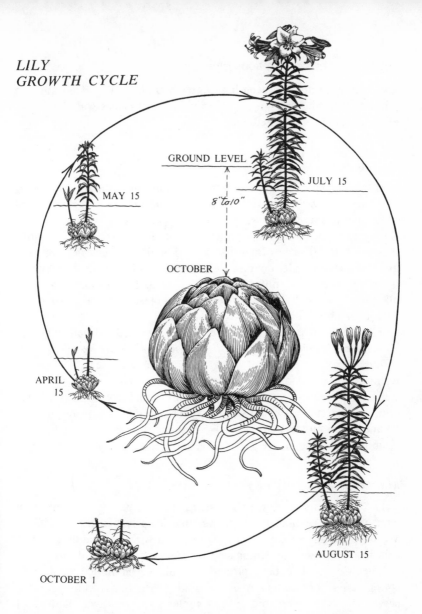

LILY
GROWTH CYCLE

GROUND LEVEL

JULY 15

8" to 10"

MAY 15

OCTOBER

APRIL 15

AUGUST 15

OCTOBER 1

the garden. Roots of the stem-rooting kinds grow quite close to the surface. For both these reasons, early spring cultivation about any lilies should be undertaken only with great care.

Lilies, more than most plants, insist on open, well-aerated soil; a hard-packed surface means poor growth, if not eventual death. The surface soil should be kept loose by shallow cultivation with a prong hoe held at an angle preventing the teeth from digging deep into the ground. After the first spring, cover plants or mulches will practically eliminate hoeing and weeding.

Feeding

Many lily species in their native habitats are found growing in meager soil. Most of them, however, respond readily to a rather generous diet in the garden. As the period of growth before blooming is a long one, we make two applications of plant food, the first after they are 6 to 10 inches high, the second as flower buds develop. We use our regular bulb mixture (Chapter 7) supplemented by wood ashes to assure a plentiful supply of potash. In soils tending to be alkaline, it would be better to secure the potash in some other form, such as a high-potash (2–8–10 or 0–10–10 formula) fertilizer. An ample supply of potash, it has been fairly well established, tends to increase resistance to diseases. *Excess nitrogen is to be avoided.* It results in soft growth and weak stems. The usual 5–10–5 garden fertilizer will provide ample nitrogen but is low in potash.

As the plants use much more food during their later growth, when two applications are made we use about one-third in spring and the balance later. In terms of a 5–10–5 formula, this would mean 1 to 2 pounds per 100 square feet in spring, and 2 to 4 pounds later on.

Mulches and Ground Covers

The use of mulches, which is so rapidly increasing in connection with all kinds of plants, has proved particularly beneficial to lilies. We have already spoken of it in connection with late planting; reference is made now to mulching as part of the year-round culture.

Lilies do not like bare ground. An all-season mulch applied in spring, after the winter-protection mulch has been removed, conserves moisture, keeps the ground cooler and does away with most weeding. Whatever the material used, it should be such as to remain open and porous to admit air and water freely. Real leafmold is excellent. We have found both pine needles and buckwheat hulls satisfactory. Peat moss, unless mixed into the soil surface, may become too packed and more or less impervious to rain or watering. In some sections, chopped straw, chopped cornstalks, or ground corncobs are available. Lawn trimmings, half-rotted leaves and other materials that may form a sodden mat should not be used.

By fall, most of these mulches will have partly decayed and settled to a thinner layer. As soon as the soil has frozen an inch or two beneath them, the winter mulch—marsh or bog hay, clean straw or evergreen boughs—is applied over varieties whose winter-hardiness may be questionable.

Ground-cover plants to be grown in combination with lilies are often recommended. Japanese spurge (*Pachysandra terminalis*) and periwinkle (*Vinca minor*) are two favorites. While serviceable in areas where lilies and other bulbs are naturalized, we have found them, under other conditions, not too practical. Pachysandra, especially, makes rather too thick a mat of foliage for any but the stronger-growing lilies, and it is an insatiable moisture-robber—a particularly serious objection with stem-rooting lilies.

For lilies grown in landscape groups and in the mixed border, there are some spreading or light-foliaged perennials and many annuals which make desirable companions for them. Among our favorites are *Phlox subulata, Iberis, Arabis, Aquilegia, Heuchera,* among the former, and *Phlox drummondii,* petunia, pansy, sweet-alyssum, among the latter.

Watering

Despite the best of care in providing ample humus in the soil, and in mulching, in prolonged periods of dry weather lilies will suffer. Even if they have bloomed, this lack of moisture will take its toll in preventing normal development of the bulbs.

To be of much use, watering must be copious enough to moisten the soil to a depth of a foot or more. Begin watering when the soil has dried out to a depth of 3 or 4 inches, and thus conserve the water lower down. We use a soil-soaker hose, laid on top of the mulch and let it run for several hours. A good method for landscape groups is to sink a 4- or 5-inch drain tile about a foot into the ground, with a couple of shovelfuls of small stones supporting the lower end. A hose stuck into this and allowed to run slowly will give a thorough subirrigation. In either of these methods, the foliage is kept dry and the watering can be done in the evening. If a sprinkler must be used, water in the early morning.

Early varieties of lilies in bloom in late June garden, with later sorts ready to take over in July and August.

Cascade strain of madonna lily (L. candidum)—*the oldest and still one of the most popular of all garden lilies.*

Cutting

Lilies are as beautiful and desirable in the house as they are in the garden, but if you wish to enjoy them both ways you will find yourself in a dilemma. Unless most of the stem is taken with the flower, its decorative value is lost. If most of the stem is taken, the bulb—having lost its lungs—will be severely injured. The only satisfactory compromise is to grow some bulbs just for cutting, and then to leave as much foliage as possible, and not to cut every year from the same bulbs. Having this supply for cutting is not difficult if one is careful to save the natural increase from offsets or to grow some from scales. Many kinds, including some of the very best for indoor decoration, increase rapidly.

In the border the flowers should be removed as they fade and no seed pods allowed to form unless they are wanted for propagation. First-year plants which for any reason seem to be weak will be helped by pinching out the flower buds and thus saving a certain amount of food for the development of the bulb.

The stalks should be cut only after the foliage has withered and begun to dry up. We leave 4 or 5 inches of stem, to mark the location of the bulb, removing this in spring as new growth emerges.

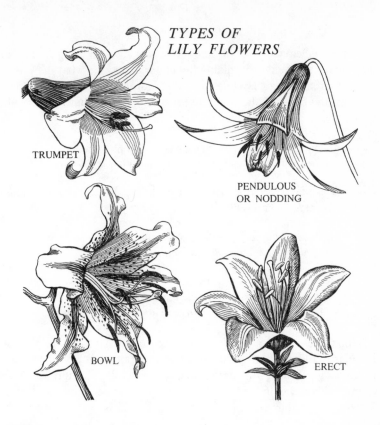

*TYPES OF
LILY FLOWERS*

TRUMPET

PENDULOUS
OR NODDING

BOWL

ERECT

Replanting

While some lilies increase slowly and may be left undisturbed for years, others will need replanting after three or four years. It is not entirely a matter of variety—congenial conditions are quite as great a factor.

Need for replanting will be evidenced by a close-crowded group of flower stalks with few or inferior blooms. The best time to replant is during the period when the bulbs are nearest to being dormant— when the seed pods are ripening, several weeks after the flowers fade.

TYPES

A few pages back we took a little journey about the garden for the purpose of selecting locations where lilies might best be placed, and got as far as leaving a lot of bamboo stakes stuck in the ground. Now let's survey the field of available lily material and see what there is.

First of all, the true lilies include four distinct types of flowers that are the basis of the many hybrids and strains that are so widely grown today. The types are:

TRUMPET OR FUNNEL-SHAPED FLOWERS: Examples—madonna (*L. candidum*); regal (*L. regale*); Easter lily (*L. longiflorum* varieties).

BOWL OR SAUCER-SHAPED BLOOMS: Examples—gold-banded lily (*L. auratum*); speciosum lily.

ERECT FLOWERS, WIDE OPEN: Examples—our native wood lily (*L. philadelphicum*); *L. concolor; L. umbellatum.*

PENDULOUS OR NODDING FLOWERS, WITH PETALS RECURVING AS FLOWERS OPEN FULLY: Examples—*L. martagon;* our native field lilies (*L. canadense* and *L. superbum*); *L. amabile; L. pumilum.*

While such species as the madonna and regal lilies retain their popularity today, the hybrids and hybrid strains are by far preferred by most gardeners for the reasons given at the beginning of this chapter. The classification below will give you a good idea of the vast selections that exist:

The Horticultural Classification of Lilies

DIVISION 1—*The Asiatic Hybrids:*
>   a   Early flowering lilies with upright flowers. For sun or partial shade. Examples: Enchantment, 2–3 feet, blazing red; Golden Chalice Hybrids, 1½–3 feet, lemon-yellow, gold and apricot-orange; Mid-Century Hybrids, 2–4 feet, red, maroon, yellow and orange.
>   b   Lilies with outward-facing flowers. Full sun or partial shade. Examples: Pastel Hybrids, 12–18 inches, miniature habit.
>   c   Lilies with pendent flowers having curled petals. Sun or partial shade. Examples: Harlequin Hybrids, 5 feet, pink, lilac, old rose, red, purple, ivory, white, yellow; 'Nutmegger', 4 feet, canary-yellow spotted reddish-brown, produces axil bulbils.

DIVISION 2—*The Martagon Hybrids:* Characteristics of *Lilium martagon* and *L. hansonii.* Flowers are pendent with recurving petal tips.

Need some afternoon shade. Example: Paisley Strain, 3–6 feet, wide color range, June.

DIVISION 3—*The Candidium Hybrids:* Hybrids of the madonna lily.

DIVISION 4—*The American Hybrids:* Hybrids of American species. Full sun or partial shade for long flowering period. Examples: Bellingham Hybrids, 6–7 feet, yellow, orange, or dark reds, with spots of red or black.

DIVISION 5—*The Longiflorum Hybrids*

DIVISION 6—*The Trumpet Hybrids:*
a   Chinese trumpets. Funnel-shaped flowers. Full sun or partial shade. Examples: Aurelian Hybrids, 4–7 feet, yellow, apricot, pink with flower shapes from trumpet to sunburst-types, July; Golden Splendor, 3–6 feet, deep gold with maroon striped exteriors, July.
b   Bowl-shaped flowers. Sun or partial shade to lengthen flower display. Examples: Heart's Desire Strain, 4–6 feet, semi-trumpet-shaped flowers, July.
c   Pendent-type flowers. Example: Golden Showers.
d   Star-shaped or sunburst-type flowers. For sun or partial shade. Examples: Golden Sunburst Strain, 4–6 feet, golden yellow, July.

DIVISION 7—*The Oriental Hybrids:* Hybrids of *L. auratum, L. speciosum, L. japonicum, L. rubellum* and their crosses with *L. henyri.*
a   Trumpet-shaped flowers.
b   Bowl-shaped flowers. Full sun in cool climates, some afternoon shade in warmer regions. Example: 'Empress of India', 4–5 feet, huge red flowers with petals edged white, August; Red-band Hybrids, 5–7 feet, crimson-red and white petals, August.
c   Flat-faced flowers. Full sun in cool areas, some afternoon shade in warm areas. Examples: Imperial Crimson Strain and Imperial Gold Strain, 5–7 feet, good fragrance, August.
d   Recurved flowers. Same exposures as above. Example: Jamboree Strain, 5–6 feet, crimson, rose or white, or red as in Red Jamboree Strain, August.

DIVISION 8—Contains all hybrids not provided for in any previous division.

DIVISION 9—Contains all true *Lilium* species and their botanical forms.

PROPAGATION—see Chapter 9.

LILY TROUBLES

Few insects are troublesome to lilies except perhaps the aphids that carry lily mosaic. More devastating is likely to be an attack by mice (see Chapter 10). Mice can be outwitted by growing lily bulbs in planters, tubs or large pots. Such container-grown lilies make a distinctive and different decoration for a sunny terrace or patio (with some afternoon shade). We do not recommend the tallest lilies for such a use, but several of the modern, lower-growing strains are perfectly suitable. (A few include Cinnabar, 2–3 feet; Sunkissed, 3 feet; Enchantment, 3 feet; Pastel Hybrids, 1–1½ feet; Connecticut Lemonglow, 2 feet.) A large lily bulb will require about 2–3 quarts of soil (about equal parts of soil, peat moss and sand). Obviously, the deeper the container the better—and all the cultural requirements given earlier apply to lilies in containers. Whether your lilies prosper after the first year depends on the care they receive: sufficient moisture but not a continuously saturated soil; protection from wind and excessive heat and extreme cold in winter.

The beginner with lilies should not be discouraged by the existence of the diseases and pests that are described below and in Chapter 10. You may grow lilies for years without encountering any of them, or you may even have them and still have lilies. A conspicuous example of a disease-tolerant lily is the popular madonna. And the many hybrid strains of lilies grown today from seed are not only resistant to diseases, but the methods of propagation used have bypassed the diseases that formerly were perpetuated by asexual increase.

Diseases

Three diseases account for most of the trouble with lilies in gardens. They are mosaic, botrytis blight and basal rot.

Lily mosaic is a virus disease which affects all parts of the plant. A few species, even though attacked, continue to grow and bloom year after year; others survive in a weakened, abnormal condition; but a great many species perish completely after a year or two.

Symptoms of mosaic include premature dying of the leaves, beginning at the base, usually accompanied by dwarfed growth; also by striping or mottling of the leaves. This occurs most commonly as circular blotches distributed over the leaf surface: in other species, as light-colored irregular spots which ultimately dry out; in others, as narrow streaks running from base to top of the leaves, which are abnormally small but not distorted. These symptoms are more discernible in spring than later in the season. Infected plants should be removed and burned.

Control measures for mosaic are not easy. Controlling the aphids that transmit this disease is a help. Fortunately it is possible to have some species without complete control. The following are resistant or immune: *Lilium amabile; L. candidum; L. hansonii; L. martagon; L. pardalinum; L. speciosum; L. testaceum; L. tigrinum; L. umbellatum;* and of course many hybrids.

Lilies grown from seed are seldom infected. If such bulbs can be planted 300 or 400 feet from any infected bulbs, they will be comparatively safe. The following lilies are easily grown from seed: *Lilium amabile; L. concolor; L. davidii; L. formosanum; L. henryi; L. pumilum (tenuifolium); L. regale.*

Botrytis blight (Botrytis elliptica), a fungous disease, is much less destructive than mosaic because it seldom injures the bulb. Most gardeners who have grown the madonna lily (*L. candidum*), its most common victim, know the characteristic "bare stems" of one season contrasted to normal leafage in others.

First symptoms of this botrytis are orangey-brown spots, circular or oval in shape, which may spread and coalesce. These are followed in about ten days by spores which develop in the form of a grayish mold. Form and coloring of the spots vary somewhat in different species. If the disease spreads to the flowers, it develops very rapidly, resulting in a messy decay similar to the familiar botrytis of tulips. The infection starts on the lower leaves and ascends. The fungus lives over the winter in diseased leaves, stems and flowers.

The standard control for botrytis blight is Bordeaux mixture, 4–2–50. This can be home-mixed, or purchased ready for use by adding water. It must be applied frequently enough—beginning when spring temperatures get up around 60 degrees—*to keep all new growth covered*. The Bordeaux spray will adhere better and longer if a "sticker" is used with it. Bordeaux dust may be used, but is generally considered less effective. Micronized copper has been claimed to be a successful preventative, but many authorities question its effectiveness. As with black spot of roses, there is no *cure;*

it can only be prevented. Plant where there is good circulation of air, with plenty of space between plants, and destroy affected parts as soon as noticed.

Basal rot. The third serious lily disease, basal rot, is responsible for the death of many lilies which simply disappear, as it attacks roots and bulbs before affecting foliage.

Aboveground symptoms are delayed emergence in spring, stunted growth and foliage that turns yellow and dies down prematurely.

Control consists in digging up any bulbs apparently affected. If examination shows that the basal plate is unaffected, remove decayed roots and tissue and sterilize by immersing bulb for thirty minutes in a solution of 1 part 40 per cent formaldehyde to 100 parts water, and replant in another place.

For gray mold blight, fusarium rot, stem rot, see Chapter 10.

INSECT PESTS

Unlike the diseases, insect pests give the lily grower little trouble in the garden. It is in storage and transit that they work havoc. The three most harmful of these are mites (related to spiders, so not strictly an insect), thrips and aphids.

The bulb mite (*Rhizoglyphus hyacinthii*), most serious lily "insect" pest, is minute, pale yellow and almost transparent. It breeds between the scales, develops rapidly under favorable conditions and may cause severe losses. Examine newly purchased bulbs, *especially if they are bruised or otherwise injured,* with a magnifying glass to make sure that they are not infested. If there is much decay, it is best to destroy them after reporting their condition to the shipper. If injury does not appear severe, they can be cleaned up by fumigating with paridichlorobenzene (obtainable from most seed stores) at the rate of 3 ounces of crystals to each cubic foot of an airtight container. Use burlap or fine mesh wire to keep bulbs from direct contact with crystals, and leave for four days, keeping at a temperature as near 60 degrees as possible. Expose to sun for a full day before planting.

The lily thrips, like the mite, completes its life cycle between the bulb scales. It is large—for a thrips—and glossy black, with wings which it does not use. Fumigate with paridichlorobenzene crystals, 3 ounces to 1 cubic foot of airtight space, for 96 hours, or dust with Sevin.

Aphids. The lily and melon aphids, most dangerous because they distribute the mosaic disease, sometimes do direct injury to new growth. Malathion, rotenone, or pyrethrum applied *promptly* will clean them out. One form, *Macrosiphum lili,* is found only on under sides of leaves. Another, *Myzus circumflexus,* attacks terminal buds and shoots.

Other insects which sometimes attack lilies are the narcissus bulb flies, lily-bulb thrips and stalk borer. For these, see Chapter 10.

CHAPTER *16. Dahlias*

Without question it is as cut flowers that dahlias have had their greatest value, but today the dahlia has become an accepted—and important—garden flower. And fanciers—and rightly so—still take pride in growing mammoth flowers (from 7 inches or more wide) for exhibiting in flower shows, but the increased popularity of the dahlia is due to the availability of numbers of smaller-flowered, low-growing varieties that can add so much color to summer's gardens. These modern bedding dahlias have the same range of flower colors and types (such as single, double or pompon, and with twisted or curled petals) and, best of all, they require neither staking nor disbudding.

INDOORS AND IN THE GARDEN

Certainly we should continue to grow dahlias for cut flowers, too, but since they are so floriferous and continue in bloom for so many weeks, it's quite possible to gather freely from plants in the display garden without resorting to having a supply in a special cut flower garden.

From two or three dozen plants in our borders, we have dahlias to gather literally by the basketful from late July until frost cuts them down. They are, incidentally, one of the most satisfactory of flowers to use as a follow-upper among or near deep-planted tulips. Potted plants set out late in May attain good size about the time the tulip foliage is mature enough to be removed. (You can grow many strains of bedding dahlias from seeds, giving them the same culture as zinnias and marigolds.)

There are many places about the garden where a small group of dahlias, *or even a single plant,* may be used to good effect. They can be used in sunny beds bordering the patio in combination with such annuals as ageratum, petunia or marigold. Or use them freely in the mixed border. Few shrubs flower after midsummer. And even those that have colorful foliage or berries in the fall go through a period when they are but masses of leaves, attractive but without color. Borders or groups of such shrubs, and also broad-leaved evergreens, make excellent backgrounds for masses of low-growing dahlias, especially those of the lovely autumn hues in which the dahlia is unequaled by any other flower except the chrysanthemum.

Another use for dahlias is to grow them as an inexpensive, temporary hedge. For this purpose the taller-growing varieties are best. The beauty of such a hedge is that while it serves as a screen, it will also provide summer-long flowers for garden display and cutting.

DAHLIA TYPES

The dahlia is an American flower, hailing from Mexico. The Mexicans used it as a garden flower before the coming of the Spaniards and probably had developed garden varieties. The original name of the species, *Dahlia variabilis,* was indeed appropriate. The species name was later changed to *D. rosea,* and now is *D. pinnata.* Although the dahlia is comparatively a Johnny-come-lately among garden flowers—the types we know having been developed since 1800—it boasts a range in size and form of bloom, in habit of growth and in coloring that has few equals in the plant world. It provides blossoms a foot and a half across, on stems like broom handles, for the exhibitor who wants the "best" flower in the show, and dainty nodding little pompons an inch in diameter.

Indeed, so rapidly do the types of the dahlia change and intermingle that the American Dahlia Society has been hard put to provide suitable classifications. Those which are "official" at the moment are as follows:

Definitions

INVOLUTE: turned inward, forward, or toward face of ray.

REVOLUTE: turned outward, toward back of ray. When fully revolute, margins of rays overlap or approximate each other.

CLASS IA. SINGLE DAHLIAS: Open-center flowers, with only one row of ray florets, with the margins flat or nearly so, regardless of the number of florets. Example: 'Ray's White'.

CLASS IB. MIGNON: Plants do not exceed about 18 inches in height. Examples: 'Nellie Geerligs'; 'Sneezy'.

CLASS II. ORCHID-FLOWERING: Flowers as in Singles, except that the rays are more or less tubular by the involution of the margins. Example: 'Marie Schnugg'.

CLASS III. ANEMONE: Open-centered flowers, with only one row of florets, regardless of form or number of florets, with the tubular-disk florets elongated, forming a pincushion effect. Examples: 'Brio'; 'Roulette'.

CLASS IV. COLLARETTE: Open-centered flowers, with only one row of ray florets, with the addition of one or more row of petaloids, usually of a different color, forming collar around disk. Examples: 'La Cierva'; 'Bride's Bouquet'.

CLASS V. PEONY: Open-centered flowers with two to five rows of ray florets, with or without the addition of smaller curled or twisted floral rays around the disk. Example: 'Bishop of Llandaff'.

CLASS VI. INCURVED CACTUS: Fully double flowers, with the margins of the majority of floral rays fully revolute for one half their length or more, tips of rays curving toward center of flowers. Examples: 'Barbie J.'; 'Silver Wedding'.

CLASS VII. STRAIGHT CACTUS: Fully double flowers, with margins of the majority of floral rays fully revolute for one half their length or more, rays straight, slightly incurved or recurved. Examples: 'Flying Saucer'; 'Tenga'.

CLASS VIII. SEMI-CACTUS: Fully double flowers with margins of majority of floral rays fully revolute for less than half their length; rays broad below. Examples: 'Golden Heart'; 'Purity'.

CLASS IX. FORMAL DECORATIVE: Fully double flowers, with margins of floral rays slightly or not at all revolute; rays generally broad, either pointed or rounded at tips, with outer rays tending to recurve and central rays tending to be cupped; all floral rays in a somewhat regular arrangement to the extent of having four or more recognizable rows of rays surrounding center. Examples: 'Jersey's Beauty'; 'Commando'.

CLASS X. INFORMAL DECORATIVE: Fully double flowers, with margins of floral rays slightly or not at all revolute, rays generally long, twisted, or pointed and usually irregular in arrangement. Examples: 'Terpo'; 'Mary Elizabeth'.

CLASS XI. BALL: Fully double flowers, ball-shaped or slightly flattened, floral rays blunt or rounded at tips and quilled or with markedly involute margins in spiral arrangement, the flowers 3½ inches or more in diameter. Examples: 'Jerry Lynn'; 'Paul Smith'.

CLASS XII. MINIATURE: All dahlias which normally produce flowers that do not exceed 4 inches in diameter, Pompons excluded, to be classified according to the foregoing descriptions: Miniature Single: 'Fugi San'; 'Prince of Bulgaria'. Miniature Peony: 'Bishop of Llandaff'; Miniature Cactus: 'Park Princess'. Miniature Semi-Cactus: 'Billy'; 'Dainty Lady'. Miniature Formal Decorative: 'Michael J.'; 'Safe Shot'. Miniature Informal Decorative: 'Red Garnet'. Miniature Ball: 'Dusky'.

CLASS XIII. POMPON: Same characteristics as Ball dahlias but, for show purposes, not more than 2 inches in diameter. Examples: 'Atom'; 'Johnny'.

The Little Dahlias

We would like to reemphasize that if you are familiar only with the big show dahlias in the "gardens" of enthusiasts that contain small forests of 6-foot stakes to which they and the dahlias are chained until show time, don't turn thumbs down on all dahlias before you have given some of the little fellows at least a trial.

First, there are the miniatures. These are merely smaller editions of the big fellows, with flowers 2 to 4 inches across, on bushy plants 2 to 4 feet tall. Again, we repeat! No need for staking or for disbudding unless you prefer to have somewhat larger and more perfect flowers. They produce blooms by the dozen over a long period, and can well be given a place in a garden of annuals and perennials or against a hedge or shrubbery, or massed around the terrace.

A favorite among the miniatures is still 'Bishop of Llandaff'—or one of its descendants, such as 'Japanese Bishop'. 'The Bishop' is a semi-double (officially classified as peony-flowered) of bright scarlet with golden stamens and distinctly bronze-maroon foliage; it is one of the most satisfactory of all flowers for cutting. Another excellent miniature is 'Park Princess'. It forms bushy plants, 3 feet high or under, and from midsummer until frost, is covered with flesh-pink flowers, superb for cutting and garden display.

Pompons

While often confused by beginners with the miniatures, pompon dahlias are entirely different. They are characterized by small, almost globular, honeycomb-like flowers, 1 to 2 inches in diameter, borne on thin, wiry stems, and produced, under favorable conditions, literally by the score. Often they can be cut in sprays that in themselves make attractive bouquets. The plants are bushy and while tall-growing varieties up to 5 feet exist, there are many varieties in the 3-foot range that will fit comfortably into most modern gardens. The colors are clear and bright and blend nicely.

Among the popular varieties are: 'Amber Queen', 5 feet; 'Doxy', 3½ feet; 'Potgeiter', 2½ feet; 'Joe Fette', 3 feet; 'Betty Ann', 3 feet.

Bedding or Dwarf

The bedding dahlias got their name from the fact that they were used extensively in England for mass plantings where large-flowered, slower-growing types were not suited to the climate. They come into flower so quickly that seed sown in the open around bean-planting time will give several weeks of bloom in late summer and fall. Started in a cold frame or indoors under artificial lights, they can be transplanted readily, being no more difficult to handle than marigolds or zinnias.

Originally most of the bedding dahlias were grown from seeds, two of the better known strains being the single-flowered Coltness and the semi-double Unwin Hybrids. Today, seeds of the single Coltness strain are still available as are improved Unwin-type strains, one being known as Early Bird. Another superior dahlia to grow from seed is Redskin. The plants from this strain grow from 12 to 14 inches high, have bronze foliage and double or semi-double flowers of many colors.

Few of these seed-grown bedding dahlias grow over 24 inches and most of them will have stems sufficiently long for cutting. We have recommended them to many gardeners—beginners and experienced alike—and have never known of anyone being disappointed. The range of colors is all that could be desired. Any plants you particularly like can be saved for another year by storing the tuberous roots over winter. You will be surprised how large the roots are by the end of the growing season.

There are still more improvements in bedding dahlias. Growing dahlias from seed can be a pleasant adventure with some variations in growth habits and unpredictable colors the results, but if you like to plan your garden effects, you will want to look into the many bedding dahlias available as tubers whose habits and flower colors are known. Among the Mignon dahlias that grow only 1–1½ feet tall are several named varieties. Some good ones are 'Nelly Geerligs', with red flowers; 'Murillo', with rose flowers; 'Sneezy', white; 'G. F. Hemerick', orange. All Mignon dahlias have single flowers. For a semi-double flower effect, there are the anemone-flowered dahlias that grow from 1–1½ feet high. Some good varieties are: 'Toto', white; 'Grisbee', yellow and pink; 'Brio', orange. Still lower growing than any of the aforementioned dahlias are lilliput or baby dahlias, only 10 inches high. Increasingly, as demand grows, there will be more of these named bedding dahlia varieties available.

PLANTING

The first rule in dahlia growing is to give the plants full sun. They are among the least tolerant of shade of all bulbous or tuberous plants.

The second is to keep them well supplied with water. The native Mexican name for dahlia was *acocotti,* which means "water pipe." In their natural habitat, the "water pipes" grew on volcanic soils in areas that never lacked for moisture during the season of active growth.

The third is to supply an abundance of plant food. The amounts suggested for bulbs in general (page 83) may safely be increased by

50 per cent. Fertilizers are best provided in several applications—about a third at planting time and the balance at intervals of two to four weeks, the last being made soon after the first flowers are open. Peat moss, compost, well-rotted manure are all suitable for mixing in the planting soil to increase its water-holding capacity.

Roots vs. Plants

When you are starting with dahlias you will have the choice of procuring "tubers" (actually tuberous roots) or "green plants," which are tuber pieces or cuttings that have been potted up long enough to form a fairly good root ball. Most mail-order dahlia specialists offer roots or tubers. A dahlia root, being literally a root and not a bulb, is much more likely to become dried out or otherwise injured in transit and handling, unless carefully packed in polyethylene bags which prevent the roots from drying out.

Once you have a supply of dahlias, it is a very easy matter to start your own plants from cuttings if the root divisions do not supply a sufficient number.

As dahlias are extremely frost-sensitive, growing plants should not be set out until after any danger of late frost—a week or so later than usual tomato-planting time. Tubers can be planted a week or so earlier. Plants grown for exhibition are often set out somewhat later —up to mid-June—as this brings the flowers on during cooler nights, which the dahlia likes, and in time for the shows.

If plants are to be supported, it is advisable to set the stakes *before* planting. For large-flowered varieties, stakes 6 to 7 feet long are generally used. In our garden—we do not grow show dahlias—we prefer the less conspicuous wire stakes if it is necessary to use any. Plants grown for show purposes are usually spaced 3 to 4 feet each way, to allow room for pruning, disbudding, and cutting. Miniatures and pompons should be allowed at least 24 inches, and the dwarf bedding kinds 18 to 20 inches.

For prize blooms, it is advisable to prepare a planting hole for each root or plant. Remove soil 10 to 12 inches deep, add compost, rotted animal manure, or fertilizer, incorporate thoroughly with the soil, and then fill back enough plain soil so that the root—which is placed horizontally—will be 5 or 6 inches below the surface level.

In early planting, the roots are at first covered only an inch or so,

Growing dahlias from seed is no trick at all. Space seeds evenly; cover ⅛ inch deep. Keep in full sun and evenly moist until ready to transplant. Seedling plant, a few weeks old, shows "tuber" already forming at base of stem.

and the remaining hole is gradually filled in as the top grows. In late planting—when the soil is thoroughly warmed up—the soil is all filled in at once.

Growing plants from pots are set about 3 inches deep, to the top of the root ball, the lower leaves being removed if necessary. For plants—and for sprouted plants from tubers—Hotkaps or similar protectors can be used to ward off injury from late frosts and to speed growth; this makes it safe to plant a week or ten days earlier. Plants which have been grown in a greenhouse or a hotbed should be well hardened off before being transferred to the open. If you grow dahlias from seeds, they can be sown indoors about the time you sow zinnias or marigolds. Grow them under fluorescent lights if you lack a sunny window. Or you can sow dahlia seeds in the open ground—again, about the same time you sow zinnias or marigolds. Indoor-grown plants will require the usual hardening off mentioned above for greenhouse plants.

CULTURE

The one outstanding necessity in the culture of dahlias is to *keep them growing*. The character of the structure of the plant is such that any serious check, from whatever source, will *cause the wood to harden*. Once that happens, they are through flowering for the season. Sometimes early-planted dahlias bloom themselves out long before frost. Plants that have gone on strike during July or early August can often be rejuvenated by cutting back the main stem, just above a new shoot at the base of the plant, or else a few inches above the lowest branches. Such a beheading—plus plenty of water if the soil is dry—may result in new growth that will give late blooms.

It is much more satisfactory, however, to prevent the check that throws the plant into semi-dormancy. Lack of moisture in the soil is the most frequent cause of premature hardening of the arteries in dahlias. Frequent but shallow stirring of the soil around plants, especially after heavy rains or packing of the soil from tying, disbudding, etc., helps to conserve moisture. Clean cultivation also eliminates weeds, insidious robbers of soil moisture.

Mulching is especially desirable for dahlias because of their need

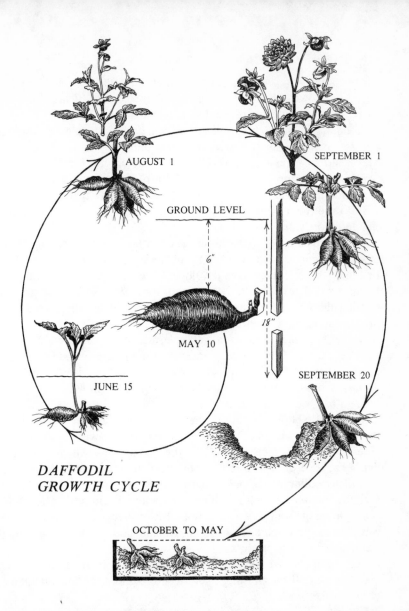

AUGUST 1

SEPTEMBER 1

GROUND LEVEL

6"

MAY 10

18"

SEPTEMBER 20

JUNE 15

DAFFODIL
GROWTH CYCLE

OCTOBER TO MAY

of moisture, their near-the-surface roots and the frequent treading on the soil between the rows in the care they require when grown for big blooms. Peat moss is a satisfactory material when water is available; if one must depend on rains, a more open substance, such as pine needles, buckwheat hulls, or clean straw, is better.

Pruning and disbudding are two operations in dahlia culture which often confuse the beginner. The former is used for controlling the shape or growth of the *plant;* the latter, for control of the *flowers*— to get larger blooms or to time them for a definite date.

A dahlia plant left to itself is likely to form a tangle of branches and foliage, with small flowers on stems but a few inches long. Or it may send up one bean-pole-like cane, subject to breakage in the wind, and bearing flowers only at the top. Those who grow dahlias for exhibition figure on supporting them by stout stakes; those who wish to use them as garden flowers want lower-growing, self-support-ing and more floriferous plants.

To get specimens of the latter type, with several branching stems low down, cut or pinch out the tip of the main stem as soon as three or four pairs of leaves have developed. Plants so grown will support themselves. They should be allowed room for horizontal growth. Cutting the flowers or removing faded ones will usually give all the additional pruning required.

To get specimen flowers, a single vertical main stem is left. When the first cluster of three buds appears at the tip, the two side ones are pinched (or "rubbed") out. This is *disbudding.* It takes from 20 to 40 days from bud formation to the opening of the flower, the average being 30.

The small shoots starting in the axils of the pairs of leaves below the terminal flower bud are also removed from several sets to pro-vide a long, unbranched stem for the big flower—which may look like a cabbage on a broomstick but still win you a coveted blue rib-bon! The axillary buds *below* the point where the stem is to be cut are left—or *one* of each alternate pairs may be removed. The lateral stems growing from these axillary buds are then treated in the same way as was the original main stem. Thus a succession of large, long-stemmed flowers is produced.

For pompons and bedding types, the original pinching back of the main stem is all the pruning likely to be required, and disbudding is not needed.

Cutting: There are few points in connection with dahlia culture on which the experts are more completely at variance than on the simple matter of cutting and keeping the blooms. A series of careful experi-ments at the Ohio Experiment Station showed pretty conclusively that the much-advocated singeing of the stem in a flame or plunging in hot water does *not* result in the blooms keeping longer after cut-

Plate 16

ABOVE: *The perfect setting for a colony of crocus. The blooms are protected from spattering soil and the foliage may be left undisturbed to mature.* BELOW: *Crocuses make an ideal succession planting with early tulips. Blooming just ahead of the tulips, they leave their attractive foliage as an edging.*

Plate 17

Plate 18

ABOVE: *The "little" spring bulbs, crocus,* Iris reticulata, *chionodoxa, puschkinia and galanthus (snowdrops), belong in rock gardens.* BELOW: *A mixed planting of tulips prolongs the spring season in the home garden. Annuals can be planted later to hide the ripening foliage.*

Plate 19

Plate 20

ABOVE: *Lilies are best planted against a protecting background of ever-greens or shrubs and kept heavily mulched rather than cultivated.* BE-LOW: Lilium centifolium, *attaining a vigorous height of 6 to 8 feet, is unsurpassed for a tall accent in the mixed border or for cutting.*

Plate 21

Plate 22

This spring garden includes a variety of bulbs including the tulips 'Holland's Glory' (deep carmine), 'Golden Apeldoorn' (yellow), 'My Lady' (salmon-orange) and the ever-popular bunch-flowered daffodil 'Geranium'. The little blue-flowered bulbs are grape-hyacinths (Muscari).

ting. One of the country's largest commercial growers cuts blooms at any time of day, prefers to have them wilt considerably, and then places them in cold water up to their necks. After they have revived, he advises, only the bases of the stems should be kept in water. This system, plus the usual precaution of changing the water daily, recutting the stems and avoiding drafts, gives him the best results.

Protection: The first touch of Jack Frost's chilly fingers will finish off the dahlias—if you let it. They are, however, readily protected against a few degrees of frost; and no flower—with the possible exception of chrysanthemums—will give greater rewards for a few minutes spent in this effort, for they frequently go on producing blooms for two or three weeks if one gets them past that first hit-and-run attack of the enemy—usually made in the full o' the moon on a starry night with no breeze stirring. We keep a supply of plant-protecting cloth (treated muslin) on hand, supplemented by old bags, curtains and sheets. Even several layers of newspapers spread over plants will give protection. It's the work of but a few moments to throw these over the plants—from which newly opened or half-opened flowers have hastily been cut. Such protection can be left on two or three days if the temperature remains low, but usually it comes off the next morning.

STORING FOR WINTER

As the dahlia "bulb" is merely an enlarged fleshy root—not even a true tuber—it is subject to drying out, or drying *up,* much more rapidly than the general run of bulbs. We have known a whole collection of valuable varieties to be completely lost in ten days' time from being stored, immediately after digging, near a heater to "dry them off."

The dual objective in winter storage of dahlias is to keep them just sufficiently moist to prevent shriveling, and just cool enough to prevent sprouting. Many different methods are employed to achieve these ends. The one which will work best *under your conditions* you will have to determine for yourself. This will mean inspecting the roots carefully at least once a month for the first winter or two. After that you can probably establish a routine that you know you can depend on, with nothing more than a quick check-up around New Year's just to be sure that all is well.

We use vegetable baskets lined with roofing paper or newspapers, and medium-coarse peat moss to pack under, around and on top of them. Some growers prefer sand, despite its greater inconvenience and the fact that it is more difficult to prevent its becoming too dry unless the storage space itself is very moist. Polyethylene bags in which to store the roots are proving to be quick and successful. Another method, described below, is the coating of roots with paraffin. The temperature should be 35 to 55 degrees. Don't just guess at storage temperatures; keep a thermometer handy.

Dahlias, in their native habitats, are not—as Hamlet's father was —cut down "grossly, full of bread"; they come to a dormant period through a *gradual* drying off at the close of the rainy season. Don't dig, then, immediately after the plants have been killed by frost. Allow a few days for the roots to absorb what they can from

Soft-pink-colored dahlia variety called 'Park Princess' grows about 3½ feet high and from midsummer until stopped by a heavy frost provides living bouquets of flowers for garden display and indoor arrangements.

the fleshy stalks and to ripen. Then—on a dry sunny day if possible —cut the stalks about 4 inches above the crowns and fasten a wired label *through* each stalk to keep varieties from getting mixed. With a spading fork, dig up a clump and let it drop, bottom down, just hard enough to jar off most of the soil, allowing what will to adhere to the roots. Clumps with large, hollow stem stubs are placed on their sides, or inverted, to prevent moisture from collecting in them.

After digging, store the clumps loosely in deep flats, allow them to dry off for a few hours, and put them in a dark, cool, moist place until they can be gone over and packed for winter storage. Some varieties, especially the first season from seed or from cuttings, make long, stringy roots which dry out quickly. These should be given special attention, if they are valued; placing them in polyethylene bags is quick and safe. Another method of protecting valuable roots is to coat them with paraffin wax. To do this, wash roots clean with a hose; fill a large pail two-thirds full of hot (about 80 degrees) water; pour in a pound of melted wax; dip tubers into water and remove slowly so the floating wax will coat them thoroughly. After wax coating hardens, pack in sawdust or peat moss. In any event, all thin or stringy roots should be examined frequently.

As planting time approaches, the roots are removed from storage and either started into growth to provide cuttings for green plants or cut up to make single-eye divisions for growing in pots or setting out directly where they are to grow. For green plants, allow 60 to 70 days to setting-out time. Placing roots in moist peat moss two or three weeks before planting will give the buds at the base of the old stem a chance to start sufficiently so that they can be divided to the best advantage—one strong eye to each root. (See page 222.)

DAHLIA TROUBLES

The most baffling of the many ills that may plague the grower of dahlias is the one commonly called "stunt." The term is used rather loosely—often applied to a plant of abnormal, undersized growth from any cause, such as insufficient plant food or insect injury. Such plants usually recover satisfactorily if the cause of poor growth is remedied or removed.

True stunt, caused by the dahlia-mosaic virus, is characterized by the typical mosaic mottling of the leaves, with yellowish stripes along the veins and curling, malformed foliage. Roots and stems are also dwarfed. There is no cure, but a regular spray program to control the green peach aphids that carry the virus is important. Immediate destruction of all sick plants may keep it under control. Growing exhibition plants under cheesecloth prevents infection by these aphids. Plants being propagated under glass can be protected by fumigation. Mosaic is *not* carried in the soil, nor transmitted by handling or tools, or through seeds; but divisions or cuttings of affected plants are almost certain to continue the infection.

Diseases

Wilt diseases, causing ring spots on foliage or rotting or browning of stems of growing plants, and decay of roots in storage are serious troubles for which there is no real cure. Dig up plants with soil about them if severely infected and destroy with quicklime. Dust roots in storage with captan or phaltan at first sign of any decaying spots. For spotted wilt and stem rot or wilt, see Chapter 10.

Powdery mildew sometimes attacks dahlias in late summer, when a powdery gray deposit appears on the foliage. Control by dusting with sulphur, Karathane or Benlate. Mildew can usually be ignored.

Insects

Among the insect pests which may attack dahlias is the potato leafhopper, a wedge-shaped sucking insect which jumps or hops when disturbed. Symptoms are the burning or browning of leaf margins, followed by stunting of the plants. Stunted plants should be destroyed, but spraying or dusting with Sevin will kill the leafhoppers if applied in time.

Other possible dahlia pests include other aphids, corn borer, stalk borer, cyclamen mite, root-knot nematodes, red spider, tarnished plant bug, and thrips. For any of these, refer to Chapter 10.

As flowers go, the gladiolus is, like the dahlia, comparatively a newcomer to gardens; and like the dahlia, also, under cultivation it has shown a surprising facility in responding to the touch of the hybridizer, crossing and crisscrossing until its devotees have finally thrown up their hands in despair at any attempt to keep the original horticultural types distinguished from each other.

Gladioli are—usually—easily grown; they provide the possibility of having bloom for three months or more by the simple expedient of making succession plantings from early April to early July, thus assuring color where and when you may want it. And they propagate so readily that from a half dozen corms of a variety one will have in a few years more than he knows what to do with.

While gladioli are hardly landscape subjects in the sense that the evergreen shrubs, rhododendrons, are, nor can they compete with the many kinds of daffodils and tulips for garden display, they are magnificent and long-lasting cut flowers, reason enough to grow them in the summer garden.

The most convenient way to grow gladioli is in rows—either in a cutting garden or perhaps at the end of the vegetable patch. If you lack this kind of growing space, you can still find a place for gladiolus. We have seen gladiolus flowers grown to perfection in a 4-foot-wide border among tall zinnias, African marigolds and yellow marguerite daisies. Use them as accents in mixed borders among perennials and annuals. Since the gladiolus possesses the advantage of growing vertically, it can relieve the monotony created by the excessive use of such rounded flowers of summer as the afore-mentioned zinnia and marigold as well as perennial phlox and chrysanthemum. A clump of six to a dozen can be tucked in among other plants with little trouble and removed at the end of the season with very slight disturbance of the roots of other plants near them. As with dahlias, the largest-flowered show varieties of gladiolus are least suited to the

'Elizabeth the Queen', *typical of the modern type of gladiolus with evenly spaced, wide-open lavender florets, facing one way.*

garden uses suggested here. Those more moderate in size of individual florets and in height of stalk give more pleasing results. Choose from among the baby, miniature or butterfly classes. If you plant in sufficient quantities and make succession plantings, as mentioned above, you will have gladiolus flowers to enjoy indoors as well as in the garden.

At this point it may be helpful to clear up the confusion which may exist in regard to the terms "miniature" and "baby" as applied to gladiolus. The miniatures are small-flowered varieties of the ordinary garden type. The babies, on the contrary, have evolved from the species *Gladiolus nanus* and possibly others, and formerly were used almost exclusively in greenhouses for late winter and spring cut flowers. They are now, however, becoming popular as garden flowers because of their diminutive flowers and stature in warmer sections of the country, and have also proved to be hardy in much of the North. They are planted between October and December and bloom in late winter in the greenhouse or in early to mid-spring outdoors. They may be left for two or three years, to form attractive groups, before being lifted and replanted. Typical varieties are 'Alba', 'Blushing Bride', 'Nymph', 'Peach Blossom', 'Amanda Mahy', 'Rubra', and 'The Bride'.

CULTURE

Soil

While commercial growers usually prefer a deep loam, slightly on the sandy side, for the growing of gladiolus, either for cut flowers or for corms, the home gardener gets wholly satisfactory results in soils ranging from almost pure sand (as near the seashore) to heavy loams. Again, while they do best with soil acidity between pH 5.5 and 6.5, another .5 point either way is not serious.

The matter of providing extremely good drainage is less important with gladiolus than with most hardy bulbs, because they do not remain in the ground over winter. If only soil that remains fairly wet is available, however, raised beds (see page 71) are advisable.

Fertilizers

While the plant-food requirements of gladiolus are in general simi-

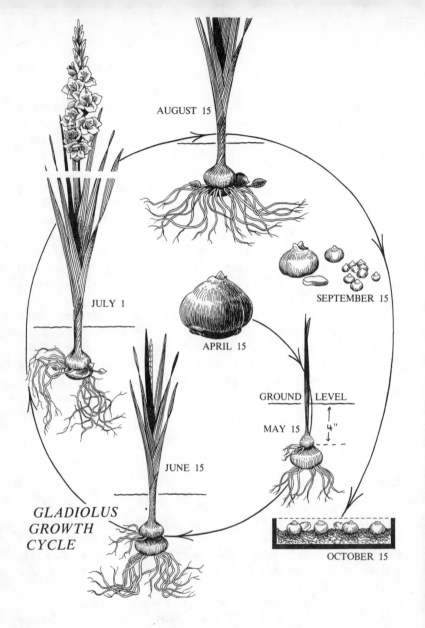

AUGUST 15

JULY 1

SEPTEMBER 15

APRIL 15

GROUND LEVEL

MAY 15   4"

JUNE 15

*GLADIOLUS
GROWTH
CYCLE*

OCTOBER 15

lar to those already recommended in Chapter 6, special attention
should be given to the time at which they are applied.

Recent experiments have demonstrated that, in soil already in
fairly good tilth, better results will be had in using all plant foods in
the form of side dressings during growth, rather than applying them

in the furrow at planting time as was formerly the practice. The reason for this is that the plants' greatest need for nutrition is during the flowering period, *and afterward,* while the new corms and cormels are forming. (See growth cycle, page 232.)

The results of these experiments emphasize again what we have reiterated throughout these pages: *the grower of bulbous plants should concentrate on producing good fat, strong bulbs, corms, or tubers; then the flowers will follow as the day the night.*

Of course if the soil is new or poor, it should be improved and fertilized before planting, with special emphasis on the addition of humus. Then, about the time the flower spike is developing, apply a 5–10–5 fertilizer, or its equivalent, at the rate of 1 to 2 pounds per 100 square feet, and follow this with 2 to 3 pounds more when the flowers have been cut. Flower heads left for garden display should be removed above the top leaf as soon as they fade.

Planting

As gladiolus are semi-hardy (I have had corms come through the winter out of doors without protection in mild winters in northern Connecticut), they may be planted as early as the ground can be worked—and from then on until the first week in July. In northern latitudes, *early* varieties (maturing in 60 to 75 days) should, of course, be used for the latest plantings.

A word on purchasing gladiolus corms may be helpful to the beginner. No. 1 size is 2 inches or more in diameter. Very large, flat bulbs with a concave upper surface are generally inferior to much smaller ones with a greater vertical diameter. These are termed "high-crowned." Corms grown from cormels are of this type, and to be preferred to those grown from old corms.

Beware of extreme bargain offers. Size Nos. 1 and 2 (1½ and 1¼ inches, respectively) will produce satisfactory flower spikes; No. 4 (1 inch) or smaller in most varieties will require another season's growth before flowering.

Gladiolus grown for cutting are planted in rows, 24 to 36 inches apart, according to the method of cultivation to be used; or, where space is at a premium, in double rows, 6 or 8 inches apart, with a 2-foot walk between. The corms are spaced 3 to 6 inches apart, the wider spacing in rich soil and for extra-fine individual spikes. Cover

3 to 4 inches deep in fairly heavy soil, an inch more in lighter soil. The first planting will start growth somewhat more quickly with an initial covering of 2 inches. Fill the trench in as growth progresses.

In flower borders, individual planting holes are readily made with a trowel. At least half a dozen bulbs of a variety should be placed in a group. As gladiolus grow straight up, with little spread of the lower leaves, they can be used for interplanting where subjects of spreading habit would not fit in.

Cultivation

Gladiolus thrive best in a soil kept open by fairly frequent cultivation and free from weeds. These conditions are particularly important during the first few weeks of growth.

If they are being grown in rows, cultivate deeply soon after planting (before they break ground) between the rows to loosen thoroughly the soil, which will have become more or less packed down in planting. Subsequent cultivating with a hoe should be shallow (1 to 2 inches), but frequent enough to prevent formation of a hard surface crust.

Watering; Mulching

Gladiolus will come through dry seasons, even drought conditions, with relatively little damage except somewhat smaller growth. Experiments have indicated that the critical need for an ample moisture supply is during the first six to eight weeks—the period until the new corm has formed and put out its own vigorous roots. In poor soil an occasional application of liquid fertilizer, just before watering, is decidedly beneficial. Any watering should be sufficiently heavy to penetrate to a depth of 6 inches or more.

As gladiolus throw comparatively little shade, mulching is particularly beneficial. Often it is not applied until fairly late in the season, but both weeding and watering can be greatly curtailed if a mulch is applied as soon as the plants are well up.

Supports

Reasonably deep planting supplemented, if necessary, by moderate hilling—such as is often used for sweet corn—will usually keep gladiolus growing in an upright position. Tall-growing varieties, especially if in very rich soil or in exposed positions, may require support. Spikes being grown for show purposes are much safer if supported, for here a crooked stem, which might well be a positive asset in using the spike in an arrangement, will practically eliminate any chance of its winning a ribbon.

Posts made of two-by-fours, driven in at intervals of 15 feet or so along the row, will serve to support wires or stout cords run along both sides of the row at the proper height. The first strand should be placed as the flower spike begins to emerge, and another, if needed, a foot or so above it.

For Exhibition

In growing especially for exhibition, ascertain (from growers' catalogues) the number of days to flowering, and make three plantings at intervals of five days, the middle date being fixed by counting back from the date, fixed or probable, of the show. (Time from planting to flowering ranges from 55 to 90 days, with the average around 80 to 85.)

Give individual plants more space than ordinarily, and support carefully. *Do not try to force by overfeeding;* this is likely to result in soft, flabby growth and failure of the florets to remain in good condition when cut. Spikes should be shown with the first three or four florets wide open. Cutting two or three days before the show and keeping in a cool or a warm temperature will help to some extent in delaying or hastening the opening.

STORING OVER WINTER

After flower spikes have been cut or faded blooms removed, the last application of fertilizer should be made, cultivated or hoed in, and the ground thoroughly watered if the weather is dry. No further care will be required until the foliage begins to turn brown—a period of 30 to 50 days, according to variety and seasonal conditions. If normal ripening is cut short by a hard frost, dig as soon as possible thereafter. It always is desirable to dig while the stems are still firmly attached to the corms.

The first thing to decide when digging is whether the cormels are to be saved. Usually the increased number of corms will provide you with all the stock you wish. In case of a favorite variety or a new high-priced one, you may wish to multiply this stock as rapidly as possible by growing the cormels on to flowering size.

If the cormels are not to be saved, digging is a very easy matter. A fork thrust into the soil near the base of the plant, with downward pressure applied to the handle, will loosen it sufficiently so that the stem, with its corms adhering, can readily be lifted out by the foliage. Then all loose soil is shaken off.

Have available a sufficient number of containers—flats, boxes, or splint baskets—so that each variety, with a substantial label, can be kept by itself. To economize on space, the tops can be cut off an inch or less above the corms immediately after lifting. The practice of twisting the tops off is not recommended; it often results in injury to corms.

The dug corms are dried for a few hours in the sun and then removed to a frostproof shed or garage to cure for a few weeks before being cleaned up for winter storage. They should have free circulation of air; a high temperature (unless the humidity is excessively low) will not be harmful.

When the corms have dried and cured sufficiently so the stems, old corms and husks may be removed readily, they are cleaned, sorted and labeled. Each lot may be placed in a stout paper bag, a small box, or a section of a flat. The temperature for winter storage should be as near 40 degrees as possible, but 10 degrees or so higher will answer. Packing in sand, sawdust, peat moss, or vermiculite will help if storage conditions are poor, but usually it is not necessary.

Immediately after cleaning is the proper time to apply any dust-control measure to combat thrips. (See page 240.)

PROPAGATION

Cormels

If it is decided to save the cormels, the corms should be lifted very carefully and placed in tight boxes, with some soil adhering. As the cormels—some of which may be little larger than buckshot—dry out much more rapidly than the corms, it is advisable to separate them as soon as possible. They may then be stored in *slightly* moist sand or peat moss. They should be examined from time to time during the winter to make sure they are in plump condition, but not starting to sprout.

As early in spring as the ground can be worked, the cormels can be planted. If dry and hard, we soak them in tepid water for two to five days until, as one of our helpers once put it, "they're just ready to bust." They are planted about 2 inches deep in rows 18 inches apart. If in quantity, they can be sown like peas; in smaller numbers, spaced 1 to 2 inches apart.

Careful weeding is essential until the grass-like foliage has attained a good start.

Cultivation, feeding and watering when necessary should be maintained during the growing season. Adequate soil moisture is especially important during the first two months. The cormel does not grow larger, but after about six weeks' growth is replaced by a corm forming just above it, at the base of the stem.

To facilitate harvesting, which is done just when the tops begin to die down, remove soil with a hoe or wheel hoe along both sides of the row and then lift the corms out carefully.

The crop of corms (known as virgin corms) will vary considerably in size. Commercial growers grade corms into six sizes, ranging from No. 1, 1½ inches or over, down to No. 6, ½ inch or smaller. Each grade is ¼ inch smaller than the one preceding it. Many of the new corms will be of flowering size—No. 3 (1 to 1¼ inches) or larger; others will require growing on for a second season before reaching flowering size.

Large Corms

Large old corms often show two or more "eyes" (growth points) —readily discernible on peeling back the husk—on the upper, concave surface. They can be cut apart with a sharp knife, dusted with a disinfectant and Rootone, a root-inducing hormone, and planted in the usual way. Each cut segment, of course, must contain an eye.

Seed

Growing gladiolus from seed is not difficult, but as garden varieties will not come true there is little point in it unless one wishes to develop new varieties. The seeds are fairly large and in appearance much like parsnip seed, with a fleshy "germ" near the center. They are gathered as the pods *begin* to open and stored in tight containers in a cool, dry place.

Seeds may be sown in a greenhouse or hotbed in February or early March, in a cold frame in March or early April, or in the open ground in April or May. Early-sown seeds often produce some flower spikes the first season. The general care of the seedlings is the same as given in Chapter 9.

OFFICIAL CLASSIFICATION OF GLADIOLUS

Formal Type—paired arrangement of florets
Informal Type—alternate arrangement of florets

Sizes

Giant	500 series	5½ inches and up (floret size)
Large	400 series	4½ to 5½ inches
Medium	300 series	above 3¼ to 4½ inches

Sizes

Small	200 series	2½ through 3¼ inches
Miniature	100 series	under 2½ inches

Color separations

White	Salmon	Lavender
Cream	Scarlet	Purple
Yellow	Pink	Violet
Buff	Red	Smoky
Orange	Rose	Any other color

GLADIOLUS TROUBLES

The gladiolus provides an interesting example of the ups and downs which a flower may undergo in popularity as a result of the ease or the difficulty of growing it. Until a few decades ago it was considered the easiest of all summer-flowering bulbs. Then suddenly along came the thrips and several diseases, and gardeners by the thousands just crossed it off their lists. Fortunately, effective—and not too difficult—controls have been found for most of these ills, and the stately gladiolus has won its way back.

Diseases

Fusarium dry rot or *brown rot* of gladiolus is a serious menace in some sections. Infection starts in the ground when small, reddish-brown lesions occur on the lower parts of corms. During the storage period the lesions enlarge and become uneven or circular brown spots, the whole corm sometimes becoming brown and hard. At digging time, corms should be inspected and any showing lesions destroyed at once. Unaffected or but slightly affected corms taken from a planting where dry rot is present should be cured as quickly and thoroughly as possible. In spring, *just* before planting, dip corms for 15 minutes in a 1 to 1,000 dilution of Busan 72; or dust corms with Benlate 50W or with Arasan. Or corms may be soaked for 3 hours in a mixture of 4 tablespoons of Lysol to 3 gallons of water.

Fusarium yellows, the commonest of gladiolus diseases, is most likely to occur in warm climates and sandy soils. First symptom is a yellowing or browning of the tips of the leaves, which gradually die back until the plant perishes. The old corm, if dug, will be found badly rotted, and the new corm forming above it will show a dark area at the base. This disease flourishes in dry weather and at high temperatures. Dig suspected corms at once and destroy. When storing for the winter, and again at planting time, carefully examine corms and destroy any with spots on their basal plates.

Botrytis shows symptoms similar to the above, but may affect any part of the plant, eventually reaching and rotting the corm, converting it to a soft, spongy mass. Its spread is favored by wet weather. Spraying foliage with Benlate (benomyl), maneb, zineb or ferbam has given some control if repeated every five days in wet weather. Burn all refuse. Diseased plants should be destroyed, as for fusarium rots. Dry harvested bulbs quickly at high temperatures if botrytis is present.

Scab, sometimes called neck-rot, as it causes the decay of several inches of the stem just above the ground, is indicated on dry corms by dark spots on the husks and circular, hard depressions on the tissue beneath. Remove the husks, cut out scabs and dust corms with thiram; or soak corms for 2 hours in a 1 to 1000 solution of mercuric chloride (deadly poison); or for 1 minute in 1 pound calomel to 5 gallons of water. Destroy badly infected corms.

For blue mold rot, see Chapter 10.

Insects

Thrips, by far the most prevalent of all gladiolus troubles, attacks the foliage, buds and flowers of growing plants, and even injures the corms in winter storage. First evidence in the garden is whitish streaks on the foliage and brownish, malformed buds. For effective control, begin spraying (or dusting) when plants are 6 inches high, with methoxychlor and repeat every week or ten days until plants, especially in the leaf sheaths, are clean under examination with a magnifying glass. Thrips on corms in storage is controlled by dusting the corms soon after digging with lindane or malathion. The dust is left on through storage.

For aphids, corn borer, mites, cutworms, wireworms and tarnished plant bugs, see Chapter 10.

For many years tuberous-rooted begonias—which can more accurately be called simply tuberous begonias—were not grown in this country, despite their popularity in Europe and in England, as generally as they deserved to be. It was a case of "give a dog a bad name"; many gardeners got the impression that they were extremely difficult and unreliable. It is true that in many sections of the United States climatic conditions are not ideal for them, but there are few areas in which they cannot be grown. They are different rather than difficult.

Gradually this fact came to be realized. No other bulbous plant during recent years has increased in favor quite so rapidly as the tuberous begonia. Today tuberous begonias are shown in gorgeous color illustrations in every seed catalogue, and the bins at local garden centers are always packed with the tubers in early spring. Americans are growing them in ever-increasing numbers.

What have tuberous begonias to offer the home gardener? First of all, they produce flowers more varied in form and color and over a longer season than any other bulbous plant. The range of blossom forms is almost unbelievable; and for purity and delicacy their coloring, especially in the lighter tints, is unsurpassed. The colors range through the entire scales of reds, pinks, yellows, and oranges, with pure crystalline whites thrown in for good measure. Blue and its associated hues are absent.

Second, tuberous begonias are incomparably the most colorful of all plants which, in northern latitudes, can be grown in part shade. At least some shade in most sections they demand; and they will tolerate a lot more of it if it is "high" shade, as from overhead trees. Around our own house we have a great deal of such shade in summer; it is part of our plan of living, and we like to be able to enjoy shade and nearby flowers at the same time. Tuberous begonias have played a big part in providing an answer for this situation.

Finally—and here we expect some gardeners will take issue with us—we grow tuberous begonias in quantity because they are easy to grow. Perhaps having tried them and failed, you are among those who will say this statement is inaccurate; but, like Bret Harte's Truthful James, "the same I arise to maintain." We have grown them for many years in several states and under widely varied conditions, in quantities ranging from a dozen or so to commercial production on a large scale.

No matter what kind of soil you have, you can grow tuberous begonias for the simple reason that if your garden soil is unsatisfactory, you can buy a suitable growing mix and grow the plants in pots. The range of shade they will tolerate is wide—every kind except dense. Starting the tubers, to get good bushy plants, is the simplest thing in the world. Growing from seed is much more difficult, but that, too, can be done if you wish.

As to pests and diseases, the only troubles we have ever encountered in growing these begonias were one infestation of cyclamen mites and occasional malformation or dropping of the buds in extremely hot, muggy weather when air circulation was poor. Overfeeding, especially after midsummer, is likely to cause soft growth that may result in stem rot.

All this adds up to a substantiation of the statement that tuberous begonias are easy to grow. Compared to many other flowers—such as roses or dahlias, for instance—they are a pushover. The one most likely source of trouble in some sections is the hot, humid weather of midsummer. This they do not like. But even this handicap can be overcome to a large degree by the proper cultural conditions—with less effort than that required for combating the usual troubles of many other flowers.

IN THE GARDEN PICTURE

No matter what your garden scheme is, you can count on these glamorous flowers to provide additional beauty and interest. There are any number of ways in which they can be used, the several types adapting themselves admirably to one purpose or another. You can try them in mass plantings to provide exceptionally colorful beds or borders; in small groups as an interesting edging-down for shrubs and broad-leaved evergreens which are often grown under overhead

The hanging or basket tuberous begonia, shown here in a lath house, bears both single and double flowers in abundance.

shade. Groups of three or four—or even individual plants—will brighten up partially shady spots such as may be found in the general planting, around house corners, or at the edge of a woodland garden. One of our favorite uses for them is along the front of the area devoted to summering house plants which, though most of them are not in bloom at this season, provide foliage that makes an attractive background.

They are ideal, too, for a shaded porch or for planter boxes on the terrace or patio and the pendent or hanging types, alone or in combination with upright forms—or with other plants which tolerate some shade, such as fuchsias, impatiens and caladiums—for various hanging baskets and a number of other kinds of containers.

Tuberous begonias are not house plants; their normal flowering season is from midsummer to frost. All in all, however, tuberous

Tuberous begonias are well suited to pot culture, and make a spectacular display over the summer months.

begonias are adapted to quite as many different uses as the most obliging of other garden flowers.

The type or types of tuberous begonias you grow will depend on the purpose for which they are to be used. For bedding or a mass-color effect to cover a considerable area, the multiflora forms are on the whole the more satisfactory. The flowers, being single, semi-double or double, are smaller and lighter than those of the standard doubles, stand up better against wind and rain and make a quicker comeback if storm damage occurs. Where the beauty of individual blossoms is the prime consideration, the large double-flowered forms are of course more glamorous and intriguing. One waits for each new plant to open its first bud, never knowing exactly what will be forthcoming.

Both the singles and doubles have a number of fairly distinct

More pots of these glamorous flowers, beneath the benign shade of a Japanese tree lilac, add color to the terrace.

flower forms. These are remarkable, especially among the doubles, for their resemblance to other flowers—so much so that the tuberous begonia may well be called the mockingbird of the floral kingdom.

Flower types among the singles include the original multiflora begonias, whose flowers are produced in great abundance and are sun-tolerant; and crispa, with ruffled-edged petals peculiarly crested like a cockscomb.

The doubles come in such flower forms as camelliaflora, with flowers startlingly like those of a camellia; rose, a fairly recent development from the foregoing; fimbriata, densely fringed, giving a carnation-like effect. The newer multiflora maxima strain has small tightly double flowers that resemble baby roses.

The hanging or pendula type is the one to use for terrace planters or window boxes, hanging baskets, atop low walls, or in any partially

Here, thriving in a window box, they receive enough late afternoon sun to keep the plants compact and floriferous.

shaded position where a flowering plant is desired and where there is fair protection from wind. Hanging begonias can be suspended from tree limbs or brackets set against the house wall of your terrace. Their flowers can be had in both double and single forms in a good range of colors. Named varieties, much used in Europe, are becoming more available here. All have much smaller flowers than the singles and doubles previously described.

GROWING METHODS

In general, there are two methods of growing tuberous begonias: planting them in ground beds or borders in the open, or carrying them through the season in pots or other containers. In either case

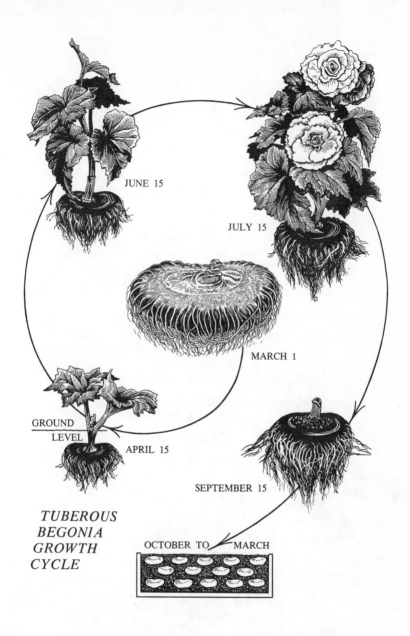

JUNE 15

JULY 15

MARCH 1

GROUND LEVEL

APRIL 15

SEPTEMBER 15

*TUBEROUS
BEGONIA
GROWTH
CYCLE*

OCTOBER TO MARCH

they may be given a running start by bringing the tubers into early growth indoors or in a greenhouse. They may, however, be planted in the open. The advantage of starting them indoors or under glass is that flowering will begin four to eight weeks earlier. Being tender plants, they cannot be set in the open until after danger of frosts— tomato-planting time in your vicinity. Unstarted tubers can be set out a week or ten days earlier than growing plants.

The tubers, as received from your seedsman or as purchased in a garden center, are rough, hairy and somewhat saucer-shaped. They may be obtained from January to May—unless the supply is exhausted before then, as can happen. If you do not have facilities for starting tubers indoors and want early bloom, you can purchase growing plants from a local florist or garden center but of course these cost considerably more than dormant tubers.

Starting the tubers yourself is a very simple matter, especially as they do not require full sunshine. While a greenhouse furnishes the

ABOVE: *Tuberous begonias are started into growth by placing the tubers in moist peat moss, concave sides up.* BELOW: *When several leaves have formed they are transplanted to pots or bulb pans; shaded from full sun. Or such plants can be set out directly in outdoor beds or planters where they are to remain, providing they have been hardened off first.*

After further growth they are removed to outdoor beds, or shifted to larger pots for flowering.

ideal conditions, any fairly light space in a room where the atmosphere is not too dry will answer. The ideal temperature for starting the tubers into growth is 55 degrees at night, with 10 to 15 degrees more during the day. However, a night temperature of 45 to 50 degrees will serve; growth will be considerably slower, but the plants as good. A hotbed or cold frame will do also for starting them a month or so in advance of outdoor planting.

The first step is to fill a box or flat, about 3 inches deep, with peat moss that has been thoroughly moistened. The tubers are pushed down into this until the tops are slightly below the surface. Place them 2 to 3 inches apart each way, *concave side up.* (Usually pink sprout buds will be showing in the hollow of the tuber.) An ordinary nursery flat, 13×21 inches, will hold from 18 to 36 tubers, according to their size.

Good light, even a few hours of sunlight or artificial light from fluorescent lamps and an occasional watering, to keep the peat moss moist *but not wet,* are the only requirements until the plants attain a height of 3 to 5 inches. Then they should be transplanted to other flats, or to pots or bulb pans sufficiently large to take the mass of roots without crowding. For this transplanting use a mixture of ½ peat moss, ½ well-rotted manure (or leafmold), plus 10 to 15 per cent coarse sand or sandy loam. *A light, porous and rapidly draining growing medium is essential for good results.* To one-half of this mixture add bone meal or cottonseed meal (we prefer a mixture of both) at the rate of one quart per bushel, and use this in the *bottoms* of flats or pots when transplanting; this is to avoid the mold that may otherwise form on the surface. Water moderately at first, increasing as growth develops. Instead of a home-prepared soil mixture, you may find it more convenient to use one of the soilless mixes, such as Redi-Earth or Jiffy Mix, available at garden centers.

Plants to be grown to maturity in pots should be shifted again to 6-, 7-, or even 8-inch size. We prefer bulb pans to standard pots, as they are much less likely to be tipped over. Most specimens of double-flowered sorts will require light bamboo stakes to hold them upright, as the heavy blooms may drag them over. Pinching out the tips of tall stalks about the time first buds show will produce stockier plants.

OUTDOOR CULTURE

The four essentials for satisfactory growth with tuberous begonias out of doors are: partial shade but good light, even a few hours of sunlight; a porous, fibrous, rich soil; perfect drainage; abundant moisture. *The soil need not be deep,* for they are surface rooters. It makes little difference what the original soil is, so long as it will drain. If it won't, you can build up a bed 6 to 8 inches deep right on the surface. In any case, the soil in which tubers are to be placed or plants set should be similar to that recommended for potting; most soils can be made so by digging in several inches of peat moss and compost or rotted manure and adding sand if necessary. Plants in pots may be plunged to the rims in a bed of peat moss.

As warm weather approaches, the critical point in culture is maintaining the moisture supply. Here the "seldom-but-thorough" formula for watering should be changed to "moderate-but-frequent"— for tuberous begonia roots require moisture in the surface soil. During excessively hot dry spells *spraying the foliage* is almost as important as watering the roots. Use a fine mist-like spray, applying it late in the afternoon.

Plants that have been flowering for several weeks will be benefited by an occasional application of liquid fertilizer—we use manure—but of course a liquid fish or a chemical solution will do.

Winter Care

With the approach of freezing weather, all watering is stopped. If plants are in pots, they can be brought indoors to finish flowering, but under no circumstance should they be subjected to a hard freeze. A *light* frost, blackening the foliage, will not harm the tubers. Plants set in the ground are taken up, *with all adhering soil,* and with the tops left on, and spread out under cover to dry off for a week or two. The tops are then cut back, leaving 3 or 4 inches of the fleshy main stem and the roots, to dry up gradually. This will take several weeks. When the stem stubs will come off at a touch, remove them, shake the tubers out of the dry soil, and pack them for winter storage in peat moss, vermiculite, or sand, and store in a temperature of 45 to 60 degrees. Polyethylene kitchen bags, to which a little slightly moist peat moss or vermiculite has been added, are convenient. With plants grown in pots, we remove the tops and store the pots, on their sides, until they have thoroughly dried out, then remove and store tubers as above. Or leave the tubers in until spring, when they should be removed from the pots and started into growth in moist peat moss, as described earlier.

SEED

The growing of tuberous begonias from seed is a ticklish proposition, but a patient and painstaking amateur can do it. (Choice plants can also be propagated from stem cuttings and by division of old tubers.) Sow not more than a packet or two for the first attempt. Sow the seed in February in a greenhouse, or indoors under fluorescent lights and you'll have—*if* you succeed—blooms during late summer and a supply of small tubers to carry over until next year.

A night temperature of 65 to 70 degrees is desirable—almost essential, in fact, for lower temperatures mean slower and poorer germination. Even in a greenhouse the seed is best started in a propagating frame, where humidity (as well as temperature) can be closely controlled.

Bulb pans or small fiber or plastic seed flats are prepared for receiving the seed by placing a 2- or 3-inch layer of gravel or broken crocks in the bottom and covering this with about 1½ inches (*not more*) of a fairly coarse, loose, growing medium. This can be made up of 2 parts leafmold and 1 part peat moss, with a pint of pulverized charcoal added to a peck of the mixture. Smooth over, *but do not pack down*. On top of this sift (through ⅛-inch mesh) a thin (not over ¼-inch) layer of the same mixture, leaving it loose. Then place in a pan or dish of water and let it soak up from below until the surface *begins* to show moisture. Or use sand and peat moss or vermiculite and peat moss or any of the packaged mixes recommended for seeds.

The seed is extremely small—almost dust. Distribute it thinly and evenly. Slip the container into a plastic bag to conserve moisture. After a few days watch carefully for germination and, at first sign of sprouting, open the bag. If temperature and moisture are kept uniform, growth will be fairly rapid. *Never let the surface dry out;* syringe with fine spray if necessary if the flat has been removed from the plastic bag. Gradually give more ventilation, but *no* direct sunshine. In six to ten weeks seedlings will be ready for transplanting. The earlier the transplanting is done, the better.

For transplanting, use similar mixtures, placed not over 2 inches deep on top of ample drainage material. No fertilizer is needed if leafmold is used; otherwise a light feeding can be given carefully following container directions. As they crowd again they will be ready to set outdoors (after hardening off) or transferred to pots—the same as for plants started from tubers.

The first transplanting is a very delicate operation; the seedlings are both tiny and brittle. Have soil in seed pans, and in flats also, moderately moist. Lift seedlings gently, a few at a time, and spread out on a flat surface. Lower roots into planting holes and press in gently; do *not* press surface of soil down hard. Syringe daily for several days. Grow under fluorescent lights or in the light of a partially sunny window.

CUTTINGS

Growing plants from cuttings is much easier and has the advantage of making it possible to increase the supply of plants which you particularly like. The general routine to be followed is the same as that which has already been described (pages 109–10).

Tuberous begonias are grown from soft cuttings, secured by removing the tops of sprouts from tubers started in flats or pots—somewhat more developed than those shown in the illustration on page 248. At least two, preferably three or four, leaves should be left below the cut, which should be made with a very sharp knife (we use a razor blade) so as not to bruise the brittle, fleshy stems. The "wings" (or leaf bracts) are removed from the lower part of the stem, and the lower leaves may be cut back a third to a half.

For a rooting medium use peat moss, or two parts peat and one of sand. Slight bottom heat is desirable but not essential. A propagating case (a flat enclosed in a tent of polyethylene sheeting) is, however, most helpful, as a humid atmosphere is even more necessary with these begonias than with most house or garden plants. Once rooted, the cuttings are transferred to 3- or 4-inch pots and shifted later to larger ones.

DIVIDING TUBERS

Begonia tubers gradually increase in size for several years, but never split up or form offsets. They do, however, send up sprouts from two or more points in the "cup" of the tuber, instead of from one point only, as is the case with younger tubers. Old tubers can be cut into two or more pieces, each with one or more "eyes" or growth points.

To do this, place the tubers in moist peat moss in February, March, or April, and when the sprouts have started sufficiently to be readily distinguished, cut the bulbs—with a sharp, thin blade, to avoid bruising—and dust the cut surfaces with Rootone, a root-inducing hormone powder available in garden centers. Then reset the pieces in peat moss, to continue root and top growth, until they are ready for potting up or setting out of doors.

BEGONIA TROUBLES

Leaf spot (*Begonia bacteriosis*) is a disease which attacks both tuberous and fibrous begonias throughout the United States. Roundish dead spots, brown with yellow translucent margins, appear on the foliage, followed by premature falling of the leaves. Sometimes the stems soften and rot. Transmitted by a yellow ooze on the infected leaves, leaf spot rapidly spreads, especially under greenhouse conditions. Control consists in watering from below to keep the foliage dry, and keeping pots widely spaced to give good circulation of air and to avoid contact. If the disease is present, spray with Bordeaux mixture.

Gray mold blight—a form of botrytis—may also attack tuberous begonias. For description and control, see Chapter 10. You may never encounter either of these diseases.

Elongated, floppy growth with few flowers means the plants are not receiving sufficient light. When and where summers are cool and moist, tuberous begonias are tolerant of full sun or many hours of it.

Pests

The only insects likely to be encountered are mealy bugs and cyclamen mites, for which see Chapter 10.

CHAPTER *19. Other Summer-Flowering and Autumn-Flowering Bulbs*

In addition to the summer-flowering bulbs discussed in the preceding four chapters, there are others, some tender and some hardy, which carry on the garden's display of bulbous flowers through the summer and well into autumn.

The more important of these are described here, as they merit somewhat fuller treatment than those included only in the general catalogue of bulbs in Part Three. So here we will take up:

Summer-flowering

Galtonia   (Summer-hyacinth)
Hymenocallis   (Ismene; Peruvian-daffodil or Basket Flower)
Polianthes   (Tuberose)
Tigridia   (Tiger-flower; Shell-flower)
Montbretia   (Crocosmia)

Autumn-flowering

Colchicum   (Meadow Saffron)
Lycoris (Autumn-amaryllis; Magic-lily-of-Japan)
Sternbergia lutea
Zephyranthes   (Fairy-lily; Zephyr-lily)

(The many lovely little autumn-flowering crocuses which add so much color and personality to the fall garden are discussed in Chapter 13.)

One of the intriguing things about growing these less well-known subjects is, of course, that they are out of the ordinary; another is that they make such excellent material for arrangements. None of them is troublesome so far as its culture is concerned.

Galtonia (cape- or summer-hyacinth), 3 to 4 feet or more in height and flowering in midsummer, is easily grown.

SUMMER-FLOWERING

Galtonia

Perhaps the most graceful and dignified of this group is tall *Galtonia candicans,* the common name of which is cape- or summer-hyacinth or just plain galtonia. The flower scape, rising to 3 or 4 feet in height above a group of long, pointed basal leaves, is set with large fragrant, bell-shaped white flowers borne in a loose raceme.

Coming late in July in the vicinity of New York City, these flowers are a welcome touch of white in the back of the summer border. We place ours behind the ismenes and acidantheras with haemanthus in

Acidanthera bicolor, *midsummer-flowering bulbs meriting much wider use. The butterfly-like flowers are fragrant and excellent for cutting.*

the foreground, thus creating an impressive bed of tender, summer-flowering bulbs. The flowering scapes of the galtonia rise well above the ismene blooms and handsome, persistent foliage, the latter hiding the less decorative leaves of the galtonia.

Galtonia bulbs should not be planted out of doors until the soil is thoroughly warm. Set 3 inches deep in rich, well-worked soil which can be kept watered in case of drought. The plants shoot up with remarkable speed after planting.

Before frost, lift the bulbs, dry and store at approximately 60 degrees.

They can be propagated by offsets from the original bulbs.

Hymenocallis (Peruvian-daffodil or isemene) has dramatic, slightly fragrant flowers which last well when cut. Blooms in early summer. Also easily forced. Shown are 'Festalis' (top) and the species, H. calathina.

Hymenocallis

This satisfactory and showy tender summer-flowering bulb has long been popular. *H. calathina,* the species usually grown, was formerly known as *Ismene calathina* and is sold commercially as ismene, sometimes as Peruvian-daffodil.

The large, fragrant white flowers have tubular crowns 4 inches long, surrounded by fringed perianth segments 2 inches long, the large trumpet-like tube giving it the common name of Peruvian-"daffodil." The other common name of spider-lily is suggested by the narrow, fringed perianth segments. 'Sulphur Queen' is a yellow hybrid, while 'Festalis', another hybrid, has extravagantly curved perianth petals. The hybrid 'Daphne' and another species, *H. speciosa,* that is grown in greenhouses when bulbs are available, are desirable for their larger flowers.

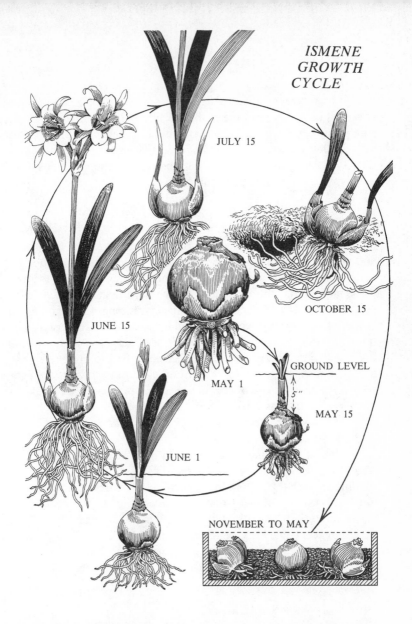

ISMENE
GROWTH
CYCLE

JULY 15

OCTOBER 15

JUNE 15

GROUND LEVEL

MAY 1

5"

MAY 15

JUNE 1

NOVEMBER TO MAY

Like galtonia, hymenocallis bulbs are planted in the open garden only after warm weather is really established. It is amazing how fast the plants grow and bloom after setting, however. We have had buds shoot up on long scapes a mere week after planting. Set the bulbs in rich, well-drained soil, in sun, planting about 3 to 4 inches deep. The extremely handsome, glossy green strap-like foliage will be decorative in the garden and useful in arrangements long after bloom is over and probably until the bulbs are lifted. This should be done before frost. Dry off in an inverted position (foliage down), not cutting off the fleshy roots. Then store at 60 degrees. Many new offsets develop each season, so you will soon have enough bulbs to give away or swap for other plant material.

Montbretia

The montbretia produces corms similar to those of the gladiolus and another near relative, tigridia, and is an excellent companion plant in the garden for both. More graceful than either of these relatives, montbretias produce a few narrow sword-shaped leaves, deeply grooved, and 1- to 3-foot flower scapes with long, simple or panicled spikes of red, orange, yellow or copper tubular flowers, or combinations of these colors. (Montbretia has been classified at various times under two genera, *Tritonia* and *Crocosmia*. At the present, montbretias, as known to commercial and home garden growers, are considered to be hybrids of *Crocosmia aurea* and *C. pottsii* and have been further classified as *Crocosmia* x *crocosmiiflora*. For *Tritonia,* see page 282, and for another species of *Crocosmia,* see "The Catalogue of Bulbs," Part III of this book.)

Monbretia corms may be ordered in mixture or in separate colors. Among these are 'Aurora', pure orange; 'Lady Oxford', pale yellow shading to peach; 'El Dorado', golden yellow; 'Vesuvius', deep red— to name but a few of many that are available.

The culture of montbretias is similar to that of gladiolus and tigridia, except that they better endure light shade although full sun is their preference. Before planting the corms, 2 to 3 inches deep, apply a generous sprinkling of 5–10–5 or a similar fertilizer over the soil.

Polianthes tuberosa

This is the old-fashioned tuberose of grandmother's garden. After many years of semi-oblivion, it has again come into favor. The spikes of waxy white flowers, which reach a height of 3 to almost 4 feet, are overpoweringly fragrant, and the plant undoubtedly came into dis-

Tigridia pavonia *or shell flower, flowering from July to frost, is brilliantly colored and dramatic. It likes full sun.*

favor in the days when unwise home gardeners brought it indoors. If placed at the back of a white border or in a landscape group at some distance from the house or terrace, the scent is really delightful, especially at night. The double form, 'Double Pearl', is the one usually grown, though the single 'Mexican Everblooming' is preferred by many. Though tuberoses are seldom planted out until early June, if you can find time to set them 3 inches deep in a well-worked sunny bed as soon as you feel sure all danger of severe frost is over, you will have earlier bloom. Or start them indoors in pots and set out in the open garden June first. Tuberoses require plenty of moisture during their growing season. Dig in autumn before the first frost. Bulbs should be stored at 65 to 70 degrees, but even when correctly carried over, they do not always bloom well the second season.

Tigridia

The Mexican tiger-flower or Mexican shell-flower is a charming irid, easy to grow and most rewarding. The straight, gladiolus-like stems, bearing but few leaves, produce in midsummer extremely showy but fleeting flowers with three wide-spreading, flared perianth segments set off by six smaller ones, forming a great spotted central cup. The colors range from flame red through orange and yellow to buff, with spotted centers. The corms are generally available in mixtures rather than in separate colors.

Placed in groups in a sunny border among plants which, like themselves, prefer sandy, well-drained soil, tigridias will give brilliant accents to the summer garden. Though the individual flowers last but a day, several appear on successive days from the same blooming stem, making them valuable for cutting as well as for garden display. Try them, too, at the seashore, where they are usually quite happy.

The culture of tigridias is similar to that of gladiolus. They are, however, considerably hardier and can, in many locations, be safely carried through outdoors with a mulch. They have been reported hardy near Boston.

AUTUMN-FLOWERING

In the autumn-flowering group we have several distinct types, running from the hardy little colchicums to the hardy-amaryllis (also known as the autumn-amaryllis) and its half-hardy sisters, *Lycoris aurea, incarnata* and *radiata.* Once a gardener has come to depend on bulbs for a good part of his bloom through the spring and summer, he will want to carry on through the fall with these later-flowering species.

Colchicums

Colchicums (meadow saffrons) are among the most charming of the little bulbs. Though they look rather like autumn-blooming cro-

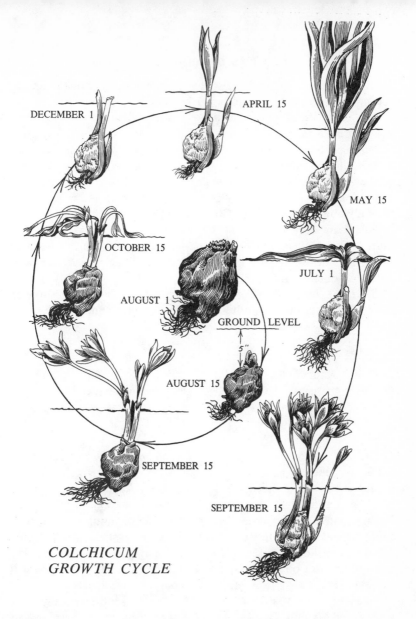

DECEMBER 1

APRIL 15

MAY 15

OCTOBER 15

JULY 1

AUGUST 1

GROUND LEVEL

5"

AUGUST 15

SEPTEMBER 15

SEPTEMBER 15

COLCHICUM
GROWTH CYCLE

cuses and in fact are commonly called autumn-crocuses, they belong
to the lily family and bloom on bare stems, unaccompanied by foliage, which does not appear until the following spring and which must
be left uncut to mature if there are to be flowers in the fall. They are
excellent material for the rock garden, for positions of light shade in

front of shrubbery or under a specimen tree which is not too greedy for moisture, or in the front of a partly shaded border.

The color range of colchicums is rather limited, running from white through the most delicate tints of lavender and orchid to deep purple-rose. It is lighter tints, however, which show up to the best advantage in the autumn garden, where they blossom brightly in September and October. *C. autumnale* is an orchid-rose, and there is a white form, *album*. 'Lilac Wonder' is violet-mauve, very late to flower, while *speciosum* 'The Giant' is rose-purple.

Colchicum corms should be planted as soon as delivered in August, as they are so anxious to come into bloom at that time of year that if they lie about for a few days the flowers begin to appear. Prepare the soil well and then plant the quite large corms only 3 or 4 inches deep. And remember next spring to keep the foliage growing until it has matured, even if it is so prolific as to be a nuisance.

Crocuses

At the head of the list of late-flowering bulbs come the autumn-flowering crocuses. These have been discussed in Chapter 13.

Lycoris

The old garden favorite, *Lycoris squamigera* (syn: *Amaryllis halli*), the autumn-amaryllis or magic-lily-of-Japan, is a fascinating garden subject. The bulbs are delivered from August on and should be planted at once, 5 inches deep, in rich, humusy soil, in part shade. Nothing more will be heard from your lycoris until early spring, when strong, handsome strap-like leaves of gray-green will suddenly shoot out of the ground, rapidly reach a height of 2½ feet, quickly mature, and dry off and disappear completely. By late June you will be able to find the location of the bulbs only by their labels.

When August arrives, keep your eyes on the spot, especially after a good soaking rain. One by one the flower spikes appear, striking up through the soil like strong green spearheads. In a remarkably short space of time, often only about a week, the solid scapes have shot up to their appointed 3 feet and are ready to open their clusters of pale orchid-pink, lily-like flowers, six to nine to a scape. Handsome for garden display or for cutting, they are enhanced by a delicate fra-

Lycoris squamigera, *called the autumn-amaryllis or magic-lily, appears suddenly in late July or August. Extremely hardy and long-lived.*

grance. Since the flower stems are so tall, select an appropriate spot in the shady garden or in front of evergreen shrubs, such as rhododendrons. Or plant them among ferns in open woodland or, through the years, develop a long shady border of them which will be a real feature when they are in bloom. One old estate not far from our house boasts a 150-foot bed of lycoris, 6 feet wide! What a sight it is at blossomtime!

Once planted, the bulbs must not be disturbed. They will probably still be blooming in the same spot when you are no longer there to enjoy them. Though often called the autumn-amaryllis, *Lycoris squamigera* blooms in August in most localities.

Lycoris radiata is a half-hardy relative, a species usually pot-grown for autumn bloom. The narrow leaves appear in spring and have the characteristic pale stripes down their centers. In September round heads of bloom appear on a solid scape. The many florets are starry red, orange, or white, with very long stamens, and are extremely showy. They are often used in flower arrangements as well as for decoration on the patio or porch. For many years *Lycoris radiata* was sold in the trade as *Nerine sarniensis,* the Guernsey-lily.

Pot the bulbs on delivery in Soil Mixture No. 4 (see Chapter 20) or an equivalent mixture, leaving the top third of each exposed. When leaves appear, give more water, sun and liquid fertilizer. After the foliage disappears in May, let them rest until late summer, giving little moisture. Then give more light, liquid fertilizer and moisture until blooms appear. Repot only when necessary, as, like many other members of the amaryllis family, *Lycoris radiata* flowers best when pot-bound.

By mulching heavily as for bulbous iris, *Lycoris radiata* can be grown out of doors in a sheltered location in the North. It is hardy to Washington, D.C.

Lycoris aurea, the golden spider-lily, with individual flowers larger than those of *radiata,* and *Lycoris incarnata,* with pink or rose lily-like blooms similar to those of *L. squamigera* but on shorter stems (to 1½ feet), are two other half-hardy sorts well worth growing. Both can be treated like *L. radiata.*

Sternbergia lutea

This is far too pretty and dainty a little flower to go by such a long name, but it seems to have no common one. Louise Beebe Wilder speaks of it as the winter-daffodil, but we have never heard it so called. Certainly it is as brightly yellow as any daffodil, but in appearance looks very much like a butter-yellow crocus surrounded by plenty of handsome, glossy foliage. Long-lasting and weather-resistant, the blooms are bright for days on end, set off by the red October leaves which drift down off the trees to lodge in their rich foliage.

Plant the bulbs 4 inches deep, as soon as they are received, in well-drained soil in sun or very light shade. We have had a slowly increasing group growing for years under a clump of gray birches. They never seem to need dividing and replanting, but fend for themselves most successfully.

Zephyranthes

Last but not least of the less well-known fall-flowering bulbs are the airy zephyranthes, zephyr-, fairy-, or rain-lilies—all, by the way, appropriate common names. Strictly speaking, some members of this group bloom in spring and summer also, but they are usually thought of as fall-blooming flowers. Natives of the Western Hemisphere, they come to us from South America, Cuba, Santo Domingo, Haiti, Mexico and the southeastern United States. The dainty, funnel-form, solitary flowers are white, yellow, red, pink, or bronze; the basal foliage is grass-like.

Z. *atamasco,* native from Virginia to Alabama and Mississippi, it is species most often grown. Flowers, white or pale pink, appear first in early spring.

Z. *candida,* hardier than the above. White flowers in August and September.

Z. *citrina* is a South American species with bright yellow blossoms.

Z. *grandiflora* blooms after rains in summer and autumn. The lily-like flowers are 4 inches across.

Z. *longifolia,* but 6 inches tall, has 1-inch yellow and copper blooms.

North of Washington, D.C., the zephyr-lilies, with the possible exception of Z. *candida,* must be treated as tender bulbs. Plant in spring in a sandy soil mixture with good humus content, 2 inches apart, with the tips of the bulbs just below the surface of the soil. Lift before frost and store like gladiolus.

They may also be forced for indoor bloom by potting six to a 5-inch bulb pan in autumn, using Potting Mixture No. 4 or an equivalent mix (see Chapter 20). Keep moist until blooms fade. Then dry off for at least 8 weeks. With this interval of rest, a second and even a third flowering may be enjoyed within the year.

CHAPTER *20.* *Bulbs for Winter Bloom*

One of the easiest and most rewarding ways of providing the home with fresh flowers during the winter months is to grow bulbs indoors for winter bloom. Bulbous plants provide welcome color and fragrance. A sunny bay window and an enclosed porch or breezeway make the ideal combination for this sort of indoor gardening; the heat-loving plants in the former, those which insist on a cool temperature in the latter.

A greenhouse is, of course, even better for the purpose, for here the temperature can be controlled to suit the preferences of most of the plants grown; but even without a greenhouse you may enjoy an almost continuous succession of flowers from early winter to spring. We use our greenhouse to grow bulbs (as well as other flowering plants) until the buds are ready to open, and then bring them into the house where we can enjoy the blossoms at close range.

A deep window sill or bay window edged with miniature ivies and with a few taller colorful foliage plants for a permanent display, can frequently be rearranged to provide a setting for bulbous plants which flower at the same time. These may include forced hardy bulbs, the "borderline" cases which must be grown very cool but which do not stand freezing, and the very tender tropical or semitropical subjects which like real warmth such as they would experience in a warm greenhouse.

Few gardening activities give greater satisfaction than bringing bulbs to bloom indoors. Of course it is easy to flower them the first year, for the embryo blossoms are already there inside the bulbs, ready to spring into growth as soon as they are planted and watered. To keep bulbous plants such as amaryllis and veltheimia blooming year after year in the window garden requires a certain groundwork of knowledge, though it is not a really difficult task.

CLASSES OF BULBS FOR WINTER BLOOM

The bulbs which may be brought to bloom indoors during cold weather can be considered in three groups, each of which must be treated differently.

1. *Hardy* spring-flowering bulbs which are forced or grown on in such a way as to produce flowers well in advance of their normal season of bloom. Examples are hyacinths and early daffodils, which are often forced for Christmas; tulips, crocuses, grape-hyacinths, and others, which can be brought to flower a little later.

2. *Half-hardy* types which cannot stand freezing but which must be grown in a very cool temperature. These are not forced but are grown indoors instead of in the open garden. Examples are freesias, ixias and ornithogalums.

3. *Tender* tropical or sub-tropical bulbs, corms, or tubers which either naturally bloom in winter or can be made to do so. As these are very tender, they must be grown as house plants the year round. Examples are members of the amaryllis family and veltheimia.

A few species from the above groups can be forced into early bloom indoors by planting them in bowls or dishes with fiber or pebbles and water. Examples are hyacinths and 'Paperwhite' narcissus, both of which can also be brought to early bloom in pots of soil, the former being hardy and the latter half-hardy or tender.

GENERAL CULTURE

Though each of the three groups mentioned above requires different treatment, and in some cases individual species have their peculiar likes and dislikes, there are general directions which apply to all.

Containers

For hardy bulbs and most of the half-hardies, bulb pans are the preferred containers. These are clay or plastic pots which are wide at the top and somewhat shallower (in proportion to the diameter) than ordinary standard pots. For some types, azalea pots—deeper than bulb pans but not so deep as standard pots—are preferable. Rose pots, extra deep, can be used for lilies.

When grown in quantity in a greenhouse or plant room, the small half-hardy corms, such as freesias and ixias, may be planted in small flats instead of pots. Many of the large tender bulbs are set with the top third of the bulb exposed, and for these, 6- to 10-inch azalea pots are the most satisfactory containers. For water culture, wide shallow ceramic bowls or containers, with a depth of at least 2 inches, may be used.

Soil Mixtures

For indoor bulb growing, the mechanical condition of the soil is even more important than its fertility, because the bulb itself contains sufficient stored-up food to produce good flowers.

You will want, however, to get the best growth possible, and for that reason it is advisable to add some plant food or dried manure to the soil. (We prefer the "organic" approach but any complete commercial fertilizer, such as 5–10–5, 5–10–10 can be used in place of bone meal and dried manure.) After the various ingredients have been combined in a bushel basket or other large container, they should be *very thoroughly* mixed and pulverized.

Since the various Potting Mixtures below have been evolved, there have been changes in potting mixes that can benefit the bulb grower. The changes are due in part to the use of light-in-weight soil substitutes, such as vermiculite and perlite, and to commercial developments in container-grown plants—developments that have spilled into the realm of the home gardener. Various potting mixes, some of them totally soilless, are now available. Some must still be prepared or partly prepared by the gardener; others are ready to use, and can be found in garden centers under such labels as Redi-Earth, Jiffy Mix, Super Soil, Pro-Mix, etc.

While we stand by our Potting Mixtures below and know from our many years' experience with them how successful they have proved, there is no doubt that these modern mixes are also satisfactory for growing bulbs. Should you decide to use them, follow the directions on the bag or container. Or try this formula, a popular one that should be suitable for container-grown bulbs: 1 part Jiffy Mix or the like, 1 part peat moss, 1 part perlite or vermiculite. Since the packaged mixes contain plant food, no fertilizer will be necessary, unless container directions are to the contrary. Another quick mix for potting bulbs can be 1 part garden soil and 1 part packaged soilless mix, such as Jiffy or Redi-Earth.

NOTE: Measurements are by *bulk,* not by weight.

POTTING MIXTURE NO. 1
  For hardy spring-flowering bulbs: daffodils, tulips, hyacinths, etc.

⅓ garden loam
If your garden loam is heavy clay, add to it ⅕ sharp sand.
⅓ pulverized peat moss
⅓ compost or well-rotted manure

Add to each bushel:
2 quarts mixed: ⅓ bone meal and ⅔ dried manure. Or use about ¾ cup of 5–10–5 fertilizer per bushel.

POTTING MIXTURE NO. 2
  For liliaceae and others: lilies, gloriosa, etc.

½ rich soil
¼ sharp sand
¼ peat moss (or leafmold)

Add to each bushel:
2 quarts mixed: ⅓ bone meal and ⅔ dried manure. Or add ¾ cup of 5–10–5 commercial fertilizer to each bushel.

OR USE

¼ loam
½ well-rotted compost
¼ sharp sand

Add to each bushel:
1 quart mixed: 1 pint bone meal and 1 pint dried manure. Or add 5–10–5 as recommended above.

POTTING MIXTURE NO. 3
  For irids: bulbous irises, moraea, etc.

⅔ rich loam
⅓ sharp sand

Add to each bushel:
1 quart bone meal

POTTING MIXTURE NO. 4
  For tender bulbs indoors: hippeastrum, veltheimia, etc.

⅓ rich loam
⅓ sharp sand
⅓ peat moss

Add to each bushel:
2 quarts mixed: ⅓ bone meal and
⅔ dried manure. Or add 5–10–5
as recommended above.

POTTING MIXTURE NO. 5
For tender bulbs which require
rich, humusy soil: tuberous begonias, achimenes, etc.

⅓ rich loam
⅙ sharp sand
⅙ peat moss or leafmold
⅓ old rotted manure

Add to each bushel:
1 pint bone meal. Or add 5–10–5
as recommended above.

OR USE

⅓ rich loam
⅓ compost
⅙ sharp sand
⅙ peat moss or leafmold

Add to each bushel:
2 quarts mixed: ⅔ dried manure
and ⅓ bone meal. Or add 5–10–5
as recommended above.

CULTURE STEP BY STEP

The Bulbs

It pays to get good bulbs for any sort of planting. For bulbs to be grown indoors, care in this particular is even more important. This does not imply that you should obtain the most expensive ones you can find listed. In hyacinths, for instance, we would much rather have first-quality medium-sized bulbs that produce graceful, some-what informal spikes than the more costly giant exhibition grade with their closely set, ramrod-like heads. Every bulb, of any sort, should be plump, sound and heavy.

Care must be exercised also in the matter of varieties. Some tulips and daffodils that are beautiful in the garden do not force well. It is advisable to follow catalogue recommendations in this respect; most dealers indicate plainly which sorts are most suitable for forcing.

If you plan to grow more than a few pots for winter bloom, secure

Here's what you need for winter bulb gardening: compost, pots or bulb pans, drainage material (broken pots), labels, and first-quality bulbs. Then you are all set for exciting adventure!

as much variety as you can. It is true that the flowering period of forced bulbs can be controlled by starting the top growth of different pots, of even the same variety, at different dates. A range of flower forms and colors, however, is much more interesting than having a succession of blooms of the same variety.

Cross section of bulb pan, with bulbs (hyacinths) in place.

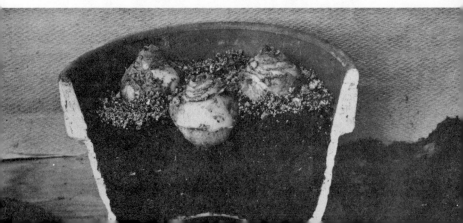

Planting

When you are ready to plant you will need to have at hand your bulbs, pots, flats, prepared soil mixtures, some broken pot shards and some coarse screenings from the compost heap.

Place several pieces of broken pot shards over the drainage hole of each pot and cover with ½ to 1 inch of coarse compost screenings. Then place enough prepared soil in the pot so that when the bulbs are set on it their tips will come to about one inch below the top. (In planting an amaryllid or some other bulb the top third of which is to be left exposed, more soil should be placed in the pot before setting the bulb.) The bulbs are then set. If several bulbs are to go in one pot, they can be placed shoulder to shoulder, but not touching. An inch to 1½ inches between bulbs is the usual distance. Pack the soil in very firmly, first jarring the pot gently against a wooden surface to settle the soil, and then pressing it in around the bulbs so there are no air spaces.

After planting, place the pots in a tray of water and let them remain there until the surface soil becomes moist. This is good practice even with bulbs which are kept on the dry side—after this initial watering—until growth starts.

When thoroughly watered, the potted bulbs are ready for their initial treatment, whatever that is to be. Hardy and half-hardy sorts requiring a period of preliminary root growth go outdoors in a trench or cold frame, or in a cold cellar. Tender species are placed under a greenhouse bench, under a table in a workroom or plant room indoors, or in a dark cool closet in the basement, until growth starts and good root development has occurred.

Flowering

When the time comes to start the potted bulbs into growth, they are brought gradually to more light and warmth. As growth develops, the amount of water is increased until the foliage is strong and of good green color. At this time they can be placed in whatever light and temperature are ideal for the particular species. At this period most of them will require frequent watering.

When buds appear, the half-hardy and tender bulbs profit by a weekly feeding of liquid fertilizer. Forced hardy bulbs will not need this booster treatment. When in flower, the blooms will last longer if the plants are kept at a reasonably cool temperature and out of direct sunshine. Water as needed when the surface soil feels dry to the touch.

And after bloom is over, remove the faded flowers but do not reduce water until the foliage shows signs of maturing. As soon as the ground can be dug, hardy sorts can be set out in a garden row to grow on for a year, when they will have recovered their vigor. Half-hardy and tender species are coaxed to keep their green foliage as long as possible, but when it matures and dries off, the bulbs or corms are rested completely, either in their pots or removed from them and dried completely, as the case may require. Species with evergreen foliage, such as amaryllis, are given just enough water to keep the foliage green until they start new growth the following fall. Types rested in their pots should have some slight moisture—just what they will get with the pots turned on their sides on the damp floor of a greenhouse or frostproof cellar.

There are a few bulbs—notably daffodils 'Paperwhite Grandiflora' and 'Grand Soleil d'Or', and sprekelia—which cannot be made to bloom satisfactorily in our northern climate a second year after being forced. These should be discarded after bloom.

FORCING HARDY BULBS

The word "forcing" used in this connection means growing to produce bloom well out of the plant's normal season for flowering. This does not imply, as many beginners are apt to assume, that the plants must be grown at a very high temperature. The more moderate the temperature, as a rule, the better the results. At no time during their growth are really high temperatures good for hardy bulbs. Keep in mind that these hardy species bloom naturally out of doors during the cool or even frosty days and nights of early spring.

In selecting varieties of hardy bulbs for forcing, use only varieties recommended for the purpose in the catalogues. Short lists of varieties are given below, but there are many others equally good.

Daffodils

TRUMPETS:
'Dutch Master'—yellow
'Joseph MacLeod'—yellow

'King Alfred'—yellow
'Magnet'—yellow trumpet, white
    perianth

'Mount Hood'—white

LARGE CUPS:
'Carlton'—yellow
'Flower Record'—white and orange
'Ice Follies'—cream cup with white perianth

SMALL CUPS:
'Barrett Browning'—white, red cup
'Verger'—white, red cup

DOUBLES:
'Van Sion'—yellow

BUNCH-FLOWERED:
'Cragford'—white, orange-scarlet
'Geranium'—white, orange-red

CYCLAMINEUS HYBRIDS:
'February Gold'—yellow

TRIANDRUS HYBRIDS:
'Silver Chimes'—white
'Thalia'—white

Tulips

SINGLE EARLIES:
'Brilliant Star'—scarlet
'Christmas Marvel'—pink
'Couleur Cardinal'—scarlet and plum
'Doctor Plesman'—orange-red
'Prince of Austria'—orange-red

DARWINS AND DARWIN HYBRIDS:
'Diplomat'—red
'Gudoshnik'—creamy-yellow
'Jewel of Spring'—yellow

COTTAGE:
'Golden Harvest'—lemon-yellow

'Rosy Wings'—salmon-pink

EARLY DOUBLES:
'Peach Blossom'—deep rose

TRIUMPH:
'Apricot Beauty'—salmon-rose
'Bing Crosby'—red
'Cassini'—brown-red
'Danton'—deep carmine
'Olaf'—red
'Paul Richter'—red
'Pax'—white

LATE DOUBLES:
'Livingstone'—cherry-pink

Hyacinths (All are fragrant)

'Amethyst'—violet
'Ann Mary'—bright pink
'Borah'—multi-flowering (fairy type), lavender-blue
'City of Haarlem'—yellow
'Delft Blue'—porcelain-blue
'Lady Derby'—shell-pink
'La Victoire'—rose-red

'L'Innocence'—white
'Ostara'—blue
'Rosalie'—miniature, pink
'Salmonetta'—salmon
'Snow Princess'—multi-flowering (fairy type), white
Also, all specially prepared hyacinths for pot or water culture

---

Minor Bulbs
Anemone, Florists'
Chionodoxa
Colchicum
Crocus

Iris reticulata
Muscari armeniacum 'Early Giant'
Muscari tubergenianum
Scilla sibirica 'Spring Beauty'
Ranunculus, Florists'

Lilies

L. *amabile*	L. *hansonii*
L. Asiatic Hybrids	L. *henryi*
L. *auratum*	L. *martagon* and hybrids
L. *candidum*	L. *pumilum*
L. *concolor*	L. *regale*
L. *formosanum*	L. *speciosum* hybrids, varieties

Potting

For large daffodil bulbs, select 6- or 7-inch bulb pans, placing three to five bulbs in each pot. Six or more tulips can be fitted neatly into a 6-inch pan. For minor bulbs, tulip and daffodil species, a 6-inch bulb pan will hold six to twelve bulbs, depending on size. Lilies are potted as soon as delivered, one bulb to a deep 6- or 8-inch pot, or several may be planted in a tub.

If old pots are used, they should be first scrubbed vigorously with a stiff brush and clear water. Pot up in Mixture No. 1, following the detailed instruction on planting given on page 274. Potting may be done any time between September and December; but with daffodils especially, the earlier the better, as they begin to develop roots early in the autumn. Place one variety only in each pot, since different varieties may mature at different dates. Use narrow, 12-inch labels to mark each pot with its species and variety name, or attach wire labels to short bamboo stakes. These long labels will greatly simplify locating the varieties you may wish to bring in when the pots are covered with mulch.

After the bulbs are potted and marked, water them thoroughly. The best way is to stand the pots in pans of water until the surface soil is uniformly moist.

Pre-rooting Period

Since hardy bulbs must undergo a period of cold in order to develop a strong root system before top growth is started, the potted bulbs must be subjected to one of the following treatments:

1. Dig a trench 12 to 15 inches deep, 18 inches wide, and long enough to hold the pots. The trench should be dug in a well-drained

Method of watering after planting. Pots are placed in an inch or so of water until moisture shows on surface.

part of the garden where there is no danger of water collecting in the bottom. In heavy clay soil, place a 4-inch layer of small stones or coarse gravel in the bottom.

Set pans and pots in the trench, shoulder to shoulder, and pack damp peat moss around and 2 or 3 inches deep over them. Just before hard freezing, place a heavy layer of straw or dead leaves over the peat moss, held down with evergreen boughs or burlap bags. This will prevent the pans from freezing hard in the peat moss so you cannot get them out. *Leave for at least six weeks,* or until roots begin to grow through the drainage holes of the pots.

2. Instead of a trench, use a well-drained cold frame, with the same packing and covering as that mentioned above. The mulching, however, will not be needed, as sash can be put on after the surface freezes.

3. Pack bulbs as above, in a *cold* cellar, omitting the covering of leaves or straw and boughs.

Wherever the bulbs are placed for this period of root development, all sorts (except daffodils) *must be protected from mice.* The simplest method is to place wire screening over the tops of the pots.

As long as the potted bulbs stay outdoors, they will be developing strong roots without making much top growth. They can therefore be brought in any time after new roots begin to grow out of the drainage holes and form a mass around the insides of the pots. This will take from six to ten weeks, according to variety and conditions. Most people bring in a few pots at a time in order to have a succession of bloom. They can stay outdoors as long as you wish to leave them

LEFT: *Pots are placed in trench, dug in shaded spot, to make root growth.* BELOW: *Pots in a cold frame. Long labels make it easy to find varieties wanted.*
Salt (marsh) hay or excelsior helps to keep soil cool. Pots showing top growth are ready to be brought in. Pot in background, having flowered indoors, has been returned to frame for foliage to mature normally.

there and will be ready to start vigorous top growth whenever you bring them in.

Bringing Indoors

When first brought indoors, start them slowly in a cool atmosphere (40 to 50 degrees if possible) and in half light. They are being shifted from darkness and a freezing temperature and must not be shocked by too much light and heat all at once. First of all, water them by setting in pans of water as before. For a week or ten days, keep them under a bench in a cool greenhouse, partly covered on a cool protected breezeway, a plant room, or under a table in a cool workroom, in half light.

At the end of this time, bring the bulbs into full sunshine, but if possible find a place for them where the night temperature never rises above 60 degrees (50 degrees is better). You will have stronger, healthier blooms if the bulbs are grown on at a cool temperature. Water them freely and give them just as much sunshine as you can until the flowers open. Then keep them out of direct sun for longer-lasting blooms. If they can be placed in a very cool room at night—even down to 40 degrees—the flowers will last longer.

Soil ball removed from pot ready to be brought in to heat: good mat of roots formed and tops started into growth.

A well-grown pot of a single early tulip variety.

Plant pests are not likely to appear except perhaps on tulips, where aphids (Chapter 10) may develop on foliage or buds.

After Care

When bloom is over, *gradually* reduce water, but give enough to keep the foliage green. Pots may then be placed in a very cool room if above freezing. As soon as the ground can be worked in spring, set the bulbs out in flower borders or in garden rows to grow on for a year, when they will be ready to replant.

HALF-HARDY BULBS

The half-hardy bulbs are just as popular as the hardies for bringing to bloom indoors. This group cannot withstand hard freezing or is at least in danger of being injured if subjected to very low temperatures, but many of its members profit by a cooling period outdoors after potting and before hard freezing. As a rule, half-hardy bulbs bear smaller but more appealing flowers than the large daffodils and tulips, which are leaders among the hardies. For more detailed information on any bulb mentioned, consult the Catalogue of Bulbs, page 287.

The Irids

Many of the half-hardy bulbs which prefer an outdoor rooting period are members of the iris family. The following species, which give attractive flowers when grown indoors, all require practically the same culture and can be potted in Soil Mixture No. 3.

Babiana	*Gladiolus tristis*	Moraea
Freesia	Iris, Bulbous	Sparaxis
	Ixia	*Tritonia crocata*
		Watsonia

The Liliaceae

Half-hardy members of the lily family which can be brought to winter bloom, using Soil Mixture No. 2, and which also require an outdoor rooting period are:

Albuca	Lachenalia	*Leucocoryne ixioides*
Brodiaea		Ornithogalum

The Amaryllids

Lycoris aurea	*Lycoris radiata*	Sprekelia
Lycoris incarnata		Zephyranthes

The above members of the amaryllis family are also half-hardy rather than tender. Nerine, sprekelia and zephyranthes can be chilled outdoors before being brought to winter bloom. *Lycoris radiata,* as a fall bloomer, should not be exposed to freezing or very cold temperatures after bloom, but brought into a cool indoor temperature to dry off after flowering. Use Soil Mixture No. 4.

Others

Narcissus 'Paper White Grandiflora'	Hyacinth, Fairy and Miniature types	Anemone, Florists'
Narcissus 'Grand Soleil d'Or'		Ranunculus, Florists'

The above two tender narcissi and the dainty hyacinths, long stand-bys for winter bloom, are treated just as the other half-hardies, potted in Soil Mixture No. 1, and placed in a frame outdoors until just before hard frost. They also lend themselves to water culture, with pebbles or plant fiber to hold the bulbs erect in the container. Hyacinths may be grown in special hyacinth glasses which can be purchased for the purpose.

Anemones and ranunculus may be forced as half-hardy or as hardy bulbs.

TENDER BULBS FOR WINTER BLOOM

The very tender bulbs, corms and tubers which must be treated as house plants the year round are among the most showy and colorful flowers available in any class. Those discussed here either normally bloom in winter or can be coaxed into blossom during the cold months. Once you develop an interest in these exotic subjects, you will find many unusual and exciting plants to choose from, some of which give a long succession of flowers at a time of year when color is most needed indoors.

The culture of many of these tropical bulbs is quite similar, with but small variations. Since the members of one flower family are apt to require pretty much the same soil and treatment, we have divided them into family groups, as follows:

The Amaryllids*

Alstroemeria	Clivia	Haemanthus
Amaryllis belladonna	Crinodonna (syn.	Nerine
Amaryllis (*Hippeastrum*)	*Amarcrinum*)	
	Crinum	
	Cyrtanthus	
	Eucharis	

Culture

The members of this group are all planted in Soil Mixture No. 4, with the upper third of the bulb exposed, in pots which tend to encourage crowding of the roots. Bloom is apt to be bigger and better if the bulb is pot-bound. Amaryllids do not like to be disturbed after they are once established and are therefore repotted only when absolutely necessary.

* For individual cultural notes, see Catalogue of Bulbs.

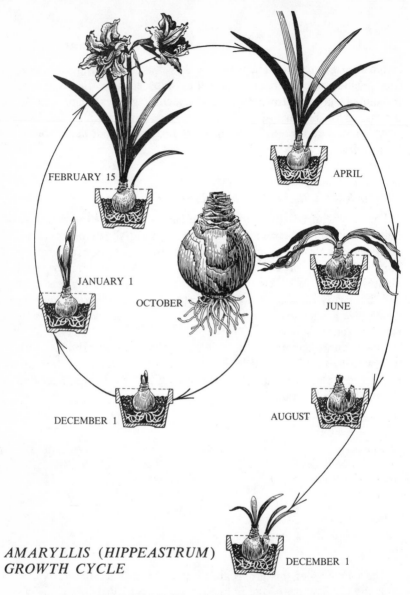

FEBRUARY 15

APRIL

JANUARY 1

OCTOBER

JUNE

DECEMBER 1

AUGUST

AMARYLLIS (HIPPEASTRUM)
GROWTH CYCLE

DECEMBER 1

From the time the bulbs are potted until growth starts, little water is given. The pots can be placed in half light, under a greenhouse bench or under a table in a workroom or plant room where they will be out of the way.

As soon as new growth appears, moisture should be increased and the pots brought to full light. When the flower scape appears, give weekly feedings of manure water or liquid fertilizer until the buds begin to show color.

After bloom, the flower scapes are cut off and water is gradually reduced until the foliage dries off (unless it is an evergreen species, in which case water sparingly during the resting period). When the foliage has withered, the bulbs are rested in their pots, which are turned on their sides under a greenhouse bench or in a damp, frost-proof cellar, until new growth begins late the following summer or early in the fall. During the summer months such pots can be stored outdoors with the bulbs in them, turned on their sides in the shade against a sheltering wall.

When repotting becomes necessary, knock the bulb out carefully without injuring or disturbing the roots. Remove what soil you can by gently dunking in a pail of water, and repot in a larger pot in Soil Mixture No. 4. Repotting is best done in late summer or early fall, before new growth begins.

Eucharis grandiflora, the beautiful white flower commonly called Amazon-lily, which rather resembles in form some of the white triandrus hybrid daffodils growing in a spray, is also an amaryllid but requires somewhat different care. See under Catalogue of Bulbs.

Araceae

Members of the arum family come from a more lush and humid habitat than the amaryllids. They include:

Arum palaestinum	*Hydrosme rivieri*
Caladium, Fancy-leaved	Zantedeschia (Calla-lily)

These prefer a very rich yet well-drained humusy soil (Mixture No. 5) and insist on high humidity and sheltering shade. Most members of this family will not do well in a centrally heated living room, though they are ideal greenhouse subjects, and the fancy-leaved caladiums are fine plants for decorating terraces and patios. If there are facilities for syringing the leaves in order to maintain humidity, some of the smaller calla-lilies, however, can be successfully grown in the window garden.

Since individual requirements of the members of this group are quite different from one another, we refer you to their cultural notes under the Catalogue of Bulbs.

Liliaceae

Members of the lily family for indoor bloom include:

Eucomis	Ornithogalum	Tulbaghia
Gloriosa		Veltheimia

All may be potted in Mixture No. 2, but as they require varying treatments to bring them into bloom, refer for details of indoor culture to the individual plants in the Catalogue of Bulbs.

Others

Other bulbs, corms and tubers which give satisfactory winter bloom indoors are:

Cyclamen	Oxalis	Schizostylis (Kafir-lily)

For culture indoors, consult the individual plants in the Catalogue of Bulbs.

Begoniaceae and Gesneriaceae

A group of tender plants, all handled in the same way as exotic pot plants, and all very showy but unfortunately summer bloomers, includes the tuberous begonias, which belong to the begonia family; and achimenes, gloxinia and some other gesneriads.

By growing from seed or starting corms or tubers out of their regular season, it is possible to bring these three fine pot plants to winter flower, but they make the finest show if started in February to April for summer bloom. For details of culture, see Chapter 18, and the individual plants in the Catalogue of Bulbs.

Interest in gesneriads has burgeoned in recent years, perhaps partially as a result of the tremendous popularity of the fibrous-rooted African-violets (*Saintpaulia*), which along with gloxinia and achimenes, remain the best known gesneriads. Among the tuberous-rooted or rhizomatous gesneriads that can be grown indoors for winter bloom are rechsteineria and the sinningia miniatures, such as 'Doll Baby', 'Bright Eyes' and 'Freckles'. These winter-blooming gesneriads do especially well under fluorescent lights. For details of culture, consult the Catalogue of Bulbs.

PART THREE
—THE CATALOGUE OF BULBS

CHAPTER 21. Descriptions and Directions for Culture

ACHIMENES [*Gesneriaceae*]

The tender scaley rhizomes of achimenes, rather resembling tiny pine cones, produce velvet-textured, long-tubed flowers in spring and summer. The flowers, in rich colors of red, pink, purple and in white, vary in size from ½ to 3 inches, and are borne in the leaf axils on 1- to 2-foot ·stems. More striking than the African-violet and smaller and more graceful than the gloxinia, achimenes have many of the virtues of both these popular plants. In common with these and other gesneriads, the achimenes, sometimes called cupid's bower, is almost solely a subject for pots and hanging containers. In fact it is in hanging baskets that the full beauty of the individual flowers can be appreciated. They can also be grown in window boxes and other planters in part shade.

Of the many species, only a few are in cultivation, but named hybrids are plentiful with annual introductions from hybridizers and commercial growers to be expected. Among the species are *Achimenes longiflora,* flowers blue-violet with long tubes; *A. patens,* with short-tubed, violet-blue flowers; *A. ehrenbergii,* with lavender-blue flowers and large woolly leaves.

Among the fine hybrids are:

Bella—white flowers with purple eye
Camillo Brozzoni—violet and white
English Waltz—salmon-pink
Evening Glow—deep salmon
Master Ingram—deep red
Purple King—purple
Wetterlow—salmon flowers, bronze foliage
Violet Night—deep purple-blue

CULTURE INDOORS: The tiny, fragile rhizomes, barely an inch long, are usually shipped from growers in late winter and spring, when they should be started into growth at a temperature between 60 and 70 degrees. The usual recommendation is to plant from 8 to 12 rhizomes in an 8-inch pot, or 5 in a 6-inch pot and usually about 5 in a 12-inch hanging basket. Use a humusy mixture (Mixture No. 5), planting the rhizomes about 1 inch deep. Water, then slip the pots in polyethylene bags to maintain a humid atmosphere, and keep in subdued light until growth appears. Embedding the rhizomes in about a 1-inch layer of milled, moist sphagnum moss placed on top of the regular soil mixture seems to encourage faster growth by the delicate roots. Still another method is to start the tubers in a mixture of peat moss and sand, then transplanting the young plants into their permanent containers. The plants respond well to fluorescent lights. During the summer when they can be kept outdoors, they produce the best floral display in a partially sunny situation. Achimenes should never be allowed to get bone dry between waterings; the result will be a slow-down in flowering and a tendency to go into premature dormancy. As with any pot-grown plant that is in profuse flower production, a regular fertilizer schedule (once a week) is a necessity to maintain the plants' vigor. A liquid fish emulsion is our choice.

When flowering ceases, usually in late fall, reduce water gradually until plants are dried off. Then remove the top of the plant and store the rhizomes in their pots in a damp cellar or under a bench in the greenhouse. When new growth appears, treat as before, bringing to light and giving ample water. Grow on in one pot through the second year, repotting when growth starts for the third time.

PROPAGATION: From division of the tubers, also by stem rhizomes formed on some varieties.

ACIDANTHERA [Iridaceae]

Acidanthera bicolor comes to us from tropical Africa. The foliage is reminiscent of that of the gladiolus but handsomer, and the delicate, fragrant white flowers with blackish centers poise like pale butterflies near the top of the 2-foot blooming stems. We usually plant them just behind the hymenocallis and in front of the galtonia in a bed of white summer-flowering bulbs.

CULTURE OUTDOORS: As for gladiolus.

PROPAGATION: From cormels.

AGAPANTHUS [*Liliaceae*]

Agapanthus africanus (blue African-lily; lily-of-the-nile) and *A. africanus variegatus* (which produces striped leaves) are usually grown in tubs or very large pots for bloom on patio or porch. They can be treated as garden subjects in the South, since they are summer bloomers. *A. orientalis* and its white variety, *alba,* are grown outdoors in California. This is a more robust species, reaching 4 feet in height.

Twelve to thirty bright blue flowers, each 2 inches in length, are borne in terminal umbels on 3-foot naked flowering stems. The basal leaves are linear, pointed, dark green in color, to 3 feet in length. There are also several named hybrids, both dwarf and tall-growing.

CULTURE INDOORS: Pot (Mixture No. 5) from February to April, with crowns at soil surface. Feed with manure water or a liquid fertilizer while buds are developing, and keep moist until bloom is over. Will flourish in sun or light shade. After blossoming, reduce water gradually. When the tuberous roots are dried off, store in pot or tub, almost dry, in a cool place over the winter.

CULTURE OUTDOORS, SOUTH: Plant outdoors in spring in rich, moist soil, covering 2 inches deep. Keep well watered. Lift the tuberous roots before hard frost. May be left out the year round where the temperature does not drop below 25 degrees.

PROPAGATION: By division.

ALBUCA [*Liliaceae*]

Albuca is a fragrant South African bulb which is grown as a border plant in California. *A. major* grows to 3 feet in height; *A. nelsonii* to 5 feet; and *A. minor* to but 1½ feet. The racemes of white or yellow flowers are large and showy, borne in late spring or early summer.

CULTURE OUTDOORS, SOUTH: As for tender ornithogalum, to which they are allied.

PROPAGATION: By offsets.

ALLIUM [*Liliaceae*]

This genus is a huge one which includes hundreds of species from many parts of the world, chiefly in the Northern Hemisphere. They vary in height from a few inches to several feet. The color range runs from white through pink to rose-red, lavender and blue, and the flowering season from spring to fall.

Garden alliums are usually hardy, and though most of them give forth an onion or garlic odor when the leaves or stems are crushed, few are objectionable in this respect if left uncut. Some of the blossoms, indeed, are pleasantly fragrant, with a heliotrope or violet scent.

The flower heads are produced in globular or flattened umbels made up of many bell-like or star-shaped flowers, each borne on its own slender stem. The umbels vary in size from 1 or 2 inches in rock-garden species to great heads 8 to 12 inches across, as in *A. christophii* (syn. *albopilosum*), commonly called stars of Persia. Leaves are sometimes tubular, sometimes strap-like, broad or narrow. Roots may be strictly bulbous or rhizomatous. *A. caeruleum* is a tall-growing species with deep blue flowers in umbels 2 inches in diameter; *A. cyaneum,* a rock-garden subject, bears nodding blue flowers on short stems, while *A. moly* and *A. flavum* are yellow. *A. ostrowskianum* bears deep pink blossoms while *A. neapolitanum* is white. All four of the last-named species grow to about a foot in height. Although there are many species to choose from, perhaps the most spectacular allium for garden display is the giant onion or allium, *A. giganteum*. Its 6- to 9-inch perfectly round balls of densely packed, lilac-purple star-shaped flowers glitter and shimmer in the early summer border, atop 3- to 4-foot stems, and always catch the attention of the most indifferent visitor. This is a fine bulb for a mixed garden of annuals and perennials, or a small colony of bulbs can be established in the foreground of a shrub planting.

All authorities agree that nomenclature is still much confused among the alliums, so the collector may encounter difficulties in obtaining species in which he is interested. This, of course, only adds to the zest of the search, especially as so many of the genus are worthwhile in the garden picture.

So keen does the competition often become to secure rare varieties and species that even the most dignified enthusiast cannot always be trusted in a strange garden. An actor friend of ours who collected alliums through the simple process of sending to a seed house that specialized in varieties for seed and growing whatever he received had a very unusual group of plants in bloom one summer. One early afternoon he was alone in the house, taking a shower, when he thought he heard the clinking of a spade outside. He threw his bath towel around him and ran to the door, to discover a former officer of the American Herb Society in the act of digging up his most precious species. "Why," he called, "I'm surprised at you." The old lady was quite unabashed. "Well, I thought you weren't at home," she excused herself.

CULTURE OUTDOORS: Plant in fall or spring in sun in well-drained, gravelly loam, with top of bulb near surface.

PROPAGATION: By seeds (many species self-seed freely) sown in spring and by offsets and bulbils taken in fall or spring.

ALSTROEMERIA [*Amaryllidaceae*]

South American members of the amaryllis family, alstroemerias are not generally hardy north of Washington, D.C., though the species *A. aurantiaca* (Peruvian-lily; Chilean-lily) can sometimes be brought through the winter outdoors as far north as Philadelphia.

The showy red, purple, or yellow flaring, tubular flowers are borne in terminal umbels on leafy stems and bloom in spring in the South where they remain in the garden the year round. Half a dozen species are generally available.

A. aurantiaca—yellow, spotted brown, tipped green

A. chilensis—mixed pastel colors

A. pulchella—red, tipped green

CULTURE INDOORS: Pot in fall (Mixture No. 4). Water sparingly until growth starts, then give more moisture. After bloom, dry off gradually, and when foliage has matured, remove roots from soil in pots and replant.

CULTURE OUTDOORS, NORTH: Plant outdoors in spring when danger of frost is past, in rich, moist, humusy soil in a shady location. After bloom, when foliage has matured, lift and store in damp sand in a cool, frostproof place.

CULTURE OUTDOORS, SOUTH: Plant in autumn as described above. Mulch for winter in upper South.

PROPAGATION: By seeds or division of roots.

AMARCRINUM—See CRINODONNA

AMARYLLIS—See HIPPEASTRUM

AMARYLLIS BELLADONNA [*Amaryllidaceae*]

The belladonna-lily (syn. *Brunsvigia rosea; Callicore rosea*) is a tender South African, a greenhouse subject. The strap-like leaves appear before or after the lovely lily-shaped blooms, rose-red and fragrant, to 3½ inches long, in umbels at the top of a 2-foot solid scape. Bloom occurs in late summer or early autumn.

CULTURE INDOORS: Pot while dormant in spring or early summer (Mixture No. 4). Use a small pot only a little larger than the bulb, the top half of which should remain exposed. When leaves appear, after bloom, give plenty of water and light until matured. Then gradually reduce water. Store bulb in pot laid on its side under greenhouse bench until new growth appears.

CULTURE OUTDOORS: As for *Hippeastrum*.

PROPAGATION: By offsets.

Anemone coronaria *of which there are several named varieties blooms in the garden in spring but is often forced into winter bloom in greenhouses. It is a popular florist's cutflower.*

AMARYLLIS hallii—See LYCORIS [squamigera]

AMORPHOPHALLUS—See HYDROSYME

ANEMONE [Ranunculaceae]

The anemone tribe includes many fine tuberous-rooted garden subjects for various uses and blooming at different seasons. The largest and handsomest are the large-flowered florists' anemones, selections from *Anemone coronaria* which can be brought to bloom outdoors or under glass. They come in white, brilliant red, rose, purple and violet. A few of the many named varieties are:

'Mr. Fokker'—blue   'Sylphide'—violet
'The Governor'—scarlet   'The Bride'—white
'The Admiral'—double rose
St. Brigid—double strain, mixed colors and de Caen—single

Tuberous-rooted hardy types, such as *A. apennina,* 9 inches, blooming in April, *A. blanda,* 8 inches, and varieties of these two species are especially suited to woodland gardens. *A. palmata,* 9 inches, yellow; *A. caroliniana,* cream to purple, and *A. fulgens,* red, are excellent in the rock garden. *A. ranunculoides,* 8 inches, the yellow wood anemone, blooming in early spring, is a somewhat tuberous-rooted sort for naturalizing. There are dozens of fibrous-rooted species and varieties.

CULTURE OUTDOORS: Florists' anemones (St. Brigid, de Caen and named selections). In the North, plant 2 inches deep and 12 inches apart in a sheltered bed or frame in humus-rich sandy loam in fall, and after first freeze, mulch with 8 inches of dead leaves. Remove mulch gradually in spring. Or plant in spring, lift roots after bloom is over and foliage matures, and store over winter.

In moist climates such as the Pacific Northwest, tubers multiply so rapidly that it is necessary to lift and to divide every year.

CULTURE INDOORS: Plant in Potting Mixture No. 2 in pots, and force as hardy bulbs. After bringing indoors, grow plants on at a cool temperature—from 35 to 50 degrees.

CULTURE, HARDY TUBEROUS-ROOTED TYPES: Plant in humus-rich, sandy, well-drained soil in sun or light shade.

PROPAGATION: By division in the spring and by seed.

ANOMATHECA—See LAPEIROUSIA

ANTHERICUM [Liliaceae]

Anthericum liliago, a native of the Alps, has been cherished in cultivation since late in the fifteenth century. This is the species known as St. Bernard's-lily. Its raceme of dainty white flowers is borne on a 1-foot stem in early summer. It is a free-flowering and satisfactory tender bulb for the rock garden.

Anthericum liliastrum (now known as *Paradisea liliastrum,* St. Bruno's-lily) is also an alpine, but is found in higher altitudes— 6,000 feet or more. It is altogether a larger plant than its relative, with white, fragrant flowers which Louise B. Wilder described as "like small slightly disheveled Madonna Lilies."

CULTURE OUTDOORS: South of Philadelphia, plant in autumn in well-drained sunny position in the rock garden. Treat as a lily.

CULTURE OUTDOORS, NORTH: Set out in spring as above. Dig and store before hard freeze in fall.

PROPAGATION: By stolons, divisions, and seeds.

ARISAEMA TRIPHYLLUM [Araceae]

Jack-in-the-pulpit or Indian-turnip is a familiar woodland plant, with its three ovate leaflets and the striped green arum-like blooms. Later in the season a heavy head of bright red berries develops. Readily transplanted into the wildflower garden, this wild tuberous-rooted subject often reaches 3 feet in height when it finds beds with good soil and abundant food.

CULTURE OUTDOORS: Plant in rather moist woodland in part shade. Leave undisturbed.

PROPAGATION: By tubers and seeds.

ARUM PALAESTINUM [Araceae]

The so-called black-calla is grown chiefly as a curiosity, since it certainly is not beautiful. Its 1-foot-tall, calla-like bloom, with a deep purple spadix and surrounding black-purple and greenish spathe, is lemon-scented, a winter bloomer. The leaves are arrow-shaped, 8 inches long.

CULTURE INDOORS: Start tuberous roots in damp peat moss, covering 1 inch deep, as the roots form near the top of the tuber. When roots develop, plant in pots (Mixture No. 5) and grow on in shade. For good bloom, the plant must be pot-bound.

PROPAGATION: By offsets.

BABIANA [Iridaceae]

Babiana is a dainty little half-hardy native of South Africa. There are a number of species bearing violet, pink, red, yellow, or white freesia-like blossoms in terminal racemes on 6- to 9-inch stems. The iris-like leaves are plicate. Hybrids are available.

CULTURE INDOORS: Pot a dozen corms in a small bulb pan in Mixture No. 3 in autumn. Keep in a very cool breezeway, plant room, garage, or cold frame until growth starts. Then grow on with plenty of water on a cool window sill or the like. Bloom appears in February or March. After foliage matures, dry off corms and store.

CULTURE OUTDOORS, SOUTH: Plant out in sandy loam 3 inches deep in full sun in autumn for spring bloom. Divide every other year.

PROPAGATION: By cormels and seeds.

BEGONIA [Begoniaceae]

Of the huge tribe of begonias, two types are of interest here, the tuberous-rooted, for which see Chapter 18, and Begonia evansiana, a hardy member of the genus, whose tubers resemble perfect little bulbs about the size of a filbert. B. evansiana produces large light green foliage, red beneath, and many tall spikes of pink blossoms on red stems in late summer. Once planted, it will increase of its own accord. It is a most valuable shade-loving perennial.

CULTURE OUTDOORS: Plant the bulb-like tubers of Begonia evan-

siana in spring in a rich, humusy soil in shade. Keep well watered in drought.

PROPAGATION: By bulblets. These will increase in the ground and distribute themselves as they choose. Or they can be dug and replanted in early spring.

BELAMCANDA [Iridaceae]

Belamcanda chinensis, commonly called the blackberry-lily because of its clusters of black seeds, is a hardy, showy member of the iris family. It produces narrow 10-inch gladiolus-like leaves on 4-foot branched, flowering stems which bear the clusters of red-spotted orange flowers. The black seed heads in autumn are prized by flower arrangers.

CULTURE OUTDOORS: Plant in fall in sandy loam in sun. Mulch after first hard freeze in the North. Leave undisturbed until bloom ceases.

PROPAGATION: By seeds or division.

BESSERA [Liliaceae]

Bessera elegans (coral drops) is a half-hardy Mexican bulb which makes a fine show forced in the window garden or grown out of doors for midsummer bloom. Growing 2 to 3 feet tall, with a few 2-foot leaves, each bulb produces several slender, naked flower scapes which bear in irregular umbels five to ten bright red 1-inch flowers marked with white. *Milla biflora* is sometimes sold as bessera.

CULTURE INDOORS: Plant several bulbs to a pot (Mixture No. 2) and force as half-hardy bulbs. (See Chapter 20.)

CULTURE OUTDOORS: As for gladiolus.

PROPAGATION: By offsets.

BRODIAEA [Liliaceae]

Brodiaeas are native American cormous plants from our far West, where they flourish in mountainous regions. Though perfectly hardy in the Pacific area and in the South, in the Northeast and Middle

West they are difficult, and are grown successfully in Zone 6 (vicinity of New York City) only by giving them the very special conditions they prefer.

The bell-shaped or starry flowers are borne in umbels at the tips of frail scapes, while the foliage is grass-like. There are red, blue, violet, white and yellow species as well as *B. volubilis,* the snake-lily, a twining species to 8 feet with rose-pink flowers.

The following are but a few of the many species available.

B. bridgesii—15 inches, violet-pink

B. crocea—9 inches, yellow

B. coronaria—12 inches, purple-blue

B. lactea—12 inches, white

B. uniflora (Spring Starflower)—*See Ipheion uniflorum.*

Brodiaeas are most useful in the rock garden.

CULTURE OUTDOORS: Plant in fall in rough, gritty, well-drained soil, in sun. Mulch in the North after first hard freeze.

CULTURE INDOORS: Pot in early fall in soil as above and treat as hardy bulbs to be forced. Blossoms will appear in early spring.

PROPAGATION: By seeds and offsets.

BRUNSVIGIA—See AMARYLLIS belladonna

BULBOCODIUM [*Liliaceae*]

B. vernum (spring meadow saffron) is a European member of the lily family, and there is but one known species in the genus. Rather like a crocus, it has narrow leaves and several large rose-violet flowers on 6-inch stems in very early spring.

CULTURE OUTDOORS: As for crocus. Lift every third year and replant.

PROPAGATION: By offsets.

CALADIUM [*Araceae*]

The fancy-leaved caladiums are becoming increasingly important decorative subjects for terraces and outdoor living areas. They are usually grown in pots but are also satisfactory in the open ground or in large boxes and other kinds of planters. Although the arrow-shaped leaves are thin and delicate in texture, their varied colorings and patterns are splashy enough to provide even bolder ornamental effects than are found in many flowering plants. Named selections are available in a variety of colors and patterns. Some good ones include:

'Blaze'—red leaves with green edges, scarlet ribs

'Candidum'—white with green veins

'Candidum Jr.'—lower growing than above

'Dr. Groover'—pink splotched with green

'Itacapus'—rust-red bordered green

'June Bride'—white with lace-like green veins

'Pink Cloud'—pink with green border and mottling

'White Christmas'—white, green veins

CULTURE, NORTH: Start tubers indoors in late winter in flats of damp peat moss at 70 to 85 degrees, covering roots 2 to 3 inches. Transfer to large pots after roots have developed using a rich, humusy soil mixture (Mixture No. 5). Plants can be moved outdoors in semi-shade when the weather is settled and warm. Caladiums tolerate shade but good light—even partial or filtered sunlight—results in the best colored foliage. Repotting may be necessary during the growing season. Keep well watered and sprayed with a fine mist in hot, dry weather. Reduce water gradually in early autumn and bring the tubers in before frost, dry off, remove from pots, and store at 60 degrees. Caladiums may also be grown under glass or for winter color in the conservatory. They need a warm greenhouse and high humidity.

CULTURE OUTDOORS, SOUTH: Plant in rich, sandy, well-drained soil to which bone meal has been added, as soon as the weather has become reliably warm. Cover 1 inch deep, placing in semi-shaded, sheltered bed. Dig before frost and dry as described above.

PROPAGATION: By division and seeds.

CALLA—See ZANTEDESCHIA

CALLICORE—See AMARYLLIS belladonna

CALOCHORTUS [*Liliaceae*]

Here are other natives of our own West. Known as Mariposa-lilies, globe-tulips, and star-tulips, several species of *Calochortus* are to be found from southern California, through the high Sierras, to the Black Hills, Colorado, and on to Oregon. Though of easy culture in the West, they are difficult to acclimate to the East and Middle West, where they seem to resent the sudden changes of temperature, with consequent thaws and "heaving" of the cormous roots. When one has seen them growing in their thousands in native mountain meadows or woods, it seems futile to plant a dozen corms in a sunny rock-garden slope in New York or Massachusetts only to watch them struggle through a few seasons to slow death. They are most decorative, however, in the northern rock garden, where they may last several years.

There are many species, varying in color from white through lavender to purple. Others are yellow and yellow-tinged with brown or orange. They are divided into three groups:

1. Star-tulips or cat's-ears. Flowers erect on slender stems, most of them low-growing. The insides of the flower petals are hairy, giving them their common name of cat's-ears. Star-tulips grow in sunny situations and better adapt themselves to northeastern conditions than the other types.

2. Globe-tulips or fairy lanterns. Flowers nodding, lantern-shaped, with glossy petals, to 2 feet in height, borne on slender stems. These endure light shade when growing conditions are right.

3. Mariposa-lilies or butterfly-tulips are the showiest of the *Calochortus* tribe. The slender stems rise from grass-like foliage from 1½ to 2 feet, bearing large (3- to 4-inch) flowers in white, red, purple, lavender, or yellow, or mixtures of these colors. Like the cat's-ears, the petals are hairy at the base. Sun-loving.

In addition to the forty or more species which make up these three groups, there are hybrids giving stronger growth, larger flowers, more varied color and greater adaptability to climatic conditions.

CULTURE OUTDOORS: Plant 2 inches deep in rather poor, light soil, porous and with perfect drainage. Though absolutely cold-hardy, they cannot stand alternate freezing and thawing. Mulch well in the North after first hard freeze. They need moisture in spring up to bloom time but prefer to be quite dry through the summer.

CULTURE INDOORS: Treat as hardy forced bulbs.

PROPAGATION: By natural increase and seeds.

CAMASSIA [*Liliaceae*]—*See Chapter 14*

CANNA [*Cannaceae*]

This old-fashioned bedding flower is coming back into favor after having been banished with Victorian houses, iron deer and stiff round or geometrical flower beds. The reason for its comeback is the introduction of many fine new hybrids which are compact in growth, with large flowers, many in pastel shades. In buying canna roots, select named varieties with green or bronze leaves and of a height— they grow 2½ to 8 feet tall—to suit the location in which they are to grow.

'Ambassador'—cherry red, bronze foliage, 4 ft.

'Chinese Coral'—deep red-salmon, green leaves, 30 inches.

'City of Portland'—orange-red flowers, green leaves.

'Florence Vaughn'—golden-yellow flowers, green leaves, 3½ ft.

'La Boheme'—rosy peach, 36 inches.

'Rigoletto'—yellow, 3 ft.

'Stadt Fellbach'—orange flowers, green leaves, 3 ft.

'The President'—scarlet flowers, green leaves, 3 ft.

CULTURE OUTDOORS: Start indoors in the North, as with tuberous begonias and caladiums, four weeks before outdoor planting date; or set rhizomes horizontally, after danger of frost is past, 1½ to 2 feet apart, according to height, 3 to 4 inches deep in rich soil with plenty of moisture and in full sun, just covering the rhizomes with soil. During growth, side-dress with 5–10–5 fertilizer at the rate of 4 ounces per square yard. When frost blackens the foliage in fall, cut to within 6 inches of root, dig the rhizomes, dry off, and store upside down in a cool place, not too dark, at a temperature of 50 to 60 degrees.

Another bulb-like flower for summer color is the canna, enjoying a revival in popularity because of the introduction of lower-growing, brighter-colored hybrids.

In March, divide rhizomes, leaving several eyes on each, and start in flats of soil and peat moss. Harden off in a cold frame or cooler room for two weeks before setting in the garden.

PROPAGATION: By seeds—soaked in warm water for forty-eight hours, or filed, before planting—and by division.

CHLIDANTHUS [*Amaryllidaceae*]

The South American bulb *Chlidanthus fragrans* (delicate-lily) has strap-like, gray-green basal leaves and bears umbels of fragrant yellow tubular flowers, each 4 inches long, on 6- to 10-inch solid scapes. Rock-garden or container subject. Late summer bloom.

CULTURE OUTDOORS, SOUTH: Treat as a garden plant.

CULTURE OUTDOORS, NORTH: Plant out 2 inches deep in early spring, in full sun, in humusy soil, well-drained and moist. Dig before frost and store bulbs above freezing; or start in small pots (Mixture No. 4) in late winter. After danger of frost is past in spring, sink pots in garden bed. Keep moist until after bloom. Then reduce water gradually until foliage matures.

PROPAGATION: By offsets.

CHIONODOXA [*Liliaceae*]—*See Chapter 14*

CLAYTONIA [*Portulacaceae*]

These gay little wild flowers of the early spring woods known as spring beauties adapt themselves well to naturalizing under shade, among ferns and in moist situations. Once a colony of their corms or tubers is established in a spot to its liking, it may be counted on to spread and increase.

C. virginica is the native species common in the northeastern United States, growing from Canada to Texas. The flowers are white, veined with pink, on 4- to 6-inch stems, the leaves grass-like and succulent. *C. rosea* and *C. megarrhiza* are both natives of the Rocky Mountains, while *C. lanceolata* and *C. nivalis* are from the Pacific Northwest. There are many species, including *C. aurea,* which is yellow.

CULTURE: Select a species native to your part of the country and naturalize in surroundings similar to those in which it grows in nature.

PROPAGATION: By natural increase.

CLIVIA [*Amaryllidaceae*]

Natives of South Africa, the clivias or Kafir-lilies are popular greenhouse subjects, where the narrow evergreen leaves and showy umbels of 2- to 3-inch orange or orange-scarlet flowers on 2-foot stems are most colorful in early spring. They may also be grown successfully as a house plant or outdoors in the South. *C. miniata* and a number of hybrids are commercially available.

CULTURE INDOORS: Pot (Mixture No. 4) June to October and leave undisturbed for several years. Keep rather dry through summer and autumn. Start in January to give more water and regular applications of liquid manure. Keep at 65 degrees. After bloom, gradually reduce water until almost none is given through the fall.

CULTURE OUTDOORS, SOUTH: Plant in fall in a shady location in a rich, humusy, but well-drained garden bed.

PROPAGATION: By division.

Plate 23

Dwarf bedding dahlias (Coltness hybrids) are as readily grown from seeds as are zinnias and marigolds. Several different seed strains are available, including Sunburst, Rigoletto and Redskin mixtures.

Plate 24

ABOVE: *Tuberous begonias, the "mockingbirds" of flowerdom, come in an almost incredible range of hues and forms. The tubers last for many years.* BELOW: *"T.B.s" in a shady nook of the author's garden, where they provide more striking color than any other shade-tolerant plant.*

Plate 25

Plate 26

ABOVE: *A group of the Buell gloxinias, an American strain far surpassing most older forms in size and variety of coloring.* BELOW: *The tiger-flower* (Tigridia) *from Mexico, which is usually available in a wide range of pleasing colors for the summer garden.*

Plate 27

Plate 28

ABOVE: *Most dramatic of the autumn-flowering bulbs are the colchicums, which suddenly appear as if by magic. 'The Giant' (illustrated) has flowers over 6 inches across.* BELOW: *"Farewell to summer" is the theme song of the sternbergias—or should it be, "Hail to another spring"?*

Plate 29

COLCHICUM [Liliaceae]—See Chapter 19

COLOCASIA [Araceae]

Commonly known as elephant's ear, this large foliage plant can grow up to 6 feet. The huge, heart-shaped leaves—to 2 feet across —for which the plant is grown, provide a screen or a tropical-looking background for smaller garden subjects. This is one of the few bulbous plants that will thrive in full shade, making it a valuable decoration for shaded terraces and porches.

CULTURE: Start as tuberous-rooted begonias and caladiums. Then transfer to shaded outdoor positions in very rich, damp soil. Dig and store before frost. May also be grown in pots or planters.

PROPAGATION: By division.

CONVALLARIA [Liliaceae]

This old-time favorite is still one of the most popular of our spring garden flowers. Flourishing and spreading as it does in deep shade, and providing masses of sweet-scented white flowers nodding like little bells on stiff flower stems, it is little wonder that the lily-of-the-valley keeps its popularity. The variety *rosea* bears pale pinkish flowers which, to us, seem rather unattractive. It is not bulbous but grows from root-stocks.

CULTURE OUTDOORS: Plant the roots in fall in rich, damp soil in partial or full shade. Leave undisturbed, but give a yearly fall application of well-rotted cow manure or compost.

CULTURE INDOORS: "Pips," for forcing indoors or under glass, may be purchased from seed houses.

PROPAGATION: By division.

COOPERIA [Amaryllidaceae]

Native to Texas and Mexico, the dainty rain-lily is often naturalized with zephyranthes in the South or Southwest. The starry white or white, pink-tinged, solitary flowers on 10-inch stems are delightfully fragrant and appear after rains throughout the summer. They are hardy to Virginia.

C. drummondii—white, tinged red in reverse
C. pedunculata—larger than preceding
C. traubii—white, tinted pink in reverse
CULTURE: As for zephyranthes.
PROPAGATION: By offsets.

CRINODONNA [*Amaryllidaceae*]

Crinodonna corsii is a bigeneric hybrid of outstanding beauty. (It is sometimes listed as x *Amarcrinum howardii*.) It produces large clusters of soft pink lily-like flowers on a thick, fleshy 2- to 4-foot stem in early autumn. At least two flower scapes are usually thrown up from a single bulb, the second appearing after the first is well along toward bloom. The trumpet-shaped blooms are long-lasting and deliciously fragrant. Because of its delicate pink color, fine form and good lasting qualities, we consider it the most beautiful of our tender flowering bulbs. Visitors are always drawn to it.

CULTURE INDOORS, NORTH: Pot the bulb in fall with the upper third above the soil level (Mixture No. 4). Grow on indoors through winter. Pots can be sunk in a shady garden bed when warm weather comes and fed occasionally with liquid fertilizer. After bloom, but before frost, bring indoors and gradually reduce water. After foliage matures, leave under bench in greenhouse or in cool cellar with pot turned on side until new growth starts. Then give more water and light, and begin feeding.

CULTURE OUTDOORS, SOUTH: Bulbs may be spring-planted in the garden for year-round growth. See crinum culture.

PROPAGATION: By offsets.

CRINUM [*Amaryllidaceae*]

Crinums, known as bengal-lilies or milk-and-wine-lilies, are usually grown in the South, where they remain out of doors the year round and in one spot for many years without needing transplanting. In spite of their beauty, they are seldom grown under glass or indoors in the North because of the space they require.

There are species with evergreen or deciduous foliage. Both throw up strong solid scapes 2 to 4 feet in height which, in September or

October, bear umbels of long-tubed, lily-like white, pink, or rose-red blooms, each 3 to 6 inches long. The following are half-hardy and may be grown as garden plants to Washington, D.C.:

C. *longifolium*—pink or white
C. x *powelli*—rose-pink

Tender varieties:

'Ellen Bosanquet'—wine red
'Louis Bosanquet'—white shading to pink, petals ruffled
C. *moorei*—pink, requires shade
C. *virginicum*—white with rose stripes, early

CULTURE OUTDOORS, SOUTH: Plant outdoors in spring in sun (except C. *moorei*) in rich, humusy, well-drained soil, covering the bulbs with 6 inches of soil. Water freely during the growing period. After bloom, reduce moisture gradually until foliage has matured in deciduous types. Less water is required after bloom in evergreen types also. Mulch tender varieties lightly in the middle South, heavily in the upper South.

CULTURE OUTDOORS, NORTH: Plant in spring, after danger of frost is past, 2 to 3 feet apart, in rich, humusy, well-drained bed. Water freely until after bloom, then reduce moisture. Lift and store before frost for deciduous types. In evergreen types, pot up before frost and keep in rather dry, semi-dormant condition until new growth starts.

CULTURE INDOORS: Pot (Mixture No. 4) as soon as delivered, with the top third of the bulb exposed. Feed with liquid fertilizer as flower scapes are thrown up and until color shows. After bloom, reduce water gradually. Repot only when necessary.

PROPAGATION: By natural offsets.

CROCOSMIA [Iridaceae]

The montbretia (*Crocosmia* x *crocosmiiflora*) is the most important member of this genus and is described in Chapter 19. The coppertip (C. *masonorum*) is sometimes offered by bulb growers. It is especially useful in a sunny border in the midsection or toward the rear. The large, bright orange-red flowers, 2 inches in length, are borne in showy, long-panicled spikes which lift their heads to 3 feet in midsummer and fall.

CULTURE: The corms can be set out in spring, about the time you plant gladiolus, 3 inches deep and 3 inches apart. Lift and store as with gladiolus; in mild climates, the corms are winter-hardy.

PROPAGATION: By offsets and seeds.

CROCUS [Iridaceae]—See Chapter 14

CYCLAMEN [Primulaceae]

The florists' cyclamen (*C. persicum*), as a universal gift plant, is familiar to all. The heart-shaped, mottled leaves look almost metallic in their crisp beauty, while the many nodding flowers, with reflexed petals, are extremely striking. Purple, cerise, rose, red, and white varieties are available.

Tiny, hardy rock-garden cyclamens are like miniature replicas of their florist relatives. *C. europaeum* is native to central and southern Europe and is perfectly hardy in the North. The leaves are mottled and the fragrant blooms rose-red. It is a summer and fall bloomer. *C. neapolitanum,* with lovely silver-marked leaves and red or white flowers, is hardy in the Northeast. The flowers appear in late summer before the leaves. The foliage of these two dainty little species remains green through the winter. *C. vernale* (syn. *repandum*) is another hardy species but differs from previous species in being a spring bloomer (April–May). The scented flowers are rosy-pink with a lilac eye, the leaves marked with silver.

CULTURE INDOORS: For florists' varieties, pot corm-like roots in a mixture of one part sifted loam, one part sand and two parts leafmold. Give light but not too much direct sun, plenty of water and a temperature not over 55 degrees. (Do not permit water to lodge and remain on leaves.) After bloom is over and foliage matures, lay pots on sides under greenhouse bench or out of doors for summer until growth starts again.

CULTURE OUTDOORS: For garden varieties, plant about 2 inches deep in a shady part of the rock garden, in the foreground of shrubs or in a woodland garden and leave undisturbed indefinitely.

PROPAGATION: By seeds or division.

CYPELLA [Iridaceae]

The cypella is a bulbous irid which comes to us from South America. The plants have basal and stem leaves and bear yellow, orange, or blue-mauve flowers in clusters on 2- to 3-foot stems throughout the summer.

CULTURE: As for gladiolus.

PROPAGATION: By seeds and offsets.

CYRTANTHUS [Amaryllidaceae]

An uncommon amaryllid from South Africa, cyrtanthus (Ifafalily) bears funnel-shaped nodding flowers in umbels on bare stalks to 1½ feet, the basal leaves being evergreen in most cultivated species.

Red, white and yellow species and varieties are known. Grown as a garden flower in the South, cyrtanthus is a summer bloomer.

CULTURE: As for *Amaryllis belladonna*.

PROPAGATION: By offsets.

DAFFODIL—See Chapter 11

DAHLIA [Compositae]—See Chapter 16

ENDYMION (Liliaceae)—See Chapter 14

ERANTHIS [Ranunculaceae]—See Chapter 14

EREMURUS [Liliaceae]

The foxtail-lily or desert-candle comes to us from Asia. It is not bulbous but produces a heavy, fibrous, star-shaped root. Its stately beauty makes it a striking subject for the back of the border where color is needed.

From rosettes of narrow leaves, flowering scapes 5 to 12 feet in height are thrown up, bearing heavy racemes, 1 to 4 feet long, of bell-shaped white, pink, yellow, or orange flowers. Several species and hybrids are available, mostly blooming in early summer, among them:

E. elwesii—white, 6–9 feet
E. himalaicus—white, 6 feet
'Himrob'—pink, 7–9 feet
'Shelford Hybrids'—pastel shades, 4–5 feet

CULTURE OUTDOORS: Plant the fleshy rootstocks in fall in rich but very well-drained soil, with the roots about 3 inches deep, but the center bud covered by only ½ inch of soil. Mulch heavily after a hard freeze, as their uncertain hardiness seems due to late frosts destroying early spring growth. Remove mulch very gradually until danger of frost is past. Water liberally during the growing season.

PROPAGATION: By division or (slow) from seed.

ERYTHRONIUM [*Liliaceae*]

Except for a single European species, *E. dens-canis,* rose-red, the erythroniums are natives of North America, where they are known under such names as adder's tongue, trout-lily, and dogtooth-violet. They are admirably hardy and most desirable rock-garden and woodland subjects, where their two basal bright green or more often dark-mottled leaves carpet the ground in early spring. The nodding, usually solitary flowers have pointed, recurved petals which give them a starry appearance. There are white, cream, yellow and purple species, varying in height from 6 to 24 inches.

E. albidum. Eastern U.S.—white, leaves green or mottled
E. americanum. Eastern U.S.—yellow, leaves mottled
E. californicum. California—cream to yellow, cluster-flowered
E. hendersonii. South Oregon—like above, but violet and maroon
E. revolutum. Pacific Northwest—white to lilac, mottled leaves, cluster-flowered
E. tuolumense. California—deep yellow, cluster-flowered, leaves green

CULTURE OUTDOORS: Plant in partly shaded location, in soil rich in humus, 3 to 5 inches apart and 3 inches deep. Set, as soon as received, in moist soil and keep well watered until bulbs are established. Leave undisturbed.

PROPAGATION: By offsets or seeds.

EUCHARIS [Amaryllidaceae]

Eucharis grandiflora (syn. *E. amazonica*), the Amazon-lily was once a popular florists' flower. It can be grown as a house plant but does best in a warm greenhouse. The blooming season is late winter and early spring.

The umbels of pure-white flowers are chastely beautiful and, in form, suggestive of some of the white triandrus hybrid daffodils.

CULTURE INDOORS: Plant in coarse, fibrous soil enriched with well-rotted or dried cow manure with a little bone meal added. Place four to six bulbs in an 8- or 10-inch azalea pot, pressing in firmly, with necks of bulbs above soil. Water sparingly until new growth begins. Then give ample moisture and humidity during the growing season, with a temperature of 70 to 85 degrees. Keep from direct sunshine. Reduce water during the resting period, but do not dry so much as to lose the foliage, which should be kept green. Like most amaryllids, the eucharis blooms best when pot-bound.

CULTURE OUTDOORS, SOUTH: Pot as above and move, in pots, to partly shaded border for blooming period. Bring indoors during the winter season.

PROPAGATION: By offsets in spring.

EUCOMIS [Liliaceae]

Eucomis, often called the pineapple-lily, is a South African bulb, easy to grow as a tender summer-flowering subject in the North, as a garden flower in the South and other mild climates, or as a pot plant indoors.

From rosettes of basal leaves rise rather coarse scapes set with dense racemes of white or greenish-white, star-shaped flowers. Leaves crowning the tip of the raceme resemble the top of a pineapple and give the plant its common name.

E. bicolor—leaves to 2 feet; greenish flowers, marked purple

E. comosa—leaves to 2 feet; brown-spotted on lower side; flowers greenish

E. undulata—leaves to 1 foot, strap-like; flowers greenish-white

CULTURE OUTDOORS: Plant in May in the North or in fall in the South in soil suitable for lily culture, with bulbs near surface. If grown outdoors in the North, dig and store before hard frost. Hardy to Washington, D.C.

CULTURE INDOORS: Pot in fall (Mixture No. 2) and treat as half-hardy forced bulb. After flowering, gradually reduce water and rest the bulbs.

PROPAGATION: By offsets.

FREESIA [*Iridaceae*]

Few winter-blooming plants give greater satisfaction when grown under glass or in a cool window than the fragrant freesia with its loose spikes of dainty, colorful, funnel-shaped flowers. Among the many hybrids there is a large range of color from white through yellow to mauve, lavender, pink, carmine, apricot and copper. (Beware of some hybrids—they lack fragrance!)

'Blue-Whimple'—violet blue

'Carmelita'—yellow

'Marie'—white

'Pimpernelle'—scarlet

'Pink Marvel'—pink

'Princess Marijke'—bronze, orange, and yellow

CULTURE INDOORS: Plant at intervals of two weeks from October to January for continuous bloom—twelve corms to an 8-inch bulb or azalea pot, using Mixture No. 3. Store pots in frame outdoors until hard frost threatens. Then grow on in a very cool temperature—45 to 55 degrees—and water freely. Full sun. Bloom will appear ten to twelve weeks after planting. Dry off after flowering and store corms through the summer. Watch for aphids.

CULTURE OUTDOORS, LOWER SOUTH: Plant in sun in well-drained sandy soil in September or October.

PROPAGATION: By offsets and seeds.

FRITILLARIA [*Liliaceae*]—*See Chapter 14*

GALANTHUS [*Amaryllidaceae*]—*See Chapter 14*

GALTONIA [*Liliaceae*]—*See Chapter 19*

GLADIOLUS [*Iridaceae*]—*See Chapter 17*

GLORIOSA [*Liliaceae*]

One of the nicest things about the gloriosa-lily is the fact that the tuberous roots can be started into growth at any season of the year after a few months' rest. A root, 5 to 6 inches long and ½ inch in diameter, started in early spring, will bloom in late summer.

The showy 4-inch red and yellow flowers with twisted petals are borne in the axils of the upper leaves, the petals being interestingly recurved in the manner of *Lilium speciosum*. The vine-like plant is supported by tendrils developed at the leaf tips, an ingenious method of climbing. The flowers are prized for arrangements and corsages.

CULTURE INDOORS: Use Mixture No. 2 and, when new eye appears on tuber, plant, one to each 6-inch pot, 2 to 4 inches deep, depending on the size of the tuber. Water well and leave undisturbed until active growth starts. Then keep consistently moist and grow on in a cool temperature which should never exceed 65 degrees. After bloom, gradually reduce water. New tuberous roots, angular in form, will have developed when the drying-off period is completed. Remove these carefully from the soil in the pot—they are very brittle— and store until a pink bud or eye is visible at end of tuber (approximately three months). Then replant as before. Two blooming periods a year may be had, as growth cycle is completed in six months.

CULTURE OUTDOORS: In southern Florida and like climates, leave in ground the year round. In the North, plant in the open ground after frost danger is past for bloom in July or August. Dig in the fall before frost.

PROPAGATION: By offsets or division of roots.

GLOXINIA [*Gesneriaceae*]—*See SINNINGIA*

HABRANTHUS [*Amaryllidaceae*]

The *Habranthus* is a small genus which until recently was confused with *Hippeastrum* and *Zephyranthes,* both of which it resembles. *H. andersonii,* but 6 inches in height, produces solitary yellow flowers veined with red; *H. robustus* is 9 inches tall with rose-red flowers 3 inches long, and *H. texanus*—a native of Texas—is yellow with copper and purple markings on the outside of the 4-inch flowers which appear in summer. Most of the species are natives of South America.

CULTURE: As for *Zephyranthes.*

PROPAGATION: By offsets and seeds.

HAEMANTHUS [*Amaryllidaceae*]

The haemanthus or blood-lily is a tender South African bulb which flowers in late summer or early fall. Most of the species are rather low-growing, with decorative leaves to 1 foot in length and almost globular flower heads produced at the tips of sturdy scapes. Made up of many tubular starry flowers of white, red, or soft salmon-orange, each with six long star-like stamens, they are further enhanced by the even longer stamens, deeper in color and each bearing a conspicuous golden anther. In the specimen before us at this writing, there are two dozen fully opened blossoms surrounding a ring of half-opened blooms which enclose a heart of another two dozen still closed buds. This particular species, *H. katharinae,* is of a delightfully soft salmon-pink color. There are a number of available species and varieties:

H. albiflos—white, to 1 foot; foliage evergreen; late summer

H. coccineus—red, to 1 foot; berries purple; late summer

H. katharinae—soft salmon-pink, leaves 3 to 5 on short separate stem, appearing with the flowers; 1½ feet; August

H. puniceus—pale red flowers followed by scarlet berries which remain in good condition for months. Wavy leaves with reddish stems.

CULTURE INDOORS: Pot (Mixture No. 4) about March 1, leaving top half of bulb exposed. Water sparingly until top growth starts, then increase moisture and feed regularly with liquid fertilizer. Place in a partly shaded garden bed during summer and give complete shade while flowering. After bloom and when foliage has matured, withhold water entirely except in evergreen varieties. Repot only when necessary.

PROPAGATION: By offsets.

HIPPEASTRUM [Amaryllidaceae]

Hippeastrum is the botanical name for our common "amaryllis"— a large tribe with glossy strap-like leaves and two to four large lily-like flowers appearing in an umbel at the tip of a hollow scape. In some species and varieties the leaves appear after the flowers, but with most, they come with the bloom. In some cases, too, the foliage is persistent, growing throughout the year.

Most amaryllis in commerce today are improved hybrids, many of them blooming several times a year. These come both in strains like the Royal Dutch and Ludwig hybrids and in named varieties, and under color. Among these are:

'Apple Blossom'—white blended pink

'Beautiful Lady'—salmon-orange

'Blizzard'—pure white

'Bouquet'—salmon

'Joan of Arc'—white with green throat

'Lucky Strike'—bright red

'Orange King'—deep orange

'Picotee'—white with red edging

'Red Master'—deep red

'Salmon Perfection'—soft salmon

Amaryllis are good subjects for the cool greenhouse, sun porch, plant room, or window garden, where they bloom in winter and early spring; or they can be used as summer-flowering bulbs in the North and as garden subjects in the South.

CULTURE INDOORS: One of the oldest and easiest of house plants to bring into bloom. Plant in early winter (Mixture No. 4) with the upper third of the bulb exposed. Water sparingly until growth begins.

Then increase water. Grow on through summer in pots in garden bed. After leaves mature in fall, dry off gradually and rest in pots until new growth again begins. Repot only when necessary.

CULTURE OUTDOORS, NORTH: Plant in shady garden beds after danger of frost is past and lift bulbs before frost, storing in damp peat moss and sand. In the far South, the bulbs may be left in garden beds the year round.

PROPAGATION: By offsets, seeds, and, with hybrids, by bulb cuttings.

HYACINTHUS [Liliaceae]—See Chapter 14

HYDROSYME [Araceae]

Grown as a curiosity, *Hydrosyme rivieri* (sometimes listed as *Amorphophallus rivieri*), is rather like a giant, dark, evil-smelling, calla-lily. The reddish spathe, often a foot long and borne on a 2- to 4-foot spotted stalk, gives the plant its common name of devil's-tongue. The broad, palm-like foliage, which appears after the flower has faded, on mottled stems (giving the common name of snake-palm), is very interesting and produces an unusually tropical effect. Well worth growing as a terrace or patio decoration.

CULTURE INDOORS: Pot 2 to 3 inches deep in very early spring (Mixture No. 5). After leaves have matured, reduce water and rest through winter in a cool greenhouse or plant room. When new growth starts, increase water.

CULTURE OUTDOORS: Set out in late May.

HYMENOCALLIS [Amaryllidaceae]—See Chapter 19

IPHEION (Liliaceae)

The spring starflower or triteleia (*Ipheion uniflorum*) is one of the little bulbs of spring and should get the same garden treatment as chionodoxa, pushkinia, grape-hyacinth and scilla. Its pale violet flowers are borne singly on 8-inch stems above grassy foliage that is faintly onion- or garlic-scented—depending on your nose sensitivity. Plant the bulbs in generous numbers for the best display, about 3 inches deep in the fall. Bulbs increase rapidly. Flowers appear in early spring. Excellent in the rock garden or among rocks, in pockets of soil on or around the terrace and among such small daffodils as 'W. P. Milner', 'Tete-A-Tete'. (The spring starflower has undergone more than its share of generic designations, having been known as *Triteleia, Milla, Leucocoryne* and *Brodiaea,* and is still often found in catalogues under *Triteleia.*)

CULTURE: As for *Muscari* and *Chionodoxa.*

IRIS, BULBOUS [Iridaceae]

The bulbous irises are separated into three main groups: the Junos, the bulbs of which keep their roots during the resting season; the xiphiums (Spanish iris) and the xiphiodes (English iris), both with smooth bulbs without roots when resting; and the reticulatas, the bulbs of which are covered with a characteristic netting.

Juno irises are not always commercially available in this country and are as a rule considered more unusual than beautiful. The plants rather resemble cornstalks with flowers in the leaf axils. They bloom with the "Dutch" bulbs in spring. The following species represent a selection of those considered of interest by iris growers:

I. bucharica—yellow with golden falls; 30 inches

I. persica—blue, purple, green, and gold; 6 inches

I. rosenbachiana—rose, purple, white, and gold; dwarf with 3-inch flowers

I. sindjarensis—blue and white; 10 inches

CULTURE OUTDOORS: Plant in well-drained sandy soil in full sun and leave undisturbed. In the North, mulch with evergreen boughs after first hard freeze.

Iris reticulata includes a number of dwarf varieties blooming in early spring. Much more decorative and appealing than the Junos, the reticulatas are beloved of rock gardeners. They produce single blossoms in shades of blue, violet, or purple with orange markings, and many are delightfully fragrant. Blooming as they do in early spring, they are often planted with *Arabis albida* and other early low-growing perennials.

I. reticulata 'J. S. Dijt' is reddish purple.

I. reticulata 'Clairette' is a light blue.

I. reticulata 'Joyce' and 'Spring Time' are deeper blue.

Also in the reticulata group is *Iris danfordiae,* a yellow species from Turkey that blooms even earlier than *I. reticulata.*

CULTURE: Plant these bulbs about 3–4 inches deep in groups of ten or more in well-drained, but moisture-holding soil in full sun. Since they bloom so early in spring, they are ideal subjects for soil pockets in the terrace or in other places near the house. In the fall, mulch well with evergreen boughs or litter after the first hard freeze.

Iris xiphium (Spanish iris) is a clan which includes many named varieties, as does also *I. xiphiodes,* or English iris. The so-called "Dutch" irises, so named because they were bred and are grown in Holland, are hybrids of *I. xiphium* and other species. They have heavier stems and larger blooms than their Spanish parent. These are the bulbous irises sold as cut flowers in florists' shops. They make fine garden flowers, too, for those who care to meet their simple requirements.

The xiphiums, xiphiodes and Dutch hybrids all produce heavy single-flower stems 1½ to 2 feet in height, the xiphiums with narrow, channeled leaves a foot in length, the xiphiodes with larger foliage equaling the stem in length, and the Dutch rather like the xiphiums but more robust in every way and with larger flowers. The flowers of all three types, in which there is a fine color range, are showy and orchid-like, with many fine porcelain blues.

There are many named cultivars of these three types of irises, but with the exception of the Dutch Hybrids, the bulbs are offered in the U.S.A. mostly in mixtures. Since the Dutch hybrids bloom in late May outdoors, the Spanish irises in early June and the English irises in late June, an extensive display of these beautiful irises is possible if all three kinds are included in the border. Some worthwhile Dutch Hybrids are:

'Blue Ribbon'—deep blue standards, bronze falls

'Bronze Queen'—blue and bronze

'Golden Emperor'—golden yellow

'Gold and Silver'—white standards, gold falls

'Golden Harvest'—yellow

'H. C. Van Vliet'—dark violet-blue
'Wedgwood'—porcelain blue
'White Superior'—white

CULTURE OUTDOORS: As for *I. reticulata,* except that xiphiums require full sun and a sheltered location with excellent drainage, while xiphiodes require summer moisture (like Japanese iris) and a rich, moist, humusy soil. Plant in fall and mulch—preferably with evergreen boughs—after the first hard freeze. *This is obligatory* in the North.

All the bulbous irises (except the Junos) may be lifted yearly after bloom and stored, to be replanted in fall; but if left in the ground and winter-mulched or grown in a frame, they need not be disturbed for six or eight years.

CULTURE INDOORS: Force as hardy bulbs.

PROPAGATION: By offsets.

ISMENE [Hymenocallis]—See Chapter 14

IXIA [Iridaceae]

Ixias (corn-lilies) are stand-bys for the Southern summer garden and in the North are often grown under glass for winter and spring bloom. They may also be planted in the open for summer color out of doors. Thin wiry flower stalks, varying in height from 1 to 3 feet, depending on the species or variety, bear hanging, bell-shaped flowers above grass-like foliage. Among the many hybrids there is a range of color from white through cream to yellow, orange, red, pink and violet. In most cases the flowers are marked with contrasting colors, as red on white, yellow with a lavender eye, etc.

CULTURE INDOORS: Plant as directed for forcing half-hardy bulbs (Chapter 20). Bring indoors before first hard freeze and keep at 55 degrees. After foliage matures, remove corms from pots, dry thoroughly in sun and store.

CULTURE OUTDOORS, SOUTH: Plant in November in moist, well-drained soil in sun or part shade; mulch after first hard freeze with 4 to 8 inches of dead leaves, depending on severity of winter climate. Remove mulch gradually in early spring.

CULTURE OUTDOORS, NORTH: Plant in garden beds in late fall. A heavy winter mulch is necessary.

PROPAGATION: By offsets.

IXIOLIRION [Amaryllidaceae]

A little-grown spring-flowering bulb from Asia, *Ixiolirion montanum,* the Siberian bluebell, sends up in late May 12- to 18-inch flowering spikes bearing sprays of true blue or lilac starry flowers.

CULTURE OUTDOORS: If planted in light, well-drained soil, 3 inches deep, ixiolirion is hardy. It cannot, however, survive poor drainage. Bulbs can be dug before frost and stored over winter.

PROPAGATION: By offsets.

LACHENALIA [Liliaceae]

Lachenalias (Cape-cowslips) form a large group of small bulbous flowers for culture indoors in a cool room or window or under glass. They are natives of South Africa.

The spikes of long tubular flowers rise from two or more basal leaves. *Lachenalia bulbifera* (syn. *pendula*) is the most satisfactory for indoor culture and has large red, yellow and purple flowers borne on stiff 12-inch peduncles.

CULTURE INDOORS: Bulbs should be potted in August (Mixture No. 2), a dozen bulbs to a 6-inch pot or bulb pan. Place in a cold frame in full sunshine until just before hard frost. Then remove to a cool room, window or greenhouse at 50 to 60 degrees and grow on in full sun, increasing the water supply. After flowering, reduce water gradually until bulbs mature. Dry off and store.

CULTURE OUTDOORS, LOWER SOUTH: Plant in September or October. After bloom and when foliage has matured, dig, dry, and store until following fall.

PROPAGATION: By offsets and seeds.

LAPEIROUSIA (Anomatheca) [Iridaceae]

The major species of this little-grown corm from South Africa are

Lapeirousia grandiflora and *L. laxa.* They are low-growing plants suitable for the summer rock garden or, forced, for bloom indoors. The bright but fleeting violet, rose, red, or white flowers are closely set in short panicles on 12-inch stems. They are half-hardy. (The generic name was formerly *Anomatheca.*)

CULTURE INDOORS: Use Mixture No. 3. Treat as freesias.

CULTURE OUTDOORS: As for gladiolus.

PROPAGATION: By seeds or cormels.

LEUCOCORYNE [*Liliaceae*]

The leucocoryne or glory-of-the-sun is a small Chilean genus producing narrow basal leaves and blue or white tubular flowers in a terminal umbel. The bulbs are tender.

L. ixioides, the species generally available, produces large, sweet-scented blue flowers, white-centered, on 18-inch stems in spring.

CULTURE INDOORS: As for freesias.

CULTURE OUTDOORS, LOWER SOUTH: As for freesias.

PROPAGATION: By offsets and seeds.

LEUCOCRINUM [*Liliaceae*]

Leucocrinum montanum (sand- or star-lily) is a single species, a hardy native of our own West, with large, pure-white, fragrant flowers in stemless clusters in early spring. Though each flower lasts but a day, many appear in succession. It is a valuble addition to the rock garden.

CULTURE OUTDOORS: Plant the rhizomes in early fall in a sunny, sandy, well-drained position in the rock garden.

PROPAGATION: By seeds.

LEUCOJUM [*Amaryllidaceae*]—*See Chapter 14*

LILIUM [*Liliaceae*]—*See Chapter 15*

LIRIOPE [Liliaceae]

Lily-turf is a common name for both the *Liriope* and the *Ophiopogon,* closely allied genera. Both are useful ground covers in sun or shade, where the tuber-like roots form mats or sods so dense as to suggest their common name.

L. muscari, the big blue liriope, has leaves to 18 inches and lilac-purple flowers. There is a variegated form with yellow-striped leaves. *L. spicata,* the creeping liriope, bears narrow grass-like leaves and pale violet or white flower spikes.

CULTURE OUTDOORS: Plant in ordinary garden soil in sun or shade. Has proved hardy with us north of New York City.

PROPAGATION: By division.

LYCORIS [Amaryllidaceae]—See Chapter 19

MILLA [Liliaceae]

Milla biflora is a bulbous species native to our Southwest, and is commonly called Mexican star. Fragrant, wax-white 2½-inch flowers are borne in spring in clusters at the top of a 1½-foot scape, while leaves are basal. It is sometimes sold commercially as *Bessera elegans.*

CULTURE INDOORS: Plant several bulbs in a bulb pan in Mixture No. 2 in fall and treat as half-hardy bulbs for forcing.

CULTURE OUTDOORS, NORTH: Plant out in early spring and lift before freezing weather. Far South it may be treated as a garden plant.

PROPAGATION: By offsets.

MONTBRETIA [Iridaceae]—See Chapter 19

MORAEA [Iridaceae]

The moraeas are popular garden plants in the South and southern California, where they are grown like irises. They may also be treated as window garden plants, especially those species which are either constant bloomers or which blossom several times a year.

Foliage is narrow and basal, while the fragrant, showy but fleeting flowers, appearing in clusters and opening successively, are white, violet, or blue, some with splotches of yellow or orange.

FOR INDOORS:

Moraea iridioides johnsonii—flowers large, white with lavender and orange; blooms several times in the summer months; 2 feet

M. polystachya—lilac with yellow markings; blooms for six weeks or more; 2 feet

FOR OUTDOORS:

M. ramosissima (syn. *ramosa*)—yellow, large; 3 to 4 feet

CULTURE INDOORS, CORMOUS TYPES: As for ixias.

CULTURE INDOORS, RHIZOMATOUS TYPES: Pot (Mixture No. 3) and keep very moist until after bloom. Then reduce, but do not withhold water.

CULTURE OUTDOORS, SOUTH: Plant out in early autumn.

PROPAGATION: By seed or division.

MUSCARI [Liliaceae]—See Chapter 14

NAEGELIA [Gesneriaceae]—See SMITHIANTHA

NARCISSUS [Liliaceae]—See Chapter 11

NERINE [Amaryllidaceae]

Nerine sarniensis, (the Guernsey-lily, so called because this South African bulb established itself in Guernsey after the bulbs were cast up there from a wrecked ship) makes a beautiful fall display indoors or under glass in the North. It produces narrow light green leaves which appear *after* the flowers. These, bright red or crimson with long bright red stamens, are produced in umbels at the top of an

18-inch solid scape and look as if sprinkled with gold dust. (For many years *Lycoris radiata* was sold as *Nerine sarniensis.*) *N. filifolia* is a smaller species, also with red flowers, and with 8-inch leaves occurring with the blossoms. Another species commercially available is *N. bowdenii,* tall-growing, with large pink flowers marked with rose.

CULTURE OUTDOORS: As border flowers in the South. Plant in early fall. Keep moist in winter, dry in summer.

CULTURE INDOORS: Pot up (Mixture No. 4) when received in autumn. Grow on through winter with plenty of water to encourage growth of foliage. As spring approaches, reduce water gradually, and when leaves turn yellow, rest completely in pots turned on their sides in dry sunny location until bloom appears in early fall. Leaves will follow bloom, and these must be kept green through winter with ample moisture.

PROPAGATION: By offsets.

OPHIOPOGON [*Liliaceae*]

A close relative of the liriopes, the ophiopogons are also commonly called lily-turf because both form dense mats of roots and foliage which create a satisfactory ground cover in sun or shade.

O. jaburan has narrow leaves to 2 feet and spikes of white flowers. There are varieties with striped leaves. (*Liriope muscari,* which has blue or violet flower spikes, is often misnamed *O. jaburan.*) *O. japonicus* is a dwarf variety with tuber-bearing roots and foot-long, very dark green leaves. Flowers are light blue. This is the best species for use as a turf substitute.

CULTURE: As for liriope.

PROPAGATION: By division.

ORNITHOGALUM [*Liliaceae*]

There are two groups of these star-like bulbous flowers, commonly known as star-of-Bethlehem: the hardy species which may be planted outdoors to give spring bloom, and the tender sorts grown under glass.

O. umbellatum, 6 to 12 inches tall, with green-margined racemes of white star-shaped flowers and grass-like foliage, makes itself so much at home in northern gardens that it often becomes a serious pest. Other hardy species are *O. pyramidale,* to 2 feet, also with green-margined white flowers and *O. nutans,* to 1 foot, with nodding white and green blossoms.

O. arabicum, a tender species for the window garden, produces racemes of white flowers with black pistils on scapes 2 feet in height. *O. caudatum,* another window-garden subject, has green-centered white flowers to 3 feet. *O. thyrsoides* produces long-lasting white or pale yellow blossoms in long, dense racemes. *O. aureum,* one of the best for indoors, has lemon yellow flowers.

CULTURE OUTDOORS: Plant as any hardy garden bulb.

CULTURE INDOORS: Plant 6 bulbs to a large bulb pan (Mixture No. 2) as soon as delivered. Keep in cold frame until roots appear in drainage holes. Then bring in to a temperature not exceeding 60 degrees. Treat as freesias.

PROPAGATION: By offsets.

OXALIS [*Oxalidaceae*]

Oxalis may be had in red, rose, pink, violet, yellow, white and striped species and varieties, which are greenhouse or indoor favorites for winter and early spring bloom. The clover-like, glossy leaves are also decorative. Native, hardy summer-blooming sorts are small-flowered.

For indoor growing or greenhouse culture, and as garden subjects in the South:

O. adenophylla—lilac-pink; spring–early summer

O. bowiei—rose-purple, large flowers; summer

O. cernua (Bermuda Buttercup)—bright yellow; spring

O. hirta—pink, large flowers, most satisfactory; winter

CULTURE INDOORS: In September or October plant bulbs near the surface, six to a 6-inch bulb pan, in Mixture No. 2. Place in dark, cool place, giving little water, until growth starts. Then bring to full light, increase water and feed with liquid fertilizer. After bloom, reduce water gradually until foliage matures. Then store in pots and let rest until early autumn. Divide and replant.

CULTURE OUTDOORS, SOUTH: Plant in fall 2 inches deep and 3 inches apart at the front of a sunny border.

PROPAGATION: By offsets, root division, or seeds.

PANCRATIUM [Amaryllidaceae]

P. maritimum is a charming summer-blooming tender bulb which comes to us from the Mediterranean region and closely resembles Hymenocallis (spider-lily or Peruvian-daffodil). The blue-green, strap-like but twisted leaves are evergreen, while the very fragrant flowers with 3-inch tubes and 1½-inch perianth-like petals make the blossoms resemble a large white daffodil. P. canariense is a species from the Canary Islands bearing six to ten flowers on long pedicles.

CULTURE OUTDOORS, SOUTH: Plant bulbs 8 to 10 inches apart, covering with 3 inches of soil in sandy, well-drained soil. Keep moist until foliage matures.

CULTURE OUTDOORS, NORTH: (Mixture No. 4.) Set pots out in late spring, on terrace or patio. (Tips of bulbs should be level with surface of soil in pot.) Bring pots indoors before first frost, keeping moist until foliage stops active growth.

PROPAGATION: By offsets and seeds.

PARADISEA LILIASTRUM [Liliaceae]—See ANTHERICUM

POLIANTHES [Amaryllidaceae]—See Chapter 19

POLYGONATUM [Liliaceae]

P. biflorum and P. commutatum are North American natives, with fleshy creeping underground stems, found in rich woods. Commonly known as Solomon's-seal, the pendent, bell-like greenish flowers in the axils of the leaves in spring are followed by shining fruits which turn rose color in autumn. There are several species native to other parts of the world.

CULTURE OUTDOORS: Naturalize in rich, fairly moist woods.
PROPAGATION: By division and seeds.

PUSCHKINIA [*Liliaceae*]

Puschkinia (striped squill) is a close relative of the scilla and is
perfectly hardy. The gray-blue flowers appearing in spring on short
(to 6 inches) stems make good rock-garden subjects. *P. scilloides*
(syn. *libanotica*) is the species offered.

CULTURE OUTDOORS: As for scilla.
PROPAGATION: By offsets.

RANUNCULUS [*Ranunculaceae*]

This is a large family, with some members scarcely 2 inches tall
(as *R. creticus*) and others 4 feet (as *R. lyallii*). Many are hardy
perennials, some suitable for the rock garden, others for the mixed
border. *R. bulbosus,* which has a bulbous root and grows to 1 foot, is
an escape from Europe which has become one of our most common
wild flowers—the buttercup.

The so-called florists' ranunculus, *R. asiaticus* (tuberous-rooted),
produces the showiest blooms. Growing to 1½ feet, it has flowers 1
to 4 inches in diameter. There are double forms with yellow, orange,
scarlet, crimson, pink and white blooms. Listed in catalogues are
Persian, French, turban and peony-flowered strains.

CULTURE: As for anemones.
PROPAGATION: By division and seeds.

RECHSTEINERIA [*Gesneriaceae*]

Rechsteineria is a tuberous-rooted gesneriad from South America
with showy, tubular flowers above hairy, soft-textured leaves that are
heart-shaped. The plants, mostly summer bloomers, are fine pot subjects for terraces and patios, often continuing to flower indoors in a
sunny window or under fluorescent lights (14–16 hours per day)
up to Christmas before requiring a rest period of a few months.
(*Rechsteineria* has been classified under *Gesneria, Corytholoma* and
Sinningia.)

The cardinal-flower (*R. cardinalis*) can be spectacular with its bright scarlet flowers, borne singly or in clusters, and 2- to 3-inch velvety-textured leaves. *R. leucotricha* grows taller, to about 10 inches, and has bright salmon-red flowers and handsome leaves, densely hairy and silvery. One species, *R. verticillata,* is mainly a winter bloomer, producing dusty-rose or peach flowers in clusters above tiers composed of three leaves. It has been given the rather uninspired common name of double-decker plant.

CULTURE: Generally as for achimenes. Pot young tubers in a 4-inch pot in a humusy mixture (Potting Mixture No. 5), increasing the pot size from year to year as necessary. Although the plants like a moist atmosphere, careful watering is needed. The foliage of *R. leucotricha* is especially sensitive to excessive water.

PROPAGATION: Seeds, stem and leaf cuttings [as with African-violets (*Saintpaulia*)] and division of large tubers.

SCHIZOSTYLIS [*Iridaceae*]

S. coccinea (crimson flag; Kafir-lily) is a member of the iris family sometimes grown indoors or under glass for winter bloom and as a cut flower. The long grass-like leaves are up to 2 feet in length, and the slender-tubed deep red flowers are borne on 1½-foot spathes in early winter.

CULTURE INDOORS: Plant in March (Mixture No. 3) and water plentifully until after bloom. Then gradually reduce moisture and rest in pots with only an occasional watering until the following spring. The potted plants may spend the summer sunk to their rims in a garden bed but should be brought in before the first frost.

PROPAGATION: By division of the rhizomes.

SCILLA [*Liliaceae*]—*See Chapter 14*

SINNINGIA [*Gesneriaceae*]

The genus *Sinningia* is not only the home of the gloxinia, one of the showiest of tender, summer-blooming tuberous pot plants, but also includes a group of species and hybrids, including some miniatures in both categories whose popularity has skyrocketed because of interest in the gesneriad family, fluorescent-light gardens indoors and in terrariums and other enclosed containers for house plants.

The gloxinia, now classified as *S. speciosa fifyana,* has great velvety leaves, suggestive in texture of giant African-violet foliage; the large bell-shaped or double flowers of violet, purple, salmon, rose, red, white and two-color combinations are startlingly beautiful. Many hybrids generally available as potted plants in full bloom from florists or as dormant tubers from garden centers and mail-order sources are imported from Europe. A few are:

'Emperor Frederick'—red flowers bordered white

'Emperor Wilhelm'—blue bordered white

'Princess Elizabeth'—blue-purple with white throat

'Switzerland'—scarlet bordered white

'Tigrina'—red or blue speckles on white

'Waterloo'—deep red

Wonderful gloxinias, known as the Buell Hybrids, have been bred by a Connecticut hybridizer, Albert Buell. Included are gloxinias in many outstanding new shades, forms and color combinations that are available directly from the hybridizer as named varieties (vegetatively reproduced) or as color-named strains or series (produced from seeds). A few named Buell gloxinias are:

'Blue Delight'—white bordered blue

'Dotted Swiss'—white speckled pink

'Mildred Louise'—red, creamy throat with red speckles

'Mrs. B.'—pink with fuchsia throat and double

'Peaches and Cream'—white suffused pink

'Pink Surprise'—pink with creamy throat speckled pink

'Trudy'—red bordered white

'White Perfection'—pure white double, short stems

From Danish hybridizers have come special gloxinia strains created especially for indoor gardeners to grow under fluorescent lights. These hybrids have smaller, more compact foliage than most gloxinias, making them more suitable for cramped shelf and window space. These hybrids are available as seed strains under such names as Robe, Glory, Peace, etc. (Gloxinias bloom from seed in six to eight months.)

Other sinningias of interest include *S. barbata,* a species from Brazil of upright habit with 6-inch-long leaves and pouch-like white flowers that are produced intermittently all year, the plant not becoming dormant in winter; *S. regina,* another species from Brazil, of compact growth, with 2- to 5-inch leaves veined white and slipper-shaped violet blooms on 2- to 4-inch stems; *S. eumorpha,* from Brazil, forming a rosette of glossy 4-inch leaves and producing nodding bell-shaped flowers in white with lilac throat in spring or summer; and last but hardly least, two remarkable little sinningias, *S. concinna,* which forms a 2-inch rosette of ¼- to ½-inch leaves and trumpet-shaped deep violet-purple flowers on 1-inch stems, and *S. pusilla,* even smaller with 1½-inch leaf rosettes and tiny lavender flowers. There are a number of named offspring from these and other species—all miniatures and suitable for small pots and terrariums. A few are: 'Doll Baby'—4-inch foliage rosette, lavender flowers, nearly everblooming; 'Freckles'—lavender and white flowers, throat speckled white; 'Little Imp'—pink; 'White Sprite'—white.

CULTURE: Gloxinias—Tubers are usually started into growth between February and May for summer and autumn flowers. One method is to handle them in the same way as tuberous begonias, setting the tubers (indented side up) in flats of moist peat moss and sand and covering with about ½ inch of the mixture. Keep at 60–70 degrees and after a few leaves have developed, pot in a coarse, fibrous, humusy soil in a 5- to 6-inch pot. Or start the tubers into growth directly in their pots, a method that eliminates further transplanting the first year. (Sometimes dormant tubers are slow to start new growth: place such tubers in a plastic bag containing a little moistened peat moss; remove the tuber as soon as roots and leaves appear.) Grow on the young plants in an eastern or southern window (or under fluorescent lamps for 14–16 hours daily) and where the night temperature never drops below 60 degrees. Though gloxinias like plenty of moisture, it is best to water thoroughly until soil in pots is moist all the way through, then not again until the surface feels dry to the touch. Avoid wetting the foliage. Feed regularly with liquid fertilizer. When summer comes, the plants will require some shade. They can remain in the window garden or on a porch or terrace well sheltered from wind and rain. In August, begin to reduce water gradually until the foliage matures and dries off. Store, in the pots, under a bench in the greenhouse or on dampish cellar floor until new growth begins. Then bring to light and increase water. Repot if necessary about every third year. For succession of bloom, start tubers at two-week intervals from February to April. For winter bloom, plant seeds in spring and grow on into the following winter, or hold tubers dormant until later in season, starting them only when new growth begins to develop.

PROPAGATION: From seed and leaf cuttings, as for African-violet.

CULTURE: Sinningias and miniature sinningias—similar to achimenes and gloxinias (above) except that the miniatures grow in small pots (1½ to about 3 inches) and in terrariums where they can be left in their pots (cover pots with moss) or planted in the growing medium.

PROPAGATION: Seeds, tubers, leaf and stem cuttings.

SMILACINA [Liliaceae]

The false Solomon's-seals are native woodland wild flowers of North America. The most common species is S. racemosa. One species, S. trifolia, is native also in Siberia, while S. stellata is found in both North America and Europe. The terminal racemes or panicles of greenish or white flowers are borne on long curving stems, to 3 feet, with alternate leaves. The round red berries which follow the flowers are also prized. Ideal subjects for naturalizing in moist, open woodland.

CULTURE OUTDOORS: Plant in drifts or colonies in woodland in part shade. S. stellata, starry false-Solomon's-seal, readily forms colonies in dry woodlands or in sandy soil in open situations.

PROPAGATION: By division and seeds.

SMITHIANTHA [Gesneriaceae]

Smithiantha (syn. Naegelia) commonly called temple bells, is a genus of plants with hairy, velvety leaves and tubular red or yellow flowers in terminal panicles up to 2 feet, although there are a few lower-growing cultivars and doubtless more will appear because of the tremendous interest in gesneriads. (Some authorities believe the correct generic name should be *Smithiana* rather than *Smithiantha*.) In *S. cinnabarina,* the foliage hairs are red and the flowers, red spotted with white, appear in spring. *S. zebrina* has leaves marked with plum or brown and red flowers, spotted yellow, in summer to fall. There are several cultivars including 'Abbey', peach and white flowers; 'Carmel', white spotted red; 'Cathedral', yellow-orange with paler spots; 'Santa Barbara', orange and pale yellow; 'Little Tudo', orange-red and yellow; 'Little Wonder', red-orange and yellow. The last two are smaller than those preceding.

CULTURE: Rhizomes are usually started into growth in late winter and early spring, although they can be planted any time you can obtain the rhizomes from a grower. Plant one root to a 5- to 6-inch pot or tub (3-inch pot is suitable for small-growing varieties such as 'Little Tudo'), using Mixture No. 5 and covering 1 inch deep. Keep moist but do not overwater until growth shows. Then increase water as needed and feed with liquid fertilizer. After bloom, reduce water gradually and rest the plants three months in their pots.

PROPAGATION: Seeds, cuttings or division of rhizomes.

SPARAXIS [Iridaceae]

Sparaxis (wand flowers) are tender cormous plants from South Africa producing in spring short spikes of yellow, purple, or rose-colored flowers rising to 1 or 2 feet from narrow basal leaves.

S. bulbifera—yellow, solitary flowers to 1 foot

S. grandiflora—yellow or purple to 2 feet

S. tricolor—purple, yellow and white to 1½ feet

Although many named cultivars are known, wand flowers are usually only available in mixtures.

CULTURE: As for freesias.

PROPAGATION: By offsets.

SPREKELIA [Amaryllidaceae]

Variously known as Aztec-lily, Jacobean-lily, and St. James-lily, this Mexican bulb is grown indoors or under glass in the North, and out of doors as a garden plant in the South. It may also be treated as a tender summer-flowering bulb in the North. *S. formosissima* produces solitary, 4-inch bright red spidery flowers on 1- to 2-foot stems. The three upper petals are erect, while the three lower ones are rolled or curled.

CULTURE INDOORS: As for *Hippeastrum* (amaryllis).

CULTURE OUTDOORS: As for *Hymenocallis* (ismene or Peruvian-daffodil).

PROPAGATION: By offsets.

STERNBERGIA [*Amaryllidaceae*]—*See Chapter 19*

TIGRIDIA [*Iridaceae*]—*See Chapter 19*

TRICYRTIS [*Liliaceae*]

Tricyrtis or toad-lilies come to us from Asia, where a number of species are native. *T. hirta,* a Japanese species which is hardy to Massachusetts, produces many creamy flowers splotched with purple. Borne on 2- to 3-foot stems, the small flowers are typical of the lily family, bell-shaped and graceful. Appearing in late September and October, they are especially welcome. *T. flava,* also from Japan, is a dwarf with yellow flowers. *T. macropoda* is another hardy species which flowers in summer. The pale violet, spotted flowers appear in a long, terminal corymb.

CULTURE OUTDOORS: Plant the rhizomes in humusy, well-drained soil in partial shade, in the rock garden or elsewhere; the dainty flowers make little show in a mixed border. After the first hard freeze, mulch lightly with salt hay or dry leaves.

CULTURE INDOORS: Pot in late winter (Mixture No. 2), and in spring sink pots in shaded garden beds. Before hard freeze, take indoors, dry off gradually, and store.

PROPAGATION: By division.

TRILLIUM [Liliaceae]

Trilliums are native to our American woods and are easily recognized because of their three whorled leaves and three-petaled flowers.

There are many species, but *T. grandiflorum,* with 3-inch white flowers, is the showiest. *T. sessile,* which bears the common name of toad trillium, has deep red-purple flowers. *T. undulatum,* the painted trillium, has 1½-inch flowers of white veined in pink or purple and is a native of the Eastern seaboard, where it is found from Canada to Georgia and west to Missouri.

CULTURE OUTDOORS: Plant thick roots in rich, moist woods soil after flowering and when foliage has matured. Once established, do not disturb.

PROPAGATION: By seeds and division of old clumps.

TRITELEIA [Liliaceae]—See BRODIAEA and IPHEION.

TRITONIA [Iridaceae]—See Chapter 19

TULBAGHIA [Liliaceae]

Tulbaghia is another South African genus grown indoors; as a tender summer bulb in the North; and outdoors in the South, where it blooms from June to September. (Hardy to North Carolina.) In California, flowers are produced in both winter and summer. Tulbaghia is a relative of both *Agapanthus* and *Allium. T. violacea* has violet, urn-shaped flowers in a terminal cluster and linear leaves from 8 inches to 1 foot in length. It is the major species available.

CULTURE INDOORS: As for *Agapanthus,* but all species must have full sun.

CULTURE OUTDOORS: Plant in sandy soil in full sun. In the North, dig and store before frost.

PROPAGATION: By offsets and seeds.

TULIPA [Liliaceae]—See Chapter 12

VELTHEIMIA [Liliaceae]

V. viridifolia has recently gained in popularity as a house plant, even though it has not as yet taken to itself a common name. Blooming in late winter, this veltheimia is decorative all through the cold weather because of its beautiful glossy basal foliage, 3 inches wide, crimped and ruffled along the edges, and growing out from the bulb in a symmetrical circle of handsome leaves, which are invaluable for use in flower arrangements.

The small tubular flowers, rather like those of the garden perennial, tritoma, but paler in color, are produced in an erect dense, tapering raceme at the top of a stalk 2 feet in height. There is something fascinating about following the rather slow development of the flower stalk and head, and we always bring the plant to a position in the window where we can watch it closely as soon as the bud appears. The flower head will keep in good condition for three weeks or longer after it first begins to show color.

CULTURE: Pot as for amaryllis (*Hippeastrum*), using Mixture No. 4. Rest plants over summer, withholding water and turning the pots on their sides. When new foliage growth starts in fall, place pots in cool, sunny window, watering as needed. Repot only as necessary.

PROPAGATION: By offsets.

WATSONIA [Iridaceae]

Watsonias, popular in California gardens, are in many ways similar to gladiolus. *W. coccinea* is scarlet; *W. pyramidata* (syn. *W. rosea*) has mauve or rose flowers. There are other species and varieties, including a group with evergreen foliage, Beatricis hybrids, with a range of color from salmon and orange to pink.

CULTURE OUTDOORS, NORTH: As for gladiolus; foliage should be encouraged to remain green as long as possible. Because more time is required for foliage to mature, watsonias cannot be planted out for succession of bloom as late in the season as gladiolus. Can be wintered over in frame.

CULTURE OUTDOORS, SOUTH: As for gladiolus. See above, but can be left in open over winter. Evergreen varieties, shipped in damp moss, are planted at once with plenty of moisture.

CULTURE INDOORS: As for *Ixia*.

PROPAGATION: By cormels.

ZANTEDESCHIA [Araceae]

The calla-lily (formerly *Richardia,* as it still is often listed) is primarily a greenhouse plant for winter blooming. It can be grown successfully in the window garden or as a tender bulb out of doors, for which use it is far too little appreciated in northern sections. The medium-sized yellow calla, Z. *elliottiana,* with spotted foliage, and the pink Z. *rehmannii* or its improved form, *superba,* dwarfs to 2 feet, are especially suitable for indoor bloom. Z. *aethiopica,* the commonly grown greenhouse species, reaches 3 feet or more. Z. *aethiopica* 'Crowborough' grows 2½ feet tall and is reputed to be winter-hardy in the North if well mulched.

In the Pacific Northwest and other mild moist climates, calla-lilies may be seen blooming in many a dooryard in spring.

CULTURE INDOORS: Plant, when received, in 6-inch pots (Mixture No. 5), the upper third of the rhizome protruding. Keep in a cool, damp, dark place until growth starts, watering sparingly. When growth begins, bring to light and warmth (65 degrees minimum) and water plentifully. Feed once a week with liquid fertilizer, such as a fish emulsion. After flowering, mature foliage gradually, then dry off bulbs and store. Repot each year.

CULTURE OUTDOORS, SOUTH: Plant in rich humusy soil, 3 to 4 inches deep, in light shade, spring or fall. Keep well watered.

CULTURE OUTDOORS, NORTH: Start indoors in March or April, or plant in open when soil is warm. Enrich bed with plenty of rotted manure, or humus plus dried manure; apply liquid fertilizer frequently. After frost, store as for tuberous begonias.

PROPAGATION: By offsets and by seeds.

ZEPHYRANTHES [Amaryllidaceae]—See Chapter 19

LISTS

BY
  Season of bloom
  Height

FOR
  Hot, dry situations
  Moist situations
  Shade
  Woodland
  Mixed borders
  Features or landscape groups

  Naturalizing
  Rock garden
  Edgings
  Terrace or patio, in pots or tubs
  Greenhouse, or as house plants
  Fragrance
  Cuttings and arrangements

WHERE TO BUY BULBS
  Mail-order sources

NOTE
  H indicates: hardy
  HH: half-hardy
  T: tender

BULBS BY SEASON OF BLOOM

SPRING	SUMMER	AUTUMN	WINTER
Achimenes T	Achimenes T	——	——
——	Acidanthera T	——	——
——	Agapanthus T	——	——
Albuca T	Albuca T	——	——
Allium H; HH	Allium H; HH	Allium H; HH	Allium H; HH
Alstroemeria HH; T	Alstroemeria T	——	——
——	——	Amarcrinum T	Amarcrinum T
——	Amaryllis bella-donna HH	Amaryllis bella-donna HH	——
Anemone HH	Anemone HH	Anemone HH	——

SPRING	SUMMER	AUTUMN	WINTER
Arisaema tri-phyllum H	Anthericum HH	——	——
——	Arum palaes-tinum HH	——	Arum pal-aestinum T
Babiana T	Begonia evan-siana H	Begonia evan-siana H	——
Bulbocodium H	Begonia, Tuber-ous T	Begonia, Tuber-ous T	——
——	Belamcanda H	——	——
——	Bessera HH; T	——	——
——	Brodiaea HH	——	——
Camassia H	Caladium T	Caladium T	Caladium T
Chionodoxa H	——	——	——
Claytonia H	Calochortus H; HH	——	——
Clivia H	Canna T	Canna T	Clivia
Convallaria H	Chlidanthus T	Colchicum H	——
——	Colocasia T	——	——
Cooperia T	Cooperia T	Crocosmia T	——
——	Crinodonna HH; T	Crinodonna T	Crinodonna T
Crinum T; HH	Crinum T; HH	——	——
Crocus H	——	Crocus H	——
Cyclamen H	——	——	Cyclamen T
——	Cypella T	——	Cyrtanthus T
——	Dahlia T	Dahlia T	——
Endymion H	Eucomis T	——	——
Eranthis H	——	——	——
Eremurus H	——	——	——
Erythronium H	——	——	——
Eucharis T	——	——	Eucharis T
Freesia T	——	——	Freesia T
Fritillaria H	——	——	——
Galanthus H	Galtonia HH	——	——
——	Gladiolus HH; T	Gladiolus HH; T	Gladiolus T
Gloriosa T	Gloriosa T	Gloriosa T	Gloriosa T

SPRING	SUMMER	AUTUMN	WINTER
Hyacinthus H	Habranthus T	——	——
——	Haemanthus T	Haemanthus T	Hippeastrum T
——	Hippeastrum T	——	——
——	Hydrosyme T	——	——
——	Hymenocallis T	——	——
Ipheion HH	——	——	——
Iris, Bulbous H; HH	Iris, Bulbous H; HH	——	——
Ixia T	Ixia T	——	Ixia T
——	Ixiolirion T	——	——
Lachenalia HH	——	——	Lachenalia HH
——	Lapeirousia HH	——	Lapeirousia HH
Leucocoryne T	——	——	——
Leucocrinum H	——	——	——
Leucojum H	Lilium H	Lilium H	Lilium H
——	Lycoris squamigera H	Lycoris radiata HH	——
Muscari H	Moraea HH	——	Moraea HH
Narcissus H	——	——	Narcissus, H 'Paperwhite' T
	——	——	Narcissus 'Soleil d'Or' T
Nerine T	——	——	Nerine T
Ornithogalum H; T	——	——	——
Oxalis HH; T	Oxalis HH; T	——	Oxalis HH; T
Polygonatum H	Pancratium T	——	——
Puschkinia H	Polianthes T	——	——
Ranunculus H; T	Ranunculus H; T	——	——
——	Rechsteineria T	——	——
Scilla H	Sinningia T	Sinningia T	Smithiantha T
Smilacina H	——	——	——
Smithiantha T	——	——	Schizostylis T

SPRING	SUMMER	AUTUMN	WINTER
Sparaxis T	Sparaxis T	Sternbergia H	——
Sprekelia T	Sprekelia T	——	Sprekelia T
——	——	——	Tulbaghia T
——	Tricyrtis H; HH	Tricyrtis H; HH	——
Tulipa H	——	——	Tulipa H
——	——	——	Veltheimia T
——	Watsonia T	——	——
Zantedeschia T	Zantedeschia T	——	Zantedeschia T
——	Zephyranthes HH; T	——	——

BULBS ACCORDING TO HEIGHT

LOW TO 1 FOOT	MEDIUM TO 2½ FEET	TALL 3 TO 8 FEET
——	Achimenes T	Agapanthus T
——	Acidanthera T	Albuca T
Allium H; HH	Allium H; HH	Allium H; HH
——	Alstroemeria T	Alstroemeria HH
——	Amaryllis belladonna T	——
Anemone H	Anemone H; HH	Anemone H; HH
Anthericum HH	——	——
Arum palaestinum T	——	——
Babiana T	Begonia, Tuberous T	Begonia evansiana H
Brodiaea HH	——	Belamcanda H
Bulbocodium H	Bessera HH; T	Bessera HH; T
——	Caladium T	——
Calochortus H	Calochortus H	——
——	Camassia H	Camassia H
Chionodoxa H	——	——
Chlidanthus T	Clivia T	Canna T

LOW TO 1 FOOT	MEDIUM TO 2½ FEET	TALL 3 TO 8 FEET
——	——	Colocasia T
——	——	Crinodonna T
Claytonia H	Crinum T; HH	Crinum T; HH
Colchicum H	——	——
Convallaria H	——	Crocosmia T
Cooperia T	Cyrtanthus T	Cypella T
Crocus H	——	——
Cyclamen H	Cyclamen T	——
——	Dahlia T	Dahlia T
Endymion H	——	——
Eranthis H	Erythronium H	Eremurus H; HH
Erythronium H	Eucomis T	——
Eucharis T	——	——
——	Freesia T	——
Fritillaria H	——	Fritillaria H
——	——	Galtonia HH
Galanthus H	Gladiolus T	Gladiolus T
——	——	Gloriosa T
Habranthus T	Haemanthus T	——
——	Hippeastrum T	——
——	——	Hydrosyme T
——	Hymenocallis T	Hymenocallis T
Ipheion	——	——
Iris H; HH	Iris H; HH	Iris H; HH
——	Ixia T	
Lachenalia HH	——	——
Lapeirousia HH	——	——
Leucocoryne T	——	——
Leucocrinum H	——	——
Leucojum H	Leucojum H	——
Liriope H	Lilium H	Lilium H
——	Lycoris radiata HH	Lycoris squamigera H

LOW TO 1 FOOT	MEDIUM TO 2½ FEET	TALL 3 TO 8 FEET
Moraea HH	Moraea HH	Moraea HH
Muscari H	——	——
Narcissus H	Narcissus H; T	——
——	Nerine T	——
Ophiopogon H	——	——
Ornithogalum H; T	Ornithogalum H; T	——
Oxalis HH; T	——	——
Puschkinia H	Pancratium T	Polianthes T
——	Polygonatum H	Polygonatum H
Ranunculus H; HH	Ranunculus H; HH	——
Scilla H	Schizostylis T	——
Sinningia T	Sinningia T	——
——	Smilacina H	——
——	Smithiantha T	——
——	Sparaxis HH	——
Sternbergia H	Sprekelia T	——
——	Tigridia HH; T	——
——	Tricyrtis H; HH	——
Trillium H	Trillium H	——
——	Tritonia HH; T	Tritonia HH; T
——	Tulbaghia T	——
Tulipa species H	Tulip H	Tulip H
——	Veltheimia T	——
——	——	Watsonia HH; T
Zephyranthes HH; T	Zantedeschia T	Zantedeschia T

FOR HOT, DRY SITUATIONS

Bessera HH; T   Brodiaea HH

Calochortus (spring moisture
  needed) H
Cooperia T
Crocosmia (Montbretia) HH; T
Gladiolus HH; T

Ixia T
Tigridia HH; T
Tulipa (species) H
Watsonia T
Zephyranthes HH; T

FOR MOIST SITUATIONS

Alstroemeria T; HH
Arisaema triphyllum H
Caladium H
Camassia H
Canna T
Claytonia H
Clivia T
Colocasia T
Convallaria H
Erythronium H

Iris xiphiodes HH
Leucojum H
Lilium canadense H
Lilium superbum H and others
Polygonatum H
Schizostylis T
Smilacina H
Trillium H
Zantedeschia T

FOR LIGHT-TO-PARTIAL SHADE

Achimenes T
Allium H
Agapanthus T
Amarcrinum T
Amaryllis belladonna HH
Anemone (woodland varieties)
  H; HH
Arisaema triphyllum H
Begonia evansiana H
Begonia, Tuberous T
Caladium, Fancy-leaved T
Camassia H
Chlidanthus T
Claytonia virginica H
Clivia T
Colocasia T
Crinum moorei HH
Endymion
  nonscripta H

Eranthis hymenalis H
Erythronium H
Eucharis T
Fritillaria H
Galanthus H
Gloriosa T
Hippeastrum T
Hydrosyme T
Ipheion uniflorum HH
Leucojum H
Lilium: Bellingham Hybrids H and
  other hybrids
  canadense H
  Henryi H
  martagon H
  philadelphicum H
Lycoris squamigera H
Muscari H
Ornithogalum H; T

Polygonatum biflorum H
Sanguinaria canadensis H
Scilla H
Smilacina H

Tricyrtis HH; T
Trillium H
Zantedeschia T

FOR WOODLAND

Allium moly H
  and others
Anthericum T
Arisaema triphyllum H
Calochortus H
Camassia H
Claytonia virginica H
Convallaria H
Endymion nonscripta H
Erythronium H
Galanthus H
Ipheion uniflorum HH
Leucojum H
Lilium H
  amabile
  auratum

  canadense
  giganteum
  Henryi
  martagon
  philadelphicum
  rubellum
  superbum
  and others, including many
    hybrids
Polygonatum biflorum H
Puschkinia H
Sanguinaria canadensis H
Scilla sibinica H
Smilacina H
Trillium H

FOR THE MIXED BORDER

Acidanthera T
Albuca T
Allium (most kinds) H; HH
Alstroemeria T
Anemone HH
  Florists'
  hortensis
  tuberosa
Belamcanda H
Bessera HH
Calochortus H
Camassia H
Canna T
Cooperia T

Crocosmia (Montbretia) T; HH
Cypella T
Cyrtanthus T
Dahlia T
Endymion
  nonscripta H
Eremurus H; HH
Eucomis T
Fritillaria imperialis H
Galtonia candicans HH
Gladiolus T; HH
Hyacinth H
Hymenocallis T
Iris, Bulbous HH

Ixia T
Ixiolirion T
Lachenalia HH
Leucojum H
Lilium H
  Aurelian Hybrids
  Auratum Hybrids
  candidum
  concolor
  Fiesta Hybrids
  Golden Chalice
  martagon
  Rainbow Hybrids and other
    hybrids
  speciosum
  tigrinum
  umbellatum
  and others

Lycoris radiata HH
Lycoris squamigera H
Moraea HH
Muscari H
Narcissus (most kinds) H
Nomocharis H; HH
Ornithogalum H; T
Oxalis T; HH
Pancratium T
Polianthes T
Ranunculus H; T
Scilla sibirica H
Sprekelia HH
Tigridia T; HH
Tritonia T
Tulipa (most kinds) H
Watsonia T; HH
Zephyranthes T; HH

FOR FEATURE PLANTINGS AND LANDSCAPE GROUPS

Acidanthera T
Anemone, Florists' HH
Anthericum T
Begonia, Tuberous T
Belamcanda H
Caladium T
Camassia H
Canna T
Clivia T
Colchicum H
Colocasia T
Crinum T; HH
Crocosmia (Montbretia) T; HH
Crocus H
Dahlia T
Eremurus HH; H
Fritillaria imperialis H

Galtonia candicans T; HH
Gladiolus T
Haemanthus T
Hippeastrum T
Hyacinth, Dutch H
Hymenocallis T
Iris, Dutch HH
  English (xiphiodes)
  reticulata H
  Spanish (xiphium)
Lilium (most kinds) H
Lycoris squamigera H
Moraea HH
Narcissus (most kinds) H
Polianthes T
Tigridia T
Tulipa (most kinds) H

FOR NATURALIZING

Allium H; HH

Anthericum

Arisaema triphyllum H
  (Jack-in-the-pulpit)
Brodiaea HH
Bulbocodium H
Calochortus H
Camassia H
Chionodoxa H
Claytonia virginica H
  (Spring Beauty)
Colchicum H
Convallaria H
Cooperia T
Crocus H
Endymion nonscriptus H
Eranthis H
Erythronium H
Fritillaria meleagris H
Galanthus H
Leucojum H
Lilium H

Bellingham Hybrids
canadense
hansonii
martagon
philadelphicum
superbum
tigrinum
and others, including many
  hybrids
Lycoris squamigera H
Muscari H
Narcissus (most kinds) H
Ornithogalum H
Polygonatum biflorum H
Puschkinia H
Sanguinaria canadensis H
Scilla sibirica H
Smalacina H
Trillium H
Tulipa, many species and their
  hybrids

FOR THE ROCK GARDEN

Allium H; HH
  moly H
  neapolitanicum H
Anemone H
  apennina
  blanda and varieties
  caroliniana
  fulgens
  palmata
  ranunculoides
Anthericum T
Arisaema triphyllum H
Babiana T
Brodiaea HH
Bulbocodium H
Calochortus HH
Camassia H

Chionodoxa H
Chlidanthus T
Claytonia virginica H
Colchicum H
Cooperia T
Crocus H
  Dutch
  Species
  Autumn fl.
Cyclamen H
  europaeum
  neapolitanum
Eranthis H
Erythronium H
Fritillaria meleagris H
Galanthus H
Ipheion HH

Lapeirousia ʜʜ
Leucocrinum ʜ
Leucojum ʜ
Lilium ʜ
 amabile
 concolor
 pumilum
Muscari ʜ
Narcissus ʜ
 asturiensis
 bulbocodium citrinus
 bulbocodium conspicuus
 cyclamineus
  'Jack Snipe'
  'February Gold'
  'March Sunshine'
  'Tete-a-Tete' and others
 gracilis
 jonquilla
odorus
rupicola
triandrus
 albus
 'Moonshine'
 'Thalia'
 Watieri
 'W. P. Milner'
Oxalis ᴛ
Puschkinia ʜ
Sanguinaria canadensis ʜ
Scilla bifolia ʜ
 sibirica and varieties
 tubergeniana
Sternbergia ʜ
Trillium ʜ
Tulipa ʜ
 Species and hybrids
Zephyranthes ᴛ

FOR TERRACES, EDGINGS OR FOREGROUNDS

Allium moly, 12 inches ʜ
Allium neapolitanum, 15 inches ʜ
Anemone blanda ʜ
Chionodoxa ʜ
Galanthus ʜ
Hyacinthus ʜ
 Dutch ʜ
 Roman ʜʜ
Ipheion ʜʜ
Leucojum ʜ
Liriope ʜ
Muscari ʜ
Narcissus ʜ
 'February Gold'
 'Horn of Plenty'
 'March Sunshine'
 'Peeping Tom'
 'Thalia'
 'W. P. Milner' and others
Oxalis ʜʜ; ᴛ
Puschkinia ʜ
Ranunculus ʜ; ᴛ
Scilla ʜ
Tulipa ʜ
 Single Earlies, species and hybrids

FOR PATIO AND TERRACE CONTAINERS AND PLANTERS

Achimenes ᴛ (hanging baskets)
Agapanthus ᴛ (tubs)
Amaryllis belladonna ᴛ (pots)
Begonia, Tuberous ᴛ (pots and
 hanging baskets)
Caladium ᴛ (pots or boxes)

Clivia T (tubs)
Crinodonna T (pots)
Crinum T (pots or tubs)
Eucomis T (pots)
Gloriosa T (pots—a climber)
Haemanthus T (pots)
Hippeastrum T (pots or boxes)

Hydrosyme T (tubs)
Nerine T (pots)
Oxalis T (boxes, hanging baskets)
Sinningia (Gloxinia) T (pots)
Smithiantha T (pots)
Zantedeschia (Calla-lily) T (tubs)

FOR GREENHOUSE OR AS HOUSE PLANTS

Achimenes
Agapanthus
Alstroemeria
Amaryllis belladonna
Arum palaestinum
Babiana
Begonia, Tuberous
Caladium
Chlidanthus
Clivia
Crinodonna
Crinum
Cyclamen, Florists'
Cyrtanthus
Eucharis
Eucomis
Freesia
Gloriosa
Haemanthus
Hippeastrum
Hydrosyme
Hymenocallis
Ixia

Lachenalia
Lapeirousia
Leucocoryne
Lilium longiflorum
Lycoris radiata
Moraea
Narcissus
    'Paperwhite'
    'Soleil d'Or'
Nerine
Oxalis
Ranunculus
Rechsteineria
Schizostylis
Sinningia
Smithiantha
Sparaxis
Sprekelia
Tritonia crocata
Tulbaghia
Veltheimia
Zantedeschia (Calla-lily)
Zephryanthes

NOTE: All tender or half-hardy. For details of culture, see Catalogue of
    Bulbs.

FOR FRAGRANCE

Acidanthera HH
Amaryllis belladonna T

Chlidanthus T
Convallaria H

Cooperia T
Crinodonna T
Crinum T
Daffodil (see Narcissus)
Freesia T
Hyacinthus H
Hymenocallis T
Ipheion HH
Iris reticulata H
Lachenalia HH
Leucocoryne T
Leucocrinum H

Lilium, in variety H
Lycoris squamigera H
Narcissus H
   Jonquil and Hybrids
   'Paperwhite'
   Poeticus and Hybrids
Ornithogalum H; T
Pancratium T
Polianthes T
Tulbaghia T
Tulipa H
   Single Earlies (many)

FOR CUTTING AND ARRANGEMENTS

Allium H; HH
Alstroemeria HH
Amaryllis belladonna HH
Anemone, Florists' HH
Belamcanda T
Bessera HH; T
Caladium* T
Canna* T
Chlidanthus T
Clivia T
Convallaria H
Crinodonna T
Crinum T
Crocosmia (Montbretia) T; HH
Cypella T
Cyrtanthus T
Dahlia T
Eucharis T
Freesia T
Gladiolus T
Gloriosa T
Haemanthus* T
Hippeastrum T
Hyacinthus H
Hymenocallis* T

Iris in variety* HH
Ixia HH
Ixiolirion T
Lachenalia T
Leucocoryne T
Lilium, in variety H
Lycoris aurea HH
Lycoris incarnata HH
Lycoris radiata T
Lycoris squamigera H
Muscari H
Narcissus, in variety H; T
Nerine T
Ornithogalum H; T
Pancratium T
Ranunculus H; T
Scilla H
Smithiantha* T
Tigridia T
Tritonia T
Tulipa, in variety H
Veltheimia* T
Watsonia T
Zantedeschia (Calla-lily)* T

* Indicates decorative foliage.

WHERE TO BUY BULBS BY MAIL

If you have been unable to find certain bulbs you want, below are listed some companies from which you can order by mail. These companies will send you, upon request, the current lists of items they have available and their prices. Where companies charge for their catalogues, this is so noted.

Blackthorne Gardens
48 Quincy St.
Holbrook, Mass. 02343
(General ornamentals including many bulbs)

Buell's Greenhouses, Inc.
P. O. Box 218
Eastford, Conn. 06242
(Gloxinias and other tuberous ges-neriads; catalogue 25¢ plus self-addressed, stamped 9½″×4″ envelope)

Burnett Bros, Inc.
92 Chambers St.
New York, N.Y. 10007
(Most kinds of bulbs)

George W. Park Seed Co.
Greenwood, S.C. 29647
(Most kinds of bulbs)

Grant E. Mitsch
P. O. Box 960
Canby, Oregon 97013
(Daffodils)

International Growers Exchange
P. O. Box 397
Farmington, Mich. 48024
(Most kinds of bulbs; catalogue $3)

John Messelaar Bulb Co.
P. O. Box 269
Ipswich, Mass. 01938
(Most kinds of bulbs)

John Scheepers, Inc.
63 Wall St.
New York, N.Y. 10005
(Most kinds of bulbs)

P. de Jager and Sons, Inc.
South Hamilton, Mass. 01982
(Most kinds of bulbs)

Rex Bulb Farms
Newberg, Oregon 97132
(Lilies)

Van Bourgondien Bros.
P. O. Box A
245 Farmingdale Road
Babylon, N.Y. 11702
(Most kinds of bulbs)

Wayside Gardens Co.
Hodges, S.C. 29695
(Most kinds of bulbs; catalogue $1)

White Flower Farm
Litchfield, Conn. 06759
(Most kinds of bulbs; catalogues $4)

Recommended Varieties of Garden Bulbs

CROCUSES

Spring-blooming, Dutch

BLUE
'Enchantress'—China blue
'Paulus Potter'—red-purple
'Pickwick'—striped lilac
'Queen of the Blues'—lilac
'Remembrance'—purple
'Striped Beauty'—blue, striped white
'The Sultan'—purple-blue

WHITE
'Jeanne d'Arc'
'Kathleen Parlow'
'Peter Pan'
'Snowstorm'

YELLOW
'Golden Yellow'
'Yellow Mammoth'

Species & Their Cultivars

biflorus (Scotch Crocus)—striped blue & white (naturalizing)
imperati—lilac
sieberi (very early) and cultivars—blue
tomasinianus and cultivars—lavender to purple
versicolor—white, feathered blue

Fleischeri

aureus—orange-yellow
chrysanthus and cultivars
Korolkowii—golden-orange
sulphureus concolor—pale yellow
susianus

Autumn-blooming Species

asturicus—purple-lilac
longiflorus—lilac
medius—lilac-purple
sativus (Saffron Crocus)—lilac, feathered violet

laevigatus
speciosus 'Albus'

speciosus—blue and
   its varieties
zonatus—lilac

DAFFODILS

Trumpet (Division 1)

YELLOW	BICOLOR	WHITE	PINK
'Arctic Gold'	'Lunar Sea'	'Beersheba'	'Mrs. R. O.
'Golden Harvest'	'Queen of Bicolors'	'Broughshane'	Backhouse'
'Golden Rapture'	'Spellbinder'	'Cantatrice'	'Pink Glory'
'Hunter's Moon'	'Spring Glory'	'Empress of Ireland'	'Rima'
'King Alfred'	'Trousseau'	'Mount Hood'	
'Kingscourt'		'Vigil'	
'Slieveboy'			

Large Cups (Division 2)

PERIANTH YELLOW, CORONA COLORED	PERIANTH WHITE, CORONA COLORED	PERIANTH WHITE, CORONA WHITE	CORONA PINK OR PINK EDGED
'Armada'	'Duke of Windsor'	'Easter Moon'	'Accent'
'Binkie'	'Festivity'	'Ice Follies'	'Louise de Coligny'
'Butterscotch'	'Green Island'	'Pigeon'	'Passionale'
'Carlton'	'Kilworth'	'Sleveen'	'Pink Rim'
'Galway'	'Signal Light'	'Stainless'	'Roseyards'
'Gigantic Star'	'Tudor Minstrel'		'Rosy Sunrise'
'St. Keverne'			'Salmon Trout'
			'Toscanini'

Small Cups (Division 3)

PERIANTH YELLOW, CORONA COLORED	PERIANTH WHITE, CORONA COLORED	PERIANTH WHITE, CORONA WHITE
'Apricot Distinction'	'Aircastle'	'Chinese White'
'Barret Browning'	'Blarney'	'Cushendall'
'Chungking'	'Firetail'	'Dream Castle'
'Edward Buxton'	'La Riante'	'Frigid'
'Irish Coffee'	'Verger'	'Polar Ice'
		'Portrush'

Doubles (Division 4)

YELLOW	BICOLOR	WHITE
'Golden Ducat'	'Irene Copeland'	'Cheerfulness'
'Inglescomb'	'Mary Copeland'	'White Lion'
'Yellow Cheerfulness'	'Texas'	

Triandrus Hybrids (Division 5)

YELLOW	WHITE
'Hawera'	'Shot Silk'
'Liberty Bells'	'Silver Chimes'
	'Thalia'
	'Tresamble'

Cyclamineus Hybrids (Division 6)

YELLOW
'Charity May'   'March Sunshine'
'February Gold'   'Peeping Tom'
'Jack Snipe'   'Tete-a-Tete'

Jonquilla Hybrids (Division 7)

LARGE AND SMALL
CUPS, VERY FRAGRANT—ALL YELLOW
'Cheri'   'Pipit'
N. jonquilla   'Suzy'
'Lintie'   'Trevithian'

Tazetta Hybrids (Division 8)

YELLOW	BICOLOR	WHITE
'Early Perfection'	'Cragford'	'Bridal Crown'
'Scarlet Gem'	'Geranium'	'Cheerfulness'
'Yellow Cheerfulness'	'Laurens Koster'	
	'Minnow'	

Poeticus (Division 9)

WHITE WITH RED-RIMMED CUPS
'Actaea'   *N. poeticus recurvus*
'Cantabile'   (Old Pheasant Eye)
                          'Red Rim'

Species and Miniature Narcissi (Division 10)

Narcissus bulboco-
   dium conspicuus
   (hoop petticoat
   daffodil)
N. gracilis
N. jonquilla
'Rip Van Winkle'
N. watieri
'W. P. Milner'

Split Cornonas (Division 11)

'Baccarat'
'Orangery'

DAHLIAS

Large Dahlias

CLASSIFICATION: ID, Informal Decorative; FD, Formal Decorative; SC, Semi-Cactus; IC, Incurved Cactus; C, Cactus; STC, Straight Cactus

RED

'Arthur Godfrey' (FD)—Orient red
'Autumn Blaze' (ID)—flame-red
'Dark Desire' (ID)—deep red
'Mary Elizabeth' (ID)—cherry-red
'The Cardinal' (SC)—cardinal-red

PINK AND ROSE

'Canby Charm' (ID)—clear pink
'D-Day' (FD)—rose
'Jersey Beauty' (FD)—pink to
  chamois
'Enchantment' (ID)—rose-pink
'Morning Kiss' (SC)—soft pink

YELLOW AND ORANGE

'Croydon Ace' (ID)—yellow
'Croydon Masterpiece' (FD)—
  salmon-orange
'First Lady' (FD)—yellow
'House of Orange' (FD)
'Moonglow' (SC)—yellow

PURPLE AND LAVENDER

'Blue River' (FD)—deep lilac
'City of Wellston' (FD)—royal-
  purple

'Lavender Perfection' (FD)—violet
'Night Editor' (ID)—royal-purple
'The Commando' (FD)—dark
  lavender

WHITE

'Alabaster' (FD)
'My Love' (SC)—creamy white
'Lula Pattie' (ID)
'Roben's White Dove' (ID)
'Snow Country' (ID)

BLENDS AND BICOLORS

'Flying Saucer' (STC)—lavender
  and white
'Grand Prix' (ID)—white and
  yellow
'Holland's Festival' (FD)—orange
  and white
'Lois Walcher' (FD)—purple and
  white
'Tartan' (ID)—maroon and white

Small Dahlias

CLASSIFICATION: A, Anemone; M, Miniature; B, Bedding; D, Dwarf; SC,
Semi-Cactus; IC, Incurved Cactus; C, Cactus; FD, Formal Decorative

RED

'Bishop of Llandaff' (MA) (Peony)—
  dark red
'Fabel' (A)—red
'Fred Springer' (B)—red
'Nelly Geerlings' (DB)—scarlet-red
'Wing' ('Wiek') (DB)—flaming red

PINK AND ROSE

'Honey' (B)—salmon-pink
'Murillo' (B)—pink
'Park Princess' (M SC)—pink
'Preference' (M C)—salmon-pink
'Siemon Doorents' (B)—pink

WHITE

'All Triumph' (M SC)
'Bride' (M C)
'Sneezy' (B)

'Toto' (A)—white with yellow
  center

YELLOW AND ORANGE

'Brio' (A)—orange
'Flashlight' (M C)—sulphur-yellow
'Irene Van Der Zwet' (B)—bright
  yellow
'Ventura's Yellow' (M FD)
'Yellow Cheer' (M FD)

LAVENDER

'Alice B. Clayson' (M FD)—
  lavender and white
'Cheerio' (M C)—Tyrian-purple
'Julie R' (M SC)—lavender
'Mrs. C. J. Robertson' (M IC)—
  lavender
'Regina' (B)—plum-purple

Pompons

RED

'Alice'—bright red
'Fuji'—red and gold
'Kochelsee'—deep red

PINK AND ROSE

'Andre Menou'—pink
'Betty Ann'—rose
'Tiki'—pink and buff blend

WHITE

'Albino'
'Celestia'
'Little Willo'

YELLOW

'Drumstick'
'Mimosa'
'Margaret John'—yellow and bronze
blend

LAVENDER

'Andrew Lockwood'
'Morning Mist'—lavender and white
'Royal Willo'—purple

GLADIOLUS

RED

'Albert Schweitzer'—scarlet
'Fire Chief'—scarlet
'Oscar'—blood-red
'Peter Pears'—shrimp-red
'Sans Souci'—scarlet

PINK AND SALMON

'Mexicali Rose'—silver-edged rose
'Miss America'—pink
'Spic and Span'—deep pink
'Spring Song'—pink
'True Love'—clear pink

SMOKIES

'Sandstorm'—rose-violet
'Stormy Weather'—dark violet

BLUES

'China Blue'—light blue
'Green Lilac'—orchid and
chartreuse
'Purple Splendor'—purple
'Salman's Blue'—violet-blue
'Sugar Plum'—purple and plum

BUFF, YELLOW AND ORANGE

'Brightside'—yellow
'Canary Bird'—deep yellow
'Orange Gold'—orange and yellow
'Pay Dirt'—golden yellow
'Sundown'—apricot blend
'Sunshine'—gold

WHITE AND CREAM

'America'—white with red blotch
'Day Dream'—creamy-white
'Glacier'
'Morning Kiss'
'White Friendship'—white and cream

GREEN AND OTHERS

'Brown Glow'—brown
'Chocolate Sundae'—brown
'Copper Lustre'—rose and copper
'Green Woodpecker'—lemon-green
'Lemon Lime'—bright green

Miniatures

RED

'Atom'—red tipped gold
'Bravo'—red with purple throat
'Red Bantam'—ruffled scarlet

WHITE

'Daintiness'—creamy-white
'Mighty Mite'—ruffled white

PINK AND SALMON

'Cutie'—light rose
'Fiesta'—salmon-orange
'Jackpot'—pink with white throat

BLUE

'Doll Dance'—lavender

YELLOW AND ORANGE

'Frolic'—yellow
'Nugget'—butter-yellow
'Papoose'—orange and salmon

GREEN

'Green Jewel'
'Greenleaf'—ruffled
'Mint Julep'—pale green

LILIES

NAME	COLOR	DATE OF BLOOM
amabile	red, spotted	June
auratum and varieties	white, spotted crimson	July–Sept.
Aurelian Hybrids	white-yellow or apricot centers	July–Aug.
Bellingham Hybrids	yellow-orange, spotted	June–July
Shuksan	yellow-orange, spotted	July
brownii	white, purple reverse	July
bulbiferum	orange-red, spotted	June
canadense and varieties	yellow-orange, spotted	July
candidum	white	June
Cascade Strain	white	June
L. *centifolium*	white, green-striped	July
Hybrids	white, flushed pink or ice-green	July
chalcedonicum	scarlet	July
Citronella Strain	yellow, spotted	July
columbianum	golden-orange, spotted	June
concolor	scarlet-orange	June
Connecticut Yankee	salmon-orange	July
davidii	red, spotted	July
elegans and varieties	apricot to red, mostly spotted	June–July
Empress of India	crimson-red edged white	August
Golden Chalice Hybrids	yellow to orange	June
Golden Sunburst Strain	golden-yellow	July
grayi	red, shaded orange, spotted	July
hansonii	yellow, spotted	June
Harlequin Hybrids	pink, rose, ivory	June–July
henryi	orange-yellow, spotted	August
humboldtii	orange-yellow, spotted	July
longiflorum and varieties	white	June–July
martagon	purple, wine-red, white	June–July
Paisley Strain	yellow, purple, orange	June
Mid-century Hybrids	salmon-buff to red	June–July
Enchantment	nasturtium-red	June
Nutmegger	yellow, spotted red-brown	July

NAME	COLOR	DATE OF BLOOM
pardalinum	orange-red to crimson, spotted	July
Giganteum	crimson to gold, spotted	July
parvum	orange-red, spotted	June
Pastel Hybrids	lilac, yellow, peach	June
philadelphicum	bright red, spotted	June
pumilum	scarlet	June
Rainbow Hybrids	yellow to red	June–July
Redband Hybrids	red and white, spotted	August
regale	white, yellow throat, rose reverse	June–July
speciosum and varieties	white to crimson	August–Sept.
superbum	orange-yellow, spotted	July–August
tigrinum and varieties	yellow, salmon, orange	August

TULIPS

* Fragrant

Single Earlies

PINK AND SALMON

'Princess Irene'—salmon and purple

ROSE

'Christmas Marvel'—cherry-pink
'Ibis'
'Le Reve'—coral-red, flushed rose

RED

'Brilliant Star'—scarlet
'Couleur Cardinal'—orange-scarlet
'Keizerskroon'—scarlet, yellow edge

WHITE

'Diana'

YELLOW

'Bellona'*
'Joffre'

ORANGE

'De Wet'*
'Doctor Plesman'*—orange-red
'Prince of Austria'*—orange-red

PURPLE

'Van der Neer'—violet-purple

Double Earlies

PINK

'Murillo Max'—white, tinged pink
'Peach Blossom'—rose-pink

YELLOW AND ORANGE

'Goya'—salmon with yellow
'Marechal Niel'—canary with orange
'Mr. Van der Hoef'—yellow
'Orange Nassau'—orange-brown

RED

'Dante'
'Electra'
'Jewel Dance' (syn. 'Willemsoord')— red, white edge
'Vuurbaak'—fiery scarlet

WHITE

'Schoonoord'

Triumphs

RED

'Elmus'—cherry-red
'Garden Party'—red and white
'La Suisse'
'Lucky Strike'—red-edged white
'Paul Richter'—scarlet-red
'Prominence'—dark red

YELLOW AND ORANGE

'Cup Final'—yellow
'Kees Nelis'—yellow

'Orange Wonder'
'Ornament'—yellow

WHITE

'Hibernia'
'Kansas'

PURPLE

'First Lady'—red-violet flushed
   purple
'Purple Star'—blue-purple

Mendels

ROSE AND RED

'Apricot Beauty'—salmon-rose
'Golden Olga'—rose-purple, edged
   gold
'Olga'—violet red, edged white
'Pink Trophy'—pink, flushed rose
'Ruby Red'—glowing scarlet

WHITE

'Athlete'
'White Sail'

ORANGE, ORANGE-RED, YELLOW

'Golden Triumph'—yellow, bronze
   base
'Sulphur Triumph'—primrose yellow

Darwin Hybrids

YELLOW

'Beauty of Apeldoorn'—yellow
   overlaid with orange
'Gudoshnik'—yellow flushed and
   veined red
'Jewel of Spring'—pale sulphur
   edged red
'President Kennedy'—yellow with
   orange undertones
'Yellow Dover'

RED

'Apeldoorn'—cherry-red
'Apeldoorn Elite'—vermillion
   edged yellow
'Holland's Glory'—warm red

'Oxford'—orange-scarlet
'Parade'
'Spring Song'—bright red, flushed
   salmon

ORANGE

'Orange Sun'

SALMON-PINK

'Elizabeth Arden'—salmon-pink

Darwins

RED

'Flying Dutchman'—scarlet
'Landseadel's Supreme'—cherry-red

WHITE

'Duke of Wellington'—white
'Magier'—white, flushed purple at
   edges

PINK AND ROSE

'Aristocrat'—magenta
'Clara Butt'—clear pink
'Dreamland'—rose
'Gander'—bright magenta
'Queen of Bartigons'—salmon-rose

YELLOW

'Golden Age'—deep yellow
'Niphetos'—lemon-yellow

'Sunkist'—golden-yellow
'Sweet Harmony'—lemon-yellow

PURPLE AND BLACK

'Queen of Night'—almost black
'Scotch Lassie'—deep lavender
'The Bishop'—blue-purple

MAUVE AND LILAC

'Bleu Aimable'—lilac
'Insurpassable'—lilac
'William Copeland'—mauve-lilac

Lily-flowered

RED

'Aladdin'
'Queen of Sheba'—deep scarlet-
   brown edged yellow
'Red Shine'

YELLOW

'Alaska'—yellow
'West Point'—primrose-yellow

WHITE

'White Triumphator'

ROSE AND PINK

'China Pink'—pink, white base
'Mariette'—deep satin-rose

VIOLET

'Maytime'—reddish-violet edged
   white

Cottage

PINK

'Artist'—salmon-rose with green
   markings
'Greenland'—rose with green
   markings
'Rosy Wings'
'Smiling Queen'—rose edged pink

RED

'Burgundy Lace'—wine-red fringed
'Halcro'—carmine-red inside orange
'Henry Ford'—cherry-red
'Renown'—carmine

WHITE

'Maureen'
'Sorbet'—white flushed rose

YELLOW

'Georgette'—yellow edged red,
   multiflowered
'Golden Harvest'—lemon-yellow
'Mrs. John D. Scheepers'—pale
   yellow
'Princess Margaret Rose'—yellow
   edged scarlet

ORANGE

'Bond Street'—yellow and orange
'Dillenburg'—salmon-orange
'Orange Bouquet'—multiflowered

VIOLET-PURPLE

'Blue Heron'—purple with fringed
   edges

Parrots

PINK

'Fantasy'

ORANGE

'Orange Favorite'

RED

'Estelle Rignveld'—white heavily
    feathered blood-red
'Firebird'—red

YELLOW

'Karel Doorman'—pale yellow
'Texas Gold'—golden-yellow

PURPLE

'Black Parrot'—maroon-black
'Blue Parrot'—lavender

WHITE

'White Parrot'

Double Late (*Peony-flowered*)

PINK

'Angelique'—pale pink
'Eros'—old rose
'May Wonder'—rose

RED

'Bonanza'—carmine-red, edged yellow
'Uncle Tom'—maroon-red

WHITE

'Mount Tacoma'

YELLOW

'Gold Medal'—golden-yellow

ORANGE

'Orange Triumph'—orange-flushed
    brown, edged yellow

Species Hybrids

'Cape Cod'—yellow and red, mottled
    foliage (*Greigii*)
'Daylight'—scarlet, mottled foliage
    (*Kaufmanniana*)
'Purissima' (syn. 'White Emperor')—
    white (*Fosteriana*)
'Red Emperor'—scarlet (*Fosteriana*)
'Red Riding Hood'—red with mottled
    foliage (*Greigii*)

'Salmon Trout'—cerise-pink
    (*Fosteriana*)
'Shakespeare'—salmon, apricot and
    orange (*Kaufmanniana*)
'Stresa'—yellow blotched red, mottled
    foliage (*Kaufmanniana*)
'Yellow Emperor'—(*Fosteriana*)

INDEX

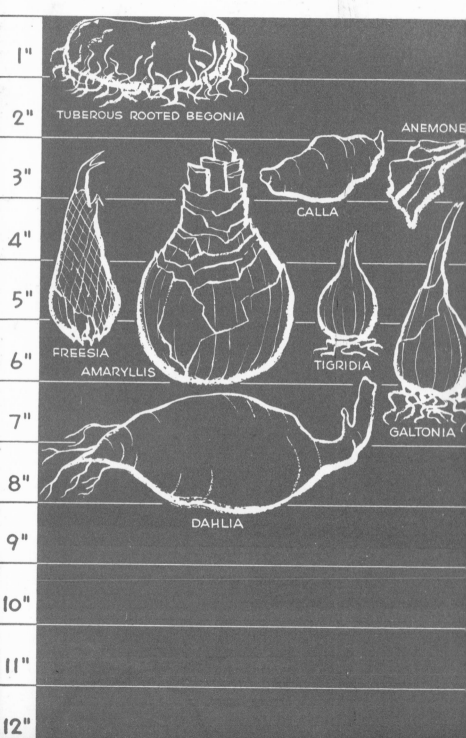

GROUND LEVEL

1"

TUBEROUS ROOTED BEGONIA

2"

ANEMONE

3"

CALLA

4"

5"

FREESIA

6"

AMARYLLIS

TIGRIDIA

GALTONIA

7"

8"

DAHLIA

9"

10"

11"

12"